Time in Fashion

Time in Fashion

Industrial, Antilinear and Uchronic Temporalities

Edited by
Caroline Evans and Alessandra Vaccari

BLOOMSBURY VISUAL ARTS
LONDON • NEW YORK • OXFORD • NEW DELHI • SYDNEY

BLOOMSBURY VISUAL ARTS
Bloomsbury Publishing Plc
50 Bedford Square, London, WC1B 3DP, UK
1385 Broadway, New York, NY 10018, USA

BLOOMSBURY, BLOOMSBURY VISUAL ARTS and the Diana logo are trademarks
of Bloomsbury Publishing Plc

First published in Italy under the title *Il tempo della moda*
© Mimesis Edizioni, Milan and Udine, Italy, 2019

First published in English, with substantial revision
and additions, by Bloomsbury Visual Arts
Copyright © Caroline Evans and Alessandra Vaccari, 2020

Research assistants: Lucy Moyse-Ferreira and Paolo Franzo

Cover image: Woman checking the time against an architectural detail backdrop at
Southdale mall in Minneapolis, MN, February 1957. (© Guy Gillette/The LIFE
Images Collection/Getty Images)

A catalogue record for this book is available from the British Library.

A catalog record for this book is available from the Library of Congress.

ISBN: HB: 978-1-3501-4694-5
PB: 978-1-3501-4693-8
ePDF: 978-1-3501-4695-2
eBook: 978-1-3501-4696-9

Typeset by RefineCatch Limited, Bungay, Suffolk

To find out more about our authors and books visit www.bloomsbury.com
and sign up for our newsletters.

Contents

Introduction

1   Industrial Time

2　Antilinear Time

3　Uchronic Time

Contents   vii

Figures

Acknowledgements

Our gratitude goes to the IUAV University of Venice where the idea for this project first took form during Caroline Evans's visiting professorship in 2016–17. A special thanks to Professor Carlo Magnani, then Director of the IUAV Department of Architecture and Arts, and Professor Maria Luisa Frisa, who founded and leads the IUAV Fashion Programme. We are also grateful to the IUAV PhD candidates and Master of Arts students in Fashion and Visual Arts who attended our seminars, for their enthusiasm and engagement with the project.

We thank Palazzo Grassi in Venice, and particularly Francesca Colasante, for inviting us in 2018 to co-curate and teach the annual 'Fashion Aperture' event and workshops at the Teatrino di Palazzo Grassi, in which we have continued to develop our thinking on fashion and time.

Caroline Evans thanks Central Saint Martins (University of the Arts) for its support on the project, in particular that of Professor Tom Corby, Associate Dean of Research, and his predecessor Professor Janet McDonnell. Alessandra Vaccari thanks the IUAV Department Director, Professor Aldo Aymonino, and the Associate Directors, Professors Laura Fregolent and Mario Lupano, for their commitment in facilitating research and teaching in fashion studies.

Thanks also go to our editors at Bloomsbury, Frances Arnold and Yvonne Thouroude, and to Merv Honeywood at RefineCatch, for their much appreciated help and enthusiasm at every stage of the work. We are grateful to Mimesis publishers in Milan for publishing the first iteration of this book in 2019.

Heartfelt thanks to our two research assistants for all their devoted work, without which this extended English-language edition could not have taken shape: Dr Lucy Moyse-Ferreira in London, and Dr Paolo Franzo in Venice. For generously allowing us to use their images, we thank Richard Maslow and Professor Judith Clark. Thanks too to Syd Shelton and Charlie Smith for their help in preparing the images for publication, and to Isabella Coraça Da Gama Vajano for help in sourcing a cover photograph.

For their rigorous, critical feedback on early drafts of the introduction, we are indebted to Dr Marketa Uhlirova and Professor Agnès Rocamora. For editorial assistance, thank you to Caitlin Storrie. We are grateful to the anonymous Bloomsbury peer reviewers whose insightful suggestions pushed us to develop our research in new directions. To all our contributors, many of whom generously allowed us to reproduce their texts at no cost, we extend our thanks.

Lastly, we thank our families and friends for all their support. Above all, warm thanks and appreciation go to our partners, Gian Paolo Chiari and Calum Storrie, indefatigable readers and critics, who gave up so much of their own time to help us put time into this book.

We have gone to every length to trace and secure rights for all the texts and images in this book. Any omissions will be acknowledged and corrected in future editions.

Introduction

Time in Fashion: An Introductory Essay

Caroline Evans and Alessandra Vaccari

Few phenomena embody the notion of time as well as fashion. Rooted in the 'now', it creates its own past through the process of rapid style change. Fast-moving, it is always on the verge of becoming something else. Uniquely poised between the past and the future, fashion has a curious affinity with unorthodox models of time. Historians, philosophers and social scientists have theorized different time regimes. In their account, time is a construct rather than a natural fact, despite our experience of it as something that just is. These various models give us ways to understand aspects of fashion that other approaches cannot describe. This is because fashion is more than an image or an object; it is also performative, which makes it a time-based and time-specific medium more than other kinds of design.

The relationship between fashion and time is at the heart of the definition of fashion itself, highlighting both its material and its immaterial aspects. The Italian philosopher Giorgio Agamben has defined 'the time of fashion' as 'an ungraspable threshold between a "not yet" [*non ancora*] and a "no more" [*non più*]', which he identifies as a caesura between 'being-in-fashion or no-longer-being-in-fashion'.[1] Agamben's definition suggests the changeability and speed of fashion. In a similar vein, Sophie Woodward and Tom Fisher have cautioned against a tendency to fix the 'fashion moment' in material culture approaches to the subject. Rather, they argue, such approaches should study the dynamic between the 'creation and dissolution of fashions'.[2] Turning to the everyday experience of fashion, Heike Jenss has maintained that fashion can be seen as a 'material mode of "making time"', perhaps as an effort of making time and present

[1]   Giorgio Agamben, 'What is the Contemporary?' in *What is an Apparatus? and Other Essays*, trans. David Kishik and Stefan Pedatella (Stanford University Press, 2009), 47 and 48.
[2]   Sophie Woodward and Tom Fisher, 'Fashioning Through Materials: Material Culture, Materiality and Processes of Materialization', *Critical Studies in Fashion & Beauty* 5, no. 1 (2014), 6.

materially graspable, of inscribing oneself into the moment'.[3] Wearing fashion is therefore a way of 'wearing time', to borrow a phrase from Tom Gunning and Marketa Uhlirova.[4]

This anthology looks at the subject of wearing time in fashion over 200 years, from the eighteenth century to the present. It also investigates many other dimensions of the relation between fashion and time, including how fashion is made in time, and at ways in which time can be crystallized or materialized in fashion. It juxtaposes well-known texts with lesser ones, in an interdisciplinary approach that includes philosophy, political economy, history, literature, media and fashion design. About half the texts are academic, but the remainder span many genres: autobiography, journalism, web posts, press releases, fiction and even an adjudication on a fashion advertisement by a UK government agency. The mix of academic and non-academic writing is in order to include texts that are not just about time, but that are exercises in their own right in writing time. The book does not set out to be an authority on, or compilation of, the standard texts on fashion and time. Instead, its selection and juxtaposition of texts constitute a proposition or, rather, a speculation: on the wider ramifications of the subject, on its implications for methodologies in fashion studies, and perhaps even for alternative ways that time and fashion can be conceptualized.

Instead of considering time in the conventional sense as a sequence of past, present and future, the book proposes three alternative ways to think about the relationships of time and fashion: industrial time, antilinear time and uchronic time.[5] The first concerns the seasonal nature of Western fashion as an industry that has impacted on workers and wearers alike. The second gives us a way of looking at fashion design as a ceaseless process of quotation, reconstruction and recombination of motifs, in which nostalgia and revivals play their part. The third construes fashion's 'imaginary', with its capacity for fantasy and myth-making, as a form of alternative history that asks 'what if?' Scrambling time, it rewrites fashion history as a kind of fiction. The term uchronia is a nineteenth-

3   Heike Jenss, *Fashioning Memory: Vintage Style and Youth Culture* (London and New York: Bloomsbury, 2015), 139.
4   Tom Gunning and Marketa Uhlirova (eds), *Wearing Time: Past, Present, Future, Dream* (London: Fashion in Film Festival Tenth Anniversary Programme, 2017), 5.
5   See too Caroline Evans and Alessandra Vaccari, *Il tempo della moda* (Milano and Udine: Mimesis, 2019).

century neologism derived from the word 'utopia', replacing place (*topos*) with time (*chronos*). It usually refers to an idealized or semi-fictional view of the past. In this book, the term is used as a way to investigate the stories that fashion tells about its past and its imagined future.

Through these analytically distinct categories, the book investigates the relative and multiple natures of fashion time. But although the categories are used to structure the book into three discrete sections, in reality they often overlap. To give just one example, vintage fashion may entail both antilinear and uchronic time: antilinear, because it brings past fashion to life through revivalism and recycling; uchronic, as it creatively reinvents the motifs of the past in the present.

Fashion time and globalization

In *Fashion History: A Global View*, Linda Welters and Abby Lillethun have challenged the dominant discourse of fashion history that identifies fashion as a purely Western phenomenon, based on rapid style change, and beginning in fourteenth-century European courts. Instead, they argue that because 'the measurement of time is a flexible concept . . . the desire for novelty existed across time and space . . . a slower arc of change than in Western capitalistic societies should not be a hindrance for conceptualizing change in styles in both premediaeval and non-Western dress as fashion.'[6] Their convincing case studies span more than 2,000 years and four continents. This 'slower arc of change' can be further nuanced – indeed problematized in some cases – by invoking Homi Bhabha's notion of the time-lag of cultural difference, which he discusses in relation to subaltern and postcolonial agency. His 'lag' is not a geographical one, but a lag in signification, and it enables Bhabha to posit 'new and hybrid agencies and articulations' on behalf of subaltern cultures as part of his critique of 'the limits of liberalism in the postcolonial perspective'.[7] It is with this in mind that this anthology begins by looking at fashion in relation to capitalist time, and

---

[6]   Linda Welters and Abby Lillethun, *Fashion History: A Global View* (London: Bloomsbury, 2018), 195. The book's argument builds on Jennifer Craik's proposal that Eurocentric accounts of fashion needed to be rethought in *The Face of Fashion: Cultural Studies in Fashion* (London and New York: Routledge, 1993).

[7]   Homi K. Bhabha, *The Location of Culture* (London and New York: Routledge, 1994), 274–76.

then goes on to consider two different models of time that may be interpreted as either complicit with, or antithetical to, the first.

Another way to conceive of these three models of time is in relation to art historian Keith Moxey's three concepts of time. The first, *chronology*, relates to industrial time. Moxey, among others, has criticized the notion of chronology as 'a motivated temporal trajectory whose significance is restricted to Euro-American culture'.[8] He has opened it up to culturally diverse and subaltern histories by adding two other concepts of time: *heterochrony*, meaning many co-existing times (relevant to antilinear time) and *anachrony*, meaning 'out of time' (relevant to uchronic time).[9] While heterochrony addresses the nature of social time, anachrony focuses on the category of individual aesthetic experience, whereby images or works of arts have 'the capacity to create their own time for attentive beholders'.[10] But the overall point to Moxey's tripartite division of time is this: his account begins with a critique of the Western-centric notion of chronological time. And this is a criticism that has also been levelled against the Eurocentric definitions of fashion that have until recently dominated fashion studies.

The first section of this book, on industrial time, shows the limits of inflexible, linear time adopted by both Western and many non-Western countries, especially the colonized, in the nineteenth century. The excerpts range from Karl Marx's critique of the 'fashion season' to what is effectively a modern-day time and motion study designed to streamline the speed of making a T-shirt in a Bangladeshi factory [*Karl Marx*] [*Ramij Howlader et al.*].[11] The two sections that follow, however, on antilinear and uchronic time, investigate the potentialities of fashion time as flexible. Just as Moxey proposes his second two categories (heterochrony and anachrony) as antidotes to the rigidity of chronology, which allow the emergence of subaltern histories, so too do the second two categories of the book make space for accounts of, for example, colonial time [*Victoria L. Rovine*], women's time [*Ilya Parkins*] and queer time [*Emma Katherine Atwood*].

---

[8]　Keith Moxey, *Visual Time: The Image in History* (Durham, NC and London, Duke University Press, 2013), 2.

[9]　Moxey, *Visual Time*, 3. Elizabeth Freeman agrees with Moxey in arguing that anachronism helps to overcome a 'notion of time as sequential and forward-moving, which is to say, without a Western, Enlightenment conceptualization of history as empty, homogeneous, and linear'. Elizabeth Freeman, 'Synchronic / Anachronic', in Joel Burges and Amy J. Elias (eds), *Time: A Vocabulary of the Present* (New York: New York University Press, 2016), 134.

[10]　Moxey, *Visual Time*, 174.

[11]　Throughout this introductory chapter, italicized names in square brackets designate a contributor to the book on the relevant topic.

These particular excerpts add to the book's overarching discourse on fashion, time and capitalism, providing some further nuances to the understanding of time in a global fashion perspective.

The section on industrial time deals with the Western fashion system and its fallout. While non-Eurocentric time is associated with flexibility, the myth of flexibility is also at the core of twenty-first-century capitalism. In 2008, Mark Fisher argued that the new 'flexibility' of post-Fordist production was if anything more pernicious than the old 'rigidity' of the Fordist production that it replaced. He associated 'flexibility' with the deregulation of capital and labour, and the casualization of the workforce, in ways that are directly applicable to mass fashion production in a globalized world. Describing twenty-first-century workers in post-Fordist economies, Fisher wrote:

> Work and life become inseparable. Capital follows you wherever you dream. Time ceases to be linear, becomes chaotic, broken down into punctiform divisions. As production and distribution are restructured, so are nervous systems. To function effectively as a component of just-in-time production you must develop a capacity to respond to unforeseen events, you must learn to live in conditions of total instability, or 'precarity', as the ugly neologism has it. Periods of work alternate with periods of unemployment. Typically, you find yourself employed in a series of short-term jobs, unable to plan for the future.[12]

This type of precarity spans most sectors of the fashion industry today, from mass fashion to high-end designer fashion.

In around 2015, high fashion brands began to experiment with 'seasonless' collections, renaming them February and September rather than spring/summer and autumn/winter. This new nomenclature highlighted the globalized nature of fashion, and signalled the beginning of the end of the Eurocentrism that was historically embedded in the idea of the fashion season. As fashion journalists Imran Amed and Kate Abnett explained in 2016, the seasonless formula was conceived 'with an eye towards global consumers who live in non-Western markets with different climatic patterns' [*Samuel Patrick Thomas*].[13] In fact the

12 Mark Fisher, *Capitalist Realism: Is There No Alternative?* (Winchester UK: Zero Books, 2009), 33–34.
13 Imran Amed and Kate Abnett, 'Burberry Aligns Runway and Retail Calendar in Game-Changing Shift', *The Business of Fashion*, 5 February 2016, https://www.businessoffashion.com/articles/news-analysis/burberry-aligns-runway-and-retail-calendar-in-game-changing-shift (accessed 21 June 2018).

incompatibility between European and Asian seasons had been raised in the 1960s when, according to Didier Grumbach, 'a new phenomenon was taking shape in the geography of international fashion: the Japanese market was opening up to Western fashion.'[14] It took another 50 years, however, and the reshaping of global fashion consumption, for the fashion industry to sit up and listen.

The claim for time as a flexible concept, then, bears further scrutiny and dissection. Any account of modern fashion time has to be rooted in an account of neoliberalism, as well as of its origins in specific, earlier moments in capitalist development, in order to avoid slipping into essentialising ways of thinking about world cultures as equally diverse. Rather, it is important to pay attention to the very real inequalities, fissures and unevenness between nations, peoples and economies that go to make up the global.[15] This is particularly so in an age of fast fashion, which Tansy E. Hoskins has discussed in relation to global as well as local inequalities in class and labour relations.[16]

At the same time however, as Moxey reminds us, there are alternative models of time with more liberatory ambitions. An important example is the concept of Afrofuturism, coined by Mark Dery in the 1990s, and since manifested in fashion and music, and which can be regarded as a parallel practice to critiques of colonial and postcolonial fashion time.[17] As well as offering an inventive reclamation of black identity through performance, self-fashioning and styling, Afrofuturism provides alternative narratives of time. As Sonja Eismann has written: 'In Afrofuturism's self-fashioned universe of alternative histories, geographies, and identities, members of the African diaspora imagine themselves as utopian space travellers with roots in Egyptian mythology as well as in space-age mysticism, unbound by the chains of slavery and racism.'[18] Eismann goes on

---

[14] Didier Grumbach, *History of International Fashion*, trans. © Roli Books (Northampton, MA: Interlink Publishing Group, 2014), 84.

[15] Michael Hardt and Antonio Negri, *Empire* (Cambridge, MA: Harvard University Press, 2000). Sabine Ichikawa, 'Creative industries: The Case of Fashion', in Helmut K. Anheier and Yudhishthir Raj Isar (eds), *Cultures and Globalization Series 2: The Cultural Economy* (London: Sage, 2008), 253–60.

[16] Tansy E. Hoskins, *Stitched-Up: The Anti-Capitalist Book of Fashion* (London: Pluto Press, 2014).

[17] Mark Dery, 'Black to the Future', in Mark Dery (ed.), *Flame Wars: the Discourse of Cyberculture* (London and Durham NC: Duke University Press, 1994), 179–222.

[18] Sonja Eismann, 'Afrofuturism as a Strategy for Decolonising the Global Fashion Archive', in Elke Gaugele and Monica Titton (eds), *Fashion and Postcolonial Critique* (Berlin: Sternberg Press, 2019), 67–68.

to cite Laura Halvin's claim that 'Time, for an Afrofuturist, is a fluid concept, and the terms past, present and future aren't necessarily linear.'[19]

Linear and cyclical fashion time

There are two principal models of time inherited from late-nineteenth and early twentieth-century modernity: the linear and the cyclical. In this book, we have drawn on these two categories to elaborate a more conceptually updated and challenging way of conceiving the relationships between fashion and time. The outcome is the triad of industrial, antilinear and uchronic time that structures the book. Of necessity, working with the themes of time and fashion brings with it a sense of history as the passage of time, and with that comes an awareness of historiography and its importance. For that reason, it is important to begin with a brief look at the traditional linear–cyclical dichotomy, in order to highlight the overlapping influences and oppositions of the book's three categories.

Since the time of Isaac Newton, and probably before, linear time – in Eugene Holland's analysis – has conventionally been depicted as a straight line in which 'each passing moment recedes behind the present, just as each approaching moment arrives from a future stretched out in front of us along the line we are travelling.'[20] The idea of the linear progression of time was pivotal in the development of the field of fashion history in the nineteenth century, which focused on the Western tradition and often adopted the standard annual calendar of the fashion industry. The proliferation of nineteenth-century European and North American fashion magazines also influenced the construction of a chronologically ordered account of fashion change. Indeed, the role of fashion magazines was so important that the French archaeologist Jules Quicherat, author of *Histoire du costume en France* (1857), claimed that the appearance of the first fashion magazines in the 1770s had rendered the fashion historian's work obsolete, and he therefore saw no reason to cover fashion after the eighteenth

---

[19] Laura Havlin, 'A History of Female Afrofuturist Fashion', *Another Mag*, 16 September 2015, n.p. Available at https://www.anothermag.com/fashion-beauty/7791/a-history-of-female-afrofuturist-fashion (accessed 28 November 2019).

[20] Eugene Holland, 'Non-Linear Historical Materialism; Or, What is Revolutionary in Deleuze & Guattari's Philosophy of History?', in Bernd Herzogenrath (ed.), *Time and History in Deleuze and Serres* (New York and London: Continuum, 2012), 22.

century in his book.[21] Timothy Campbell has argued that the consumer revolution of eighteenth-century Britain was linked to the rise of a new kind of historical self-consciousness, in which fashion and its imagery played a key role. His thesis is that, in a modern society, fashion inculcates a sense of history, including of the recent past.[22] The speed of fashion in the late eighteenth century, he argues, gave people a sense of how to see themselves in history.

The overlap between linear and industrial time recurred in twentieth-century fashion journalism that replaced the notion of the century with the concept of the decade as a key element in the construction of chronology. Against those writers who uncritically embraced this new regimentation of time, the fashion historian Christopher Breward has argued that the historian needs to make a 'distinction between "decadism" as a reflection of market and media demands, and its use as an artificial organizational device, unconnected to historical events'.[23]

The introduction of the model of cyclical time to fashion studies stems mainly from early twentieth-century social and economic sciences. In a seminal study of 1919, the North American anthropologist Alfred L. Kroeber applied a quantitative approach to measure changes in Western women's dress through the centuries. The outcome of his research was a model of time represented by 'simple geometrical curves', and characterized by a 'repeated return of what had receded into the past'.[24] Fashion magazines were a privileged source for Kroeber, who held them in great esteem because, he stated, 'they are exactly dated; and they bring together in each volume a considerable number of examples to which rule and calipers can be applied without hindrance'.[25] For him, the images furnished by magazines enabled a better understanding of fashion change than the 'knowledge of real dress'.[26]

---

[21] Jules Quicherat, *Histoire du Costume en France depuis les temps les plus reculés jusqu'à la fin du XVIIIe siècle* (Paris: Hachette, 1875).

[22] Timothy Campbell, *Historical Style: Fashion and the New Mode of History, 1740–1830* (Philadelphia: University of Pennsylvania Press, 2016), 14–16 and 24–27.

[23] Christopher Breward, *The Culture of Fashion: A New History of Fashionable Dress* (Manchester and New York: Manchester University Press, 1995), 185.

[24] Alfred L. Kroeber, 'On the Principle of Order in Civilization as Exemplified by Changes in Fashion', *American Anthropologist*, New Series, 21 (3), 1919, 235; Agata Zborowska, 'Invoking the Spirit of Fashion', *Czas Kultury*, no. 173 (2013): 151. Available at http://czaskultury.pl/en/wp-content/uploads/2017/02/AZborowska_InvokingTheSpiritOfFashion_CzasKultury_2_2013.pdf (accessed 6 November 2019).

[25] Kroeber, 'On the principle of order', 238.

[26] Ibid.

Kroeber, however, viewed fashion change in an abstract and universal form, and took no account of its historical, social or cultural diversity. Nor did Agnes Brooks Young, in her analysis of fashion cycles in the 1930s.[27] Kroeber and Young both aimed to reveal the recurrence of Western styles of the past, in order to create data sets conducive to trend forecasting. This vision is in some respects consistent with the concept of industrial time in so far as, according to Young, the cyclical approach endorses the idea of fashion as 'evolution without destination'.[28]

In an entirely different vein, Julia Kristeva has proposed the concept of cyclical time as 'women's time', and as the time of 'female subjectivity' in opposition to the model of time as linear and progressive. Conceived of as existing outside the dominant histories made by men, women's time is a 'future perfect' tense that leads to the rediscovery of something forgotten, as projections of the past resurface in the future.[29] Drawing on Kristeva, Granata has applied the concept of cyclicality to fashion, in order to reflect on the 'subject-in-process', and on experimental fashion as a dynamic of transformation [*Francesca Granata*].[30] Parkins has analysed turn-of-the-century 'time consciousness' as highly gendered, and tending to polarize between men and women, but she has argued that the relationship between the two was, in fact, subtly imbricated [*Ilya Parkins*].[31] Both these writers are included in the section on antilinear time, therefore, because they break the mould of thinking about fashion cycles as repetitive and inherently predictable.

The notion of time as either linear or cyclical was criticized as redundant in 2000 by Zygmunt Bauman in his account of 'liquid modernity'.[32] He argued that modern time consists of a series of arbitrary, unpredictable moments which are

[27] Agnes Brooks Young, *Recurring Cycles of Fashion, 1760–1937* (New York and London: Harpers & Bros, 1937).

[28] Young, *Recurring Cycles*, 5.

[29] Julia Kristeva, 'Women's Time', trans. Alice Jardine and Harry Blake, *Signs* 7, no. 1 (1981): 14; Alice Jardine, 'Introduction to Julia Kristeva's "Women's Time"', *Signs* 7, no. 1 (1981): 5.

[30] Francesca Granata, 'Fitting Sources – Tailoring Methods: A Case Study of Martin Margiela and the Temporalities of Fashion'. In Heike Jenss (ed.), *Fashion Studies: Research Methods, Sites and Practices* (London and New York, Bloomsbury, 2016), 148–59; Kristeva, 'Women's Time', 13–35.

[31] Ilya Parkins, 'Fashion as Methodology: Rewriting the Time of Women's History', *Time and Society* 19, no. 1 (2010): 98–119; Ilya Parkins, *Poiret, Dior and Schiaparelli: Fashion, Femininity and Modernity* (London: Bloomsbury, 2013), 25–46.

[32] Zygmunt Bauman quoted in Agnès Rocamora, 'New Fashion Times: Fashion and Digital Media' in Sandy Black et al. (eds), *The Handbook of Fashion Studies* (London and New York: Bloomsbury, 2013), 64.

hard to make sense of in the instant. And in his 2010 article on fashion as a 'perpetuum mobile' he compared fashion to an endless cycle of change in which novelty constantly replaces the old, which would suggest that fashion is more of a vicious circle than a repetitive cycle.[33] If liquid modernity was all about constant change, then the fashion principle for Bauman was an unchanging constant. Bauman's critique is of fashion as a consumer industry, and here the notion of industrial time comes into its own.

Industrial time

The concept of 'industrial time' identifies the seasonal nature of fashion as an industry, and shows how this has impacted on workers and wearers alike. It corresponds with the period of post-Enlightenment modernity and the nineteenth-century colonial expansion of global capitalism. Accordingly, this section of the book deals with Western fashion in relation to dominant nineteenth-century ideologies concerning time and cultural value. It looks at both the production and the consumption of fashion, but focuses more on the former. Starting with Marx's critique of the 'meaningless, murderous caprices of fashion', it reflects primarily on the ways of measuring time that were created by the fashion system in the nineteenth century, with its historical relation both to the rhythms of industrial production and to the social season.[34] In Marx's analysis, fashion played a crucial role 'as motor, product, and metaphor of the capitalist system', as pointed out by the cultural theorist Esther Leslie.[35] What was or was not fashionable, according to Marx, was determined by the social season. The social season set the pace for a biannual cycle of production that existed at all levels of the garment industry, from home dressmakers to large-scale factories.

---

[33] Zygmunt Bauman 'Perpetuum Mobile', *Critical Studies in Fashion and Beauty* 1, no. 1 (2010): 55–63. With grateful thanks to Marketa Uhlirova for these ideas. See too Zygmunt Bauman, *Legislators and Interpreters: On Modernity, Post-Modernity, Intellectuals* (Ithaca, NY: Cornell University Press, 1987), 165, where Bauman writes that 'Fashion seems to be the mechanism through which the "fundamental order" (market dependency) is maintained by a never ending chain of innovations; the very perpetuity of innovations renders their individual (as inevitable) failures irrelevant and harmless to the [overall] order.'

[34] Karl Marx, *Capital Volume I* [1867] trans. Ben Fowkes (Harmondsworth: Penguin 1976), 365.

[35] Esther Leslie, 'The Murderous, Meaningless Caprices of Fashion': Marx on Capital, Clothing and Fashion', in *Culture Matters*, 4 May (2018). Available at https://www.culturematters.org.uk/index.php/culture/clothing-fashion/item/2809-the-murderous-meaningless-caprices-of-fashion-marx-on-capital-clothing-and-fashion (accessed 4 January 2020).

As a result, Marx wrote, workers were cruelly over-worked for half the year, and equally cruelly unemployed for the other half.

Industrial time is 'clock time', as the British Marxist historian E. P. Thompson pointed out.[36] It is rationalized time, first standardized at the 'International Meridian Conference' in Washington DC in 1884 on the basis of Greenwich meantime, and then agreed by the Western powers in Paris in 1913, when the Eiffel Tower sent the first time signal transmitted around the world and, as Steven Kern has argued, 'the independence of local times began to collapse once the framework of a global electronic network was established'.[37] Thompson emphasized how 'mature industrial societies of all varieties are marked by time-thrift' and the creation of the 'industrial man went necessarily through the exercise of a 'time-discipline'.[38] Industrial time is the duration of the workday: the factory time between clocking on and off. It is the disciplined time of the workplace. It is the driver of the early twentieth-century time and motion studies pioneered by the American engineer Frank Bunker Gilbreth, and follows the principles of the scientific management of labour pioneered by Frederick Wilmslow Taylor in 1911.

Industrial time is also modernist time, and without it the fashion industry could not have expanded internationally in the twentieth century.[39] As Anja Aronowsky Cronberg has pointed out, its 'universal temporal framework, with time zones, seasonal changes and accurate clocks' created new technology and goods as well as new tastes and sensibilities.[40] According to Cronberg, the 'previous more subjective understanding of time had to make way for expedience and the hustle of modern life'.[41] One quotidian example of this inflexible temporal framework was the rigid differentiation of the personal wardrobe into day,

---

[36] E. P. Thompson, 'Time, Work-Discipline, and Industrial Capitalism', *Past & Present*, 38 (3), 1967, 56–97.

[37] Stephen Kern, *The Culture of Time and Space 1880–1918* (Cambridge, MA and London: Harvard University Press, 2nd ed. 2003), 14.

[38] Thompson, 'Time, Work-Discipline, and Industrial Capitalism', 93. On E.P. Thompson's conception of time, see too Arjun Appadurai, *Modernity at Large*, vol. I (Minneapolis: Minnesota University Press, 2003), 79.

[39] Caroline Evans, *The Mechanical Smile: Modernism and the First Fashion Shows in France and America, 1900–1929* (New Haven and London: Yale University Press, 2013), 57–58 and 221. On how the organization of time and space in the early twentieth century accelerated 'the turnover time of capitalist production' Evans cites David Harvey, *The Condition of Postmodernity: An Inquiry into the Origins of Cultural Change* (Oxford: Basil Blackwell, 1989), 266.

[40] Anja Aronowsky Cronberg, 'Editor's Letter', *Vestoj*, 5, 2014: 9–12. Available at: http://vestoj.com/issues/issue-five-on-slowness/ (accessed 24 June 2018).

[41] Cronberg, 'Editor's Letter', *Vestoj*, 9.

afternoon and evening wear: 'like an imaginary 24-hour assembly line', as Alessandra Vaccari has written, fashion imposed 'the rhythms of an ideal modern day' upon the individual.[42]

Yet it is important to remember that the idea of seasonal fashion originated long before the standardization of time. It lay in seventeenth-century France, in the reign of Louis XIV, when fashion was featured in the periodical *Le Mercure Galant*. Van de Peer explains its origins [*Aurélie Van de Peer*], and Chrisman-Campbell describes the rapidly accelerated pace of fashion change in the eighteenth century [*Kimberly Chrisman-Campbell*]. Between the 1860s and the 1920s, the seasonal structure of the modern Western fashion system was cemented by the production of biannual collections, which survive in today's autumn/winter and spring/summer collections. No other industry has had quite such a rigidly prescribed annual timetable, although the American automotive industry had yearly collections.

Twice a year, these collections are shown at fixed times in the 'fashion weeks' held in the major fashion capitals of Paris, New York, Milan and London; they are augmented by the addition of mid-season collections. And, apart from the big four, today there are other fashion weeks in cities throughout the time zones of the world – over one hundred at the time of writing, and still rising. The idea of strictly scheduled fashion collections that set the agenda for the international fashion business originated with the French haute couture union in 1911. Before then, both haute couture and women's ready-to-wear were represented by the same union, the *Chambre Syndicale de la confection et de la couture pour dames et fillettes* (founded in 1868). In 1910 a splinter group broke away, and in 1911 the *Chambre syndicale de la couture Parisienne* was formed, which clearly demarcated haute couture as a separate trade from ready-to-wear.[43]

Although foreign buyers from all over Europe and the Americas had travelled to Paris seasonally to purchase luxury goods and accessories since the nineteenth century, it was really with the centralized management of French haute couture in the twentieth century that the modern fashion calendar evolved.[44] In Paris

---

[42] Alessandra Vaccari, 'The Daily Wardrobe – The Chronometer of Fashion', in Mario Lupano and Alessandra Vaccari (eds), *Fashion at the Time of Fascism: Italian Modernist Lifestyle 1922–1943* (Bologna: Damiani, 2009), 64.

[43] Grumbach, *History*, 31–32.

[44] On nineteenth-century Paris fashion sales, see Françoise Tétart-Vittu, 'Naissance du couturier et du modèliste', in Françoise Tétart-Vittu and Jean-Pierre Vittu (eds), *Au paradis des dames: Nouveautés, modes et confections 1810–1870* (Paris: Paris-musées, 1992), 36.

and New York, seasonal fashion shows had begun to be staged from the 1890s. They became well established from the early 1900s, and from 1911 the *Chambre Syndicale* stipulated that haute couture houses had to present biannual collections in spring and autumn.[45] Gradually, these seasonal collections in Paris began to be held on the fixed dates of 1 February and 1 August, in order to facilitate the travel arrangements of the foreign buyers who flocked to Paris twice a year to buy export models.[46] The biennial shows were augmented by the introduction of mid-season shows in the 1920s, so that a couture house might be producing four collections a year to sell to overseas buyers at set times.

As Nancy Green has shown, early twentieth-century Paris couture was an export trade that dealt not in mass-produced fashion but in design ideas and prototypes, called 'models', and the right to reproduce them.[47] The transaction was dependent on an idea promulgated by all parties that French fashions were superior and world-leading in taste and originality. Between the 1930s and the 1950s, Italian couture, *alta moda*, developed along similar lines to the French.[48] Despite a few changes over the twentieth century, this seasonal pattern of international sales persisted as the dominant model of Western fashion time. The *Chambre Syndicale*'s edicts also impacted on the rhythms of the ready-to-wear industry, which depended on the cultural capital of haute couture for its marketing and sales. The *Chambre* decided the fashion show biannual schedules, and the delivery dates of the first models to the buyers; it controlled the release of promotional materials to journalists, specified the first dates on which they could publish their copy, and ruthlessly banned any journalist who broke this rule by withdrawing the press card that gave them vital access to the collections.[49]

The *Chambre*'s control was absolute and, throughout the twentieth century, this annual timetable dominated the working routine of fashion designers across the board, who had to learn to work six months ahead of time, and to keep two seasons' collections in mind simultaneously. The section of the book devoted to industrial time therefore pays special attention to the figure of the designer, to

[45] Evans, *Mechanical Smile*, 30–32 and 77–78.
[46] Evans, *Mechanical Smile*, 33.
[47] Nancy L. Green, *Ready-to-Wear, Ready-to-Work: a Century of Industry and Immigrants in Paris and New York* (Durham and London: Duke University Press, 1997), 120.
[48] Grumbach, *History*, 82. See too Maria Luisa Frisa, Anna Mattirolo, Stefano Tonchi (eds), *Bellissima: l'Italia dell'alta moda, 1945–1968* (Milan: Electa, 2014), which argues that Italian *alta moda* began in 1945.
[49] Grumbach, *History*, 92–96. See too Alexandra Palmer, *Couture & Commerce: The Transatlantic Fashion Trade in the 1950s* (Vancouver: UBC Press, 2001).

whom, since the nineteenth century, Western fashion narratives had given the task of embodying fashion change and representing the *zeitgeist*.[50] Even the starriest of designers has always had to submit to the authority of the fashion calendar. In her autobiography, the ready-to-wear London designer Mary Quant grumbles that she always had to keep two parallel timetables in mind [*Mary Quant*]. One was the schedule of the collection which she was working on that she had to keep secret; the other was the current collection that she had to pretend to the press was fresh and new, even though she had designed it six months previously.

Quant thus distances herself from the narrative of the long periods of inspiration, concentration and lonely retreats so peculiar to French haute couturiers such as Christian Dior and Yves Saint Laurent. The former habitually retired to his family country home in Granville to design the new collections, while the latter used to leave Paris and take refuge in his Marrakech house. The contrast between Quant (with her love for the chaos of the city) and the two couturiers highlights two different approaches to time: the hectic rhythms of youth-oriented ready-to-wear fashion on the one hand, and the extended time and labour of custom-made haute couture on the other. This mythologizing persists in the present, as when a design company promotes the aura of each luxury dress by listing the thousands of hours of hand-sewing that went into it (as in Valentino's haute couture spring/summer 2016 press release).

Even today, designer-led fashion remains linked to the nineteenth-century model of biannual collections that are shown six months ahead. Designers complain, just as Quant did 50 years earlier, of the time constraints and anxiety induced by their production schedules [*Anja Aronowsky Cronberg and Christophe Lemaire*]. A well-known example is Raf Simons, the Belgian designer who resigned in 2015 from his post as creative director at Dior, where he had a workload of six shows per year. He explained his decision by saying, 'I'm not the kind of person who likes to do things so fast' and that he needed more time to design his own brand, to follow his cultural interests and, particularly, to have more 'incubation time for ideas'.[51] The fashion journalist Suzy Menkes has spoken out about the increase of fashion shows – 'Ten shows a year' and 'a show nearly

---

[50]   Alessandra Vaccari, *La moda nei discorsi dei designer* (Bologna: CLUEB, 2012), 62.
[51]   Quoted in Cathy Horyn, 'Why Raf Simons Is Leaving Christian Dior', *The Cut*, 22 October 2015. Available at https://www.thecut.com/2015/10/raf-simons-leaving-christian-dior.html (accessed 22 June 2018).

every month' – which she connected to the increasing pace of fashion. She speculated that 'the pace of fashion was part of the problem behind the decline of John Galliano, the demise of Alexander McQueen', and concluded that 'nonstop shows seem a high price to pay for the "newness" demand of fashion now. The strain on both budgets and designers is heavy'.[52]

Menkes was discussing high-end designer fashion in the twenty-first century. But the speed of mass market fashion production had accelerated a century earlier, in both Europe and North America, due to progressive standardization [*Georg Simmel*]. As the century advanced, the industry produced increasingly efficient responses to market demand by reducing the length of the design, production and distribution phases. In the 1950s the concept of 'just-in-time' production was elaborated in Japan where it was first adopted by Toyota, and then by the global automobile industry, from where it spread to a number of industrial fields, including the fashion industry. The use of the 'quick response' system in the supply chain allowed ready-to-wear fashion to speed up the distribution between producers and retailers, thus accelerating retail sales flows.[53] This concept was specifically developed for the North American apparel industry by Kurt Salmon Associates, whose 1986 study of the old distribution system had shown that it took an average of 66 weeks from manufacture for a product to reach the store.[54]

By contrast, in 2012 it took Spanish brand Zara no more than 13 days to take a product from the factory to the shop floor.[55] Zara provided an example of progressive time compression through 'vertical integration' which allowed it to control every stage of the supply chain from manufacture to distribution. In 2013 the sociologist Agnès Rocamora argued that 'modernity has entered a new phase, characterized by the intensification of speed and the valuing of immediacy and real time . . . with the rise of new technologies fashion time has speeded up; a new fashion time has emerged defined by acceleration and immediacy'.[56]

[52] Quoted in Valerie Steele, 'Fashion Futures', in Adam Geczy and Vicki Karaminas (eds), *The End of Fashion: Clothing and Dress in the Age of Globalization* (London: Bloomsbury, 2019), 11.
[53] See Leopoldina Fortunati and Elda Danese, *Manuale di comunicazione, sociologia e cultura della moda*, 3: *Made in Italy* (Rome: Meltemi, 2005). See too https://mainstaymfg.com/just-in-time-manufacturing-eliminate-waste-improve-productivity/ (accessed 2 November 2019).
[54] Liz Barnes and Gaynor Lea–Greenwood, 'Fast Fashioning the Supply Chain: Shaping the Research Agenda', *Journal of Fashion Marketing and Management: an International Journal* 19, no. 3 (2006): 259–71.
[55] Alice Payne, 'Counting the Cost of Fast Fashion', *The Conversation*, 16 February 2012. Available at http://theconversation.com/counting-the-cost-of-fast-fashion-5297 (accessed 27 November 2019).
[56] Rocamora, 'New Fashion Times', 61.

One of the defining characteristics of the relatively recent phenomenon of 'fast fashion' (cheap, disposable and mass produced garments, made for Western consumers in non-Western factories, with scant regard for ethics or sustainability) was that it no longer obeyed the dictates of the biannual fashion seasons, instead bringing new designs to the stores on a rolling programme throughout the year.[57] This time compression was augmented by the Internet, and it became an ongoing process. By 2017, online retailers like Boohoo, Asos and Missguided took no longer than a week or two to bring products from the design studio to the market, wrote the market analyst Deborah Weinswig, who emphasized how these brands were 'faster than traditional fast-fashion retailers' and dubbed the phenomenon 'ultrafast fashion'.[58]

With its aspiration to constant novelty, lower retail prices and instant availability, fast and ultrafast fashion has had dramatic consequences for workers. Trade unions called the catastrophic collapse of the Rana Plaza complex in Bangladesh in 2014 a 'mass industrial homicide', as 1,134 workers lost their lives and another 2,500 were injured.[59] The case of this notorious outsourcing hotspot for fast fashion brands recalls, on a giant scale, the overwork and poor working conditions the led to the death of the milliner Mary Anne Walkley, as described by Marx, and the Triangle Shirtwaist Factory Fire in New York in 1911, when 147 workers perished and a further 78 were injured.

Rocamora has highlighted the ways in which fashion communication and marketing had speeded up as a consequence of the newly accelerated pace of fashion design and sales [*Agnès Rocamora*]. New fashion media had effectively abolished the boundaries between work time and leisure time, as could also be seen in the ways that the 'immaterial labour' of fashion modelling in the twenty-first century had changed.[60] Similarly, Jonathan Crary has argued that production and consumption had become round-the-clock activities, effectively abolishing

[57] Rocamora, 'New Fashion Times', 67.
[58] Deborah Weinswig, 'Fast Fashion Speeding Toward Ultra Fast Fashion', *Fung Global Retail and Technology*, 19 May 2017. Available at: https://www.fungglobalretailtech.com/research/fast-fashion-speeding-toward-ultrafast-fashion/ (accessed 4 July 2018).
[59] Michael Safi and Dominic Rushe, 'Rana Plaza, Five Years On: Safety of Workers Hangs in Balance in Bangladesh', *Guardian*, 24 April 2018. Available at: https://www.theguardian.com/global-development/2018/apr/24/bangladeshi-police-target-garment-workers-union-rana-plaza-five-years-on (accessed 7 July 2018). See too Tansy E. Hoskins, *Stitched Up*.
[60] Elizabeth Wissinger, 'Modelling a Way of Life: Immaterial and Affective Labour in the Fashion Modelling Industry', *Ephemera*, 7 (1), 2007: 250–69. See too Maurizio Lazzarato, 'Immaterial Labour', in Paolo Virno and Michael Hardt (eds), *Radical Thought In Italy: A Potential Politics* (Minneapolis, MN: University of Minnesota Press, 1996).

the regular alternation of night and day, including the metabolic patterns of sleep. It was, he wrote, 'a time without sequence or recurrence . . . a hallucination of presence'. Nowhere is this demonstrated more clearly than in the way that fashion began to circulate as data. In Crary's words, 'no moment, place, or situation now exists in which one can *not* shop, consume, or exploit networked resources, there is a relentless incursion of the non-time of 24/7 into every aspect of personal or social life'. Crary called this a 'systemic colonization of individual experience'.[61] When designers live-streamed their collections, and influencers and bloggers commented on the collections the moment they appear on the catwalk and the web (often ahead of the traditional press) the institutional idea of the fashion season was effectively dismantled, as the conventionally agreed time-lag between showing fashion on the runway, reporting on it in print, producing the garments and selling them in shops no longer existed.

In the 2010s, Burberry, Tom Ford, Moschino and Versace (Versus) were among the early adopters of a new way of selling directly from the catwalk, the 'see now, buy now' model, also known as 'instant runway-to-shop'.[62] It meant that a customer could buy a look as soon as it appeared on the runway, rather than having to wait six months for it to appear in the shops. This strategy effectively mimicked fast fashion as it dramatically reduced the time between the fashion show and the in-store availability of the new collection. It was made possible by the new public access to fashion shows (which had previously been elite, private affairs), enabled initially through websites such as style.com, created by Condé Nast in 2000, and then, at the end of the first decade, through live-streaming.[63] As fashion designer and creative director Tom Ford explained in the press release of his men's and womenswear collections for autumn/winter 2016, 'The current way of showing a collection four months before it is available to customers is an antiquated idea and one that no longer makes sense. We have been living with a fashion calendar and system that is from another era. Our customers today want a collection that is immediately available'.[64]

[61] Jonathan Crary, *24/7: Late Capitalism and the Ends of Sleep* (London: Verso, 2013, 2014), 4, 29–30 and 52.

[62] Sarah White, 'Fashion Firms Dither over Instant Shopping on the Catwalk', in *Reuters*, 20 February 2018. Available at https://uk.reuters.com/article/us-fashion-retail/fashion-firms-dither-over-instant-shopping-on-the-catwalk-idUKKCN1G40RY (accessed 27 November 2019).

[63] Caroline Evans, 'Yesterday's Emblems and Tomorrow's Commodities: The Return of the Repressed in Fashion Imagery Today', in Stella Bruzzi and Pamela Church Gibson (eds), *Fashion Cultures Revisited: Theories, Explorations and Analysis* (London and New York: Routledge, 2nd ed. 2013), 78.

[64] Tom Ford, press release autumn/winter 2016, available at https://www.tomford.com/TFBrand_AW16_Presentation_2.html?fdid=brand (accessed 27 June 2018).

The 'see now, buy now' model was not universally accepted, however, and the luxury brands belonging to the powerful LVMH and Kering groups opposed it. Young independent designers who produce on a much smaller scale also complained about it, arguing that this new distribution strategy only worked for large, established firms.

To sum up, the retail forms of twenty-first-century fast fashion, as well as of designer-led fashion, have thus dramatically overturned the traditional fashion calendar derived from haute couture that dominated mass fashion for most of the twentieth century. All this points to the fact that, since the beginning of the twenty-first century, the fashion industry has had to profoundly reorganize its calendar, and to revise the ideas of seasonal fashion and of fashion weeks. In a broader context, many designers have claimed that the stranglehold of the nineteenth-century fashion system no longer works, and that fashion is 'broken'. In 2014 the respected trend forecaster Li Edelkoort wrote a pamphlet on these topics titled 'Anti-Fashion: Ten Reasons Why the Fashion System is Obsolete'.[65] Yet no-one seemed to have a solution. Meanwhile, further criticism of the system came from two other arenas: slow fashion and fashion activism.

If the new millennium began with an unprecedented growth of the fast fashion sector, 'slow fashion' emerged as a backlash phenomenon. It was part of a wider social movement promoting slow values in many fields. The expression came from the 'slow food' movement that started in Italy in the 1980s as a protest against the spread of fast food chains such as McDonald's in a country with a strong tradition of regional cuisines and small scale, family-run restaurants.[66] Like slow food, slow fashion was not just about speed, it was also about values, especially the need for better, and more ethical, patterns of work and consumption [*Kate Fletcher*]. In 2008 Hazel Clark explored some possible contradictions in the term, asking whether slow fashion really was a sustainable solution, or an oxymoron engendered by the contradictions of the modern fashion industry.[67]

[65]   https://mycourses.aalto.fi/pluginfile.php/243780/course/section/70823/anti_fashion_
        manifesto011.pdf (accessed 28 November 2019). Also BoF https://www.businessoffashion.com/
        articles/voices/li-edelkoort-anti-fashion-manifesto-fashion-is-old-fashioned
[66]   Kate Fletcher and Mathilda Tham, 'Clothing Rhythms', in Ed van Hinte (ed.), *Eternally Yours: Time
        in Design* (Rotterdam: 010 Publishers, 2004), 254–74. Kate Fletcher, 'Slow Fashion: An Invitation for
        Systems Change', *Fashion Practice*, 2 (2), 2010: 259–65. See also https://www.slowfood.com/
        (accessed 7 July 2018).
[67]   Hazel Clark, 'Slow + Fashion – an Oxymoron – or a Promise for the Future . . .?', *Fashion Theory* 12,
        no. 4 (2008): 427–46.

Nevertheless the 'slow fashion' movement attracted a mix of environmentally conscious people, activists, niche brands and fashion designers. Among the latter was the designer Carol Christian Poell who, from the beginning of his career in 1994, adopted a radical, slow approach to fashion design, *à rebours* when compared with sweatshops, and to the deadlines decreed by fashion buyers and fashion editors.[68]

From the 2010s, there emerged an increasingly organized form of fashion activism that was opposed to the speed and staggering wastefulness of fashion, and its polluting effects. Campaigns were led by organizations that included Fashion Revolution and Extinction Rebellion, with its #Boycottfashion initiative.[69] Paradoxically, there is a close relationship between activism and speed, because these groups are motivated by a sense of urgency that something has to be done fast before it becomes too late to halt or reverse the effects of climate change.

Antilinear time

'I was thinking that if I could design time it would be very nice,' said the Japanese fashion designer Yohji Yamamoto in the film directed by Wim Wenders, *Notebook on Cities and Clothes* (1989). From the 1990s and 2000s, a few designers made time itself the theme of their collections, notably two. The Belgian designer Martin Margiela endlessly reversed, condensed, accelerated and even invented time in his designs [*Francesca Granata*]. The British designer Hussein Chalayan often worked with the themes of memory and archaeology, layering his design references like palimpsests. His *One Hundred and Eleven Collection* of 2007 is in some ways an exemplar of the concept of antilinear time, not because he altered traditional fashion history or chronology, but because he compressed both. The 111 years of his title referred to the lifespan of the sponsoring company, Swarovski, from 1895–2006. The press release for the show described the first of a series of mechanically controlled transformation dresses that morphed between decades:

[68] See Jan Brand and José Teunissen (eds), *Fashion and Imagination: About Clothes and Art* (Arnhem: ArtEZ Press, 2009).

[69] For Fashion Revolution see https://www.fashionrevolution.org (accessed 30 November 2019); for the #Boycottfashion initiative see https://rebellion.earth/event/fashion-costs-the-earth-xr52-boycott-new-clothing/ (accessed 30 November 2019).

1895 is the starting point for the collection, a full-length skirt with a tightly pulled in waist on a gown with a high, frilled neckline. This transforms into a looser fitting dress with a hemline that has risen to the calf in 1910-style. In turn, this seamlessly morphs mechanically into a loose, layered knee-length skirt with a plunging neckline, which is unmistakably a 1920s flapper dress.[70]

In this way, in the words of Alessandra Vaccari, each of these technologically inventive morphing dresses 'concentrate[d] a century of fashion within a time span of a few seconds'.[71]

Aptly, the show's backdrop was an enormous square clock with water running down its face that was, in fact, a Swarovski crystal watermill. Chalayan wrote that: 'The fluidity of time is explored using the relationship between light, water and crystals'.[72] The clock's face was un-numbered, and its hands, which turned like an analogue timepiece, were not actually hands but a single, elongated hour glass that revolved like a sparkling *memento mori*, as glittering 'sand' trickled from one chamber to the other. Vaccari writes, 'The clock, like a time machine, is always a double image in fashion as it represents both compulsory change, and the fluid and relentless time of its history. The notion that, in fashion, seasons don't exist anymore has become a cliché that has contributed to our perception of the progressive sense of the annulment of time'.[73]

The idea of time as fluid is critical for the definition of antilinear time, which is the antithesis of clock time. The concept of antilinear time goes beyond the straightjacket of industrial and postindustrial capitalism, including work time, to focus instead on how fashion design can actually represent time, how theorists can think about it, and how photographers can picture it [*Siegfried Kracauer*] [*Alistair O'Neill*]. The concept is thus helpful for speculating on how fashion design and image-making can enable the formulation of alternative models of time, due to fashion's proclivity for stylistic quotation, its revivals, its speed and mutability, and what it leaves behind in the form of the recently outmoded.

[70] Cited in Alessandra Vaccari, 'Hussein Chalayan. Morphing the Century', *ZoneModa Journal* 1, no. 1 (2009): 16.
[71] Vaccari, 'Hussein Chalayan', 16. See too Lianne Toussaint and Anneke Smelik, 'Memory and Materiality in Hussein Chalayan's Techno-Fashion'. In Lászlo Munteán, Liedeke Plate and Anneke Smelik (eds), *Materializing Memory in Art and Popular Culture* (New York and London: Routledge, 2017), 89–105.
[72] Quoted in Vaccari, 'Hussein Chalayan', 17.
[73] Vaccari, 'Hussein Chalayan', 17.

The idea is not new. In the 1960s and 1970s, retro fashion (today known as vintage) harked back to the styles of the 1920s and 1930s to subvert linear time [*Heike Jenss*]. As the exhibition maker Judith Clark has written:

> Fashion, by definition, has a promiscuous memory; it locks into things and it locks out with surprising speed. Uncanny recognitions and unpredictable conjunctions are integral to the fashion machine. Fashion can't afford to get stuck, but it also can't afford to be predictable. The question is: how does fashion keep unlocking itself? In this compulsive love affair with the past, the past is alternatively familiar and alien.[74]

In the 1980s, postmodern fashion quoted and re-mixed a plurality of historical styles, from antiquity to modernism. In 1989, Martin and Koda curated one of the first fashion exhibitions about postmodernism [*Richard Martin and Harold Koda*] [*Angelo Flaccavento*]. Paying homage to this exhibition, in 2015 the writer and curator Maria Luisa Frisa referred to history as 'a vast collection of images', and 'a tank of styles and shapes that are reused in a random way, and interpreted without nostalgia', pointing out how fruitful this approach is in fashion exhibitions.[75]

While it is hard to pin down exactly when the concept of antilinear time first emerged in Western culture (perhaps it is implicit in Elizabethan drama and poetry, as literary scholars have suggested), a fundamental turning point came with debates about postmodernism in the 1980s, with their rejection of 'master narratives' and of Enlightenment beliefs about progress.[76] Since then, scholars have emphasized the particular contribution of fashion to the postmodern moment in intellectual history, due to fashion's propensity for parody, pastiche and fragmentation, and its nostalgic ambiguity between the new and the old.[77] As Elizabeth Wilson wrote:

---

[74] Judith Clark, *Spectres: When Fashion Looks Back* (London: V&A Publications, 2004), 28.

[75] '[V]asta collezione di immagini'; 'serbatoio di stili e forme che vengono ripresi in modo randomico e interpretati senza nostalgia'. Maria Luisa Frisa, *Le forme della moda. Cultura, industria, mercato: dal sarto al direttore creativo* (Bologna: Il Mulino, 2015), 30.

[76] On time in Elizabethan drama see, for example, Jonathan Gil Harris, *Untimely Matter in the Time of Shakespeare* (Philadelphia: University of Pennsylvania Press, 2009). On the concept that 'time is out of joint' see Jacques Derrida, *Specters of Marx: The State of the Debt, the Work of Mourning, and the New International*, trans. Peggy Kamuf (New York and London: Routledge, 1994).

[77] Hal Foster (ed.), *The Anti-Aesthetic: Essays on Postmodern Culture* (Port Townsend, Washington: Bay Press, 1983); Jean Baudrillard, *Seduction*, trans. Brian Singer (New York: St. Martin's Press, 1990); Jean Baudrillard, *Symbolic Exchange and Death*, trans. Iain Hamilton Grant (Thousand Oaks, CA: Sage Publications, 1993); Juliet Ash and Elizabeth Wilson (eds), *Chic Thrills* (London: Pandora, 1992).

Postmodernism, with its eclectic approach to style, might seem especially compatible with fashion; for fashion, with its constant change and pursuit of glamour enacts symbolically the most hallucinatory aspects of our culture, the confusions between the real and the not-real, the aesthetic obsessions, the vein of morbidity without tragedy, of irony without merriment, and the nihilistic critical stance towards authority, empty rebellion almost without political content.[78]

Disavowing the idea of origins and chronology, postmodern design was a quintessential example of the antilinearity of time, through its eclecticism, its promiscuous quotation of past styles, and in the way that it scrambled historical references.

These tactics might also offer a blueprint for antilinear methods in fashion studies, challenging the idea of simple chronologies, time lines and teleology, in favour of a recursive account. This account might ask which new historical models of events, time, continuity and change could produce alternative fashion histories. Here, there are some possible lessons to be learnt from a different field, media archaeology, to which fashion historians have not generally paid attention. As the film and media scholar Wanda Strauven has written, media archaeological methods allow one to question orthodox periodization. By looking closely at what is often overlooked in traditional approaches, a new narrative can emerge. It can lead to 'excavations of hidden, forgotten, and imaginary' forms. Strauven writes that in these methods 'history is the study not only of the past, but also of the (potential) present and the possible futures . . . [and hence allows] a rethinking of temporalities'. Such an approach, which suggests an alternative historiography drawing on the German philosopher Walter Benjamin's ideas, may involve finding the old in the new, the new in the old, or in identifying ruptures and discontinuities as well as unexpected commonalities between events that are not proximate in time.[79]

Indeed, this type of approach has gained some traction in academic fashion studies since approximately 2000. In the same period that the designers Margiela and Chalayan were working with the theme of time, a number of fashion historians began to work with a new idea of fashion history and chronology,

[78]   Elizabeth Wilson, *Adorned in Dreams; Fashion and Modernity* [1985] (London: I.B. Tauris, revised edition 2003), 63–64.
[79]   Wanda Strauven, 'Media Archaeology: Where Film History, Media Art, and New Media (Can) Meet'. In Julia Noordegraaf, Cosetta G. Saba, Barbara Le Maître and Vinzenz Hediger (eds), *Preserving and Exhibiting Media Art. Challenges and Perspectives*, (Amsterdam: Amsterdam University Press, 2013), 64 and 67–68. Available at https://www.academia.edu/37493500/Media_Archaeology_Where_ Film_History_Media_Art_and_New_Media_Can_Meet (accessed 31 December 2019).

often drawing on Benjamin's ideas.[80] Drawing on the ideas of the Russian formalist writer Mikhail Bakhtin, Francesca Granata has written about new, and progressive ways forward for fashion scholarship through the avoidance of unquestioning chronological narrative in ways compatible with this approach [*Francesca Granata*].

The concept of antilinear time owes much to Benjamin's writing on history and time, in particular to his critique of progress-oriented temporal narratives that are typical of post-Enlightenment modernity. For Benjamin, fashion was closely bound up with temporality, due to its ephemeral and changeable nature, alongside its proclivity for promiscuous historical citation. The philosopher and critic Andrew Benjamin has noted that fashion operates in two ways in Benjamin's writing: as a phenomenon which registers change, and as a marker of time.[81] Philipp Ekardt has analysed Walter Benjamin's concept of fashion as 'a *chronotechnics* – i.e. a distributed, collectively reactualised technique for operationalising time.' As such, Ekardt proposes that Benjamin's model of fashion is not only a 'mechanism for handling and articulating time' but also an object that allows for the 'wider production of knowledge.'[82] In its complexity, his writing offers a rich and flexible set of methodological tools to think about time in fashion, particularly in its use of metaphor. These include *Jetztzeit*, or 'now-time', the tiger's leap, the labyrinth, the telescope and the concept of dialectical images [*Walter Benjamin*].

Benjamin argued that the historian 'establishes a conception of the present as the 'time of the now'.[83] Hence the usual translation of *Jetztzeit* as 'now-time' rather than 'the present'; it enables an understanding of 'the emptiness of simple chronology', and of 'the potential [of] moments of the past' which are activated in the present, as Andrew Benjamin has argued.[84] Walter Benjamin also explored the relationship between time, fashion and mortality in *The Arcades Project*,

---

[80] Ulrich Lehmann, *Tigersprung: Fashion in Modernity* (Cambridge, MA: MIT Press, 2000); Paola Colaiacomo and Vittoria Caterina Caratozzolo, *Cartamodello: antologia di scrittori e scritture sulla moda* (Rome: Sossella, 2000); Caroline Evans, *Fashion at the Edge: Spectacle, Modernity and Deathliness* (New Haven and London: Yale University Press, 2003); Patrizia Calefato, *Gli intramontabili. Mode, persone, oggetti che restano* (Rome: Meltemi, 2009).

[81] Andrew Benjamin, *Style and Time: Essays on the Politics of Appearance* (Evanston, IL: Northwestern University Press, 2006), 25.

[82] Philipp Ekardt, *Benjamin on Fashion* (London and New York: Bloomsbury Academic, 2020), 7 and 18.

[83] Walter Benjamin, 'Theses on the Philosophy of History'. In *Illuminations: Essays and Reflections*, trans. Harry Zohn, ed. and introduction by Hannah Arendt, preface Leon Weiseltier (New York: Schocken Books, 1969), 263. First published in *Neue Rundschau*, 61, 3, 1950, 'Theses on the Philosophy of History' is translated as 'On the Concept of History' in Benjamin, *Style and Time*, 25–38.

[84] Andrew Benjamin, *Style and Time*, 29.

using a line from Giacomo Leopardi's 'Dialogue between Fashion and Death' (1824) as the epigraph to *Konvolut B*, on fashion.[85] The literary scholar Paola Colaiacomo has argued that Leopardi's association of immortality with caducity anticipated Benjamin's concept of *Jetztzeit* by over a century.[86]

Jetztzeit also helps to enrich the understanding of Benjamin's concept of the 'tiger's leap'. The tiger springs over historically congruent moments to seize others from 'the thickets of long ago'. Benjamin wrote that '[t]he past can be seized only as an image which flashes up at the instant when it can be recognized and is never seen again ... For every image of the past that is not recognized by the present as one of its own concerns threatens to disappear irretrievably'.[87] In his 2000 book *Tigersprung: Fashion in Modernity* Lehmann discussed three different historical iterations of the 'tiger's leap' in relation to the writing on fashion of Charles Baudelaire, Théophile Gautier, Stéphane Mallarmé, Georg Simmel and, obviously, Benjamin [*Ulrich Lehmann*].

The tiger's leap is more than a vivid metaphor for historical citation in fashion. Lehmann writes that, with the tiger's leap, 'Benjamin brought together various splintered parts of modernity to form a new concept of history, a political ideal, and an aesthetic credo'.[88] The term references Marx's *18th Brumaire of Louis Bonaparte* (1852), and contains within it Benjamin's concept of the dialectical model of history, which requires some explanation in order to understand its potential 'offer' for fashion historians. Benjamin rejected the idea of history as a linear narrative of causes and effects, and instead argued for the need to 'explode' the historical continuum.[89] He proposed a form of historical writing that would create a 'constellation' of the historical present and a specific moment in the past, as opposed to a teleological or chronological account of historical events. This is the basis of his concept of dialectical images, that he called 'constellations of past and present'.[90] His writing on dialectical images informed much of Caroline Evans's method in *Fashion at the Edge* (2003), which also used his ideas about the labyrinth and the telescope to understand the 'historical relay between past and present in 1990s fashion'.[91]

[85] Walter Benjamin, *The Arcades Project*, trans. Howard Eiland and Kevin McLaughlin (Cambridge, MA and London: The Belknap Press of Harvard University Press, 1999), 62.
[86] Paola Colaiacomo, 'Introduzione'. In Colaiacomo and Caratozzolo, *Cartamodello*, 6–19.
[87] Benjamin, 'Theses on the Philosophy of History', 255.
[88] Lehmann, *Tigersprung*, xvi.
[89] Benjamin, 'Theses on the Philosophy of History', 261 and 263.
[90] On the use of the concept of dialectical images in fashion studies, see Evans, *Fashion at the Edge*, 29–35.
[91] Evans, *Fashion at the Edge*, 22.

The main difference between antilinear time and the concept of cyclical time lies in the fact that the former lacks sequential order and relies instead on the discontinuities of history. Evans associated this peculiarity of antilinear time with 'ragpicking', taking inspiration from Benjamin's writing on the figure of the nineteenth-century ragpicker who sifted through the detritus of the city.[92] Building on the work of historian Irving Wohlfarth, Evans argued that 'historical scavenging' constituted a key methodological tool for the contemporary fashion designer as well as for the cultural historian.[93]

In the field of fashion exhibition-making, the concept of the dialectical image was interpreted in three dimensional form by Judith Clark in her exhibition *Malign Muses* (MoMu (ModeMuseum), Antwerp 18 September 2004–30 January 2005 and, under the title of *Spectres*, Victoria & Albert Museum, London 24 February–8 May 2005), for which she built a moving model consisting of three enormous revolving turntables fitted with gigantic interlocking cogs. As the wheels turned, the mannequins on each turntable passed each other in ever-changing constellations, to demonstrate the constantly shifting relationships between past and present in fashion.[94] In part a visual and material response to Evans's theoretical framework in *Fashion at the Edge*, the exhibition's scenography and sets referenced more than one of Benjamin's temporal metaphors, including the labyrinth that folded back on itself, and the idea of optical devices that visualized historical distance.[95]

Besides Benjamin, other twentieth-century writers have theorized different models of time in reaction to nineteenth-century historiographies which have been taken up in the field of fashion studies. Gilles Deleuze's and Michel Serres's reflections on time, in particular, have been used to develop alternative approaches to linear and cyclical accounts of fashion history, and to investigate the relationship between clothing and memory. These include the metaphors of the fold, the pleat and the crumpled handkerchief.

The concept of the fold as matter-time (*matière-temps*) enabled Deleuze to formulate subjectivity as a process of infinite becoming.[96] The fold is a relational

[92] Evans, *Fashion at the Edge*, 11, citing Walter Benjamin, *The Arcades Project*, trans. Howard Eiland and Kevin McLaughlin (Cambridge, MA and London: The Belknap Press of Harvard University Press, 1999), 860.

[93] Irving Wohlfarth, 'Et cetera? The Historian as Chiffonnier', in *New German Critique* 39 (fall 1986): 142–68, cited in Evans, *Fashion at the Edge*, 11.

[94] See the section 'Locking In and Out', in Judith Clark, *Spectres: When Fashion Turns Back* (London: Victoria & Albert Museum, 2004), 28.

[95] See the section 'Reappearances: Getting Things Back' in Clark, *Spectres*, 18 and 22.

[96] Gilles Deleuze, *The Fold, Leibniz and the Baroque*, trans. Tom Conley (London: Athlone Press, 1993), 7.

concept, as evidenced by its etymological relationship to the term implicate (from the Latin *in-plicare*), literally to envelop, wrap up and, hence, involve. It means, according to Deleuze, eliminating binary oppositions by establishing a dialogue between the inner and the outer, the deep and the superficial.[97] In her writing on fashion, Anneke Smelik has adopted the morphing characteristics of Deleuze's notion of the fold to highlight the fluidity of the silhouette of the modern clothed body, in order to investigate the transformation of identity in modern and postmodern fashion design.[98]

For Michel Serres, time is 'pleated', 'sporadic' and 'lacunary'.[99] In his claim that '[a]ll is folded', Serres made explicit reference to Deleuze; but in addition, he has adopted the textile metaphors of the 'crumpled handkerchief' and the 'badly stitched tatter' to express the multidimensionality of time.[100] The image of the crumpled, as opposed to the ironed, handkerchief suggests history as complex and non-linear, as opposed to the Cartesian concept of time as a straight line. According to Serres, past and present can meet, or are folded together. Therefore, one cannot experience an isolated historical moment, as time does not 'filter or eliminate' the past; rather, time simultaneously receives and encompasses multiple eras.[101]

Ellen Sampson has written about the relationship between Serres's crumpled handkerchief and the way in which memory is materialized in clothing. For her, the act of ironing 'renders a garment amnesiac, it forgets the previous day's creases and gestures'.[102] Jack Gann has applied Serres's concept of 'pleated time' to

[97]   Kevin Clayton, 'Time Folded and Crumpled: Time, History, Self-Organization and the Methodology of Michel Serres', in Bernd Herzogenrath (ed.), *Time and History in Deleuze and Serres* (New York and London: Continuum, 2012), 39.
[98]   Anneke Smelik, 'Fashioning the Fold: Multiple Belonging', in Rosie Braidotti and Rick Dolphijn (eds), *This Deleuzian Century: Art, Activism, Life* (Leiden and Boston: Brill-Rodopi, 2015), 37–55; Anneke Smelik, 'Gilles Deleuze: Bodies-without-Organs in the Folds of Fashion' in Agnès Rocamora and Anneke Smelik (eds), *Thinking Through Fashion: A Guide to Key Theorists* (London: I.B. Tauris, 2016), 165–83.
[99]   Michel Serres, *Genesis*, trans. Geneviève James and James Nielson (Ann Arbor: University of Michigan Press, 1995), 115; Michel Serres, *Atlas* (Paris: Éditions Julliard, 1994), 49.
[100] Serres, *Atlas*, 49; Serres, *Genesis*, 115. See too Clayton, 'Time Folded and Crumpled', 31.
[101] Serres, *Genesis*, 115.
[102] Ellen Sampson, 'Creases, Crumples, and Folds', *Fashion Studies*, 2017, available at: http://www. fashionstudiesjournal.org/2-visual-essays-2/2017/4/2/creases-crumples-and-folds-maps-of-experience-and-manifestations-of-wear (accessed 10 July 2018). See also the exhibition *Fashion Unraveled*, curated by Colleen Hill, The Museum at FIT, New York, May 25, 2018–November 17, 2018, and the associated oral history project *Wearing Memory*. Available at https://www.fitnyc.edu/museum/events/special-projects/wearing-memories.php (accessed 9 September 2018); Caroline Evans, 'Materiality, Memory and History: Adventures in the Archive', in Alistair O'Neill (ed.), *Isabella Blow: Fashion Galore!* (Milan: Rizzoli, 2013), 137–41.

Alexander McQueen's tailored tartans in his neo-Victorian collection *The Widows of Culloden* to exemplify how the 'perception of our place in time is simultaneously of multiple eras'.[103] The metaphor of the crumpled handkerchief also appears in Wendy Ligon Smith's writing on the Italian designer Mariano Fortuny's pleated Delphos dress (1909), but she puts the handkerchief in dialogue with Marcel Proust's treatment of time in his novel *Remembrance of Things Past* (1913–1927).[104] To conclude, the antilinear approach provides the methodological tools to understand and interpret the traces of the past in the present — as in Proust — and the mysterious romance that fashion plays with the new in the old, as explained by Ilya Parkins. That approach opens up the fundamental question of what thinking about time really means. The theoretical physicist and writer Carlo Rovelli claimed that time is 'entirely in the present, in our minds, as memory and as anticipation'. This entails, for Rovelli, the idea that '[w]e are stories'.[105]

Uchronic time

The final section of the book is an exploration of fashion's 'imaginary' and its capacity for fantasy, myth-making and innovative thinking, as well as its propensity for predicting future trends and playing tricks with the passage of time [*Angelo Flaccavento*]. The concept of uchronia means an impossible or fictional time. It allows the invention of possible futures, and the rewriting of the past. Many of the subjects or authors of this section are, therefore, fabulists in some way, and they are included not because they write objectively about uchronic time but because their texts or actions exemplify or materialize it [*Elsa Schiaparelli*] [*Miuccia Prada*] [*Karl Lagerfeld*] [*Paola Colaiacomo*] [*Ilaria Vanni*].

The concept of uchronia moves away from the rigours of linear and antilinear time and towards more playful and creative possibilities, albeit ones that may be shaped by the exigencies of the fashion industry. It is predicated on a different

---

[103] Jack Gann, 'Stitching Pleats in Time: Multi-temporality in Alexander McQueen's "Savage Beauty" Exhibition, 2015', Leeds Centre for Victorian Studies, 27 August 2017. Available at: http://www. leedstrinity.ac.uk/blogs/leeds-centre-for-victorian-studies/stitching-pleats-in-time-multi-temporality-in-alexander-mcqueens-savage-beauty-exhibition (accessed 27 November 2019).

[104] Wendy Ligon Smith, *Reviving Fortuny's Phantasmagorias*, PhD diss., University of Manchester, UK, 2015; Walter Benjamin, 'Some Motifs in Baudelaire', in *Charles Baudelaire: A Lyric Poet in the Era of High Capitalism* (London: Verso, 1983), 143.

[105] Carlo Rovelli, *The Order of Time*, trans. Erica Segre and Simon Carnell (London: Allen Lane, 2018), 158, 163.

model of time from the other two sections, and uchronic time is perhaps the most speculative and experimental concept of fashion time that the anthology covers. The term uchronia encompasses a variety of phenomena: utopian heritages; trend-forecasting and other commercially motivated predictions; forward-looking fantasies set in an imagined future; and activism motivated by a real sense of urgency and political engagement. All help to illuminate fashion's complex relationships with time. The section also reveals the power of uchronic narratives in twentieth- and twenty-first-century fashion and media.

The word utopia was coined by Thomas More in the early sixteenth century, to describe a fictional island inhabited by an ideal society. Just as the term u-topia (no place) indicates an imaginary place and a good society, so u-chronia (no-time) refers to a non-existent time with multiple potentialities. Here activism comes into play, be it via queer theory or the inventive reclamation of black identity such as the case of the above-mentioned Afrofuturism, or in forms of protest for a better future [*Emma Katherine Atwood*] [*Ilaria Vanni*].[106] And just as utopia has its opposite in the concept of dystopia, so too uchronia has its corollary, dys-chronia. A nineteenth-century example of this is included in the book [*Charles Dickens*].

Writing about the relation between history and fiction, the Italian semiologist and novelist Umberto Eco has argued that there is more truth to fiction than to history, because historical writing is always open to interpretation and doubt, whereas the veracity of the fictional text is unquestionable.[107] Uchronia emerges when story-telling poses as history, and the past or future is continually rewritten through the lens of the present [*Greg French*]. Time becomes enmeshed with narrative, and is subverted by the category of the uchronic. Since the nineteenth century, the term uchronia has been used to designate alternative histories: the 'what if?' of fiction. Philip K. Dick's *Man in the High Castle* (1962) is a well-known contemporary example of a novel which is an alternative history (made into a multi-version TV series in 2015). The earliest example of alternative history, however, is the French writer Louis Geoffroy's *Napoléon et la Conquête du monde* (1836), republished as *Napoléon apochryphe* (1841), a work of political fiction that adopted a utopian view of history – history not as it was but as it

---

[106]   Caroline Evans and Alessandra Vaccari, 'Il tempo della moda. A Dialogue on Fashion and Time', *ZoneModa Journal* 9, no. 2 (2019): 169–72.
[107]   Umberto Eco, *The Book of Legendary Lands*, trans. Alistair McEwen (London: MacLehose Press, 2013), 440–41.

might have been.[108] The neologism 'uchronia' was first coined by Charles Renouvier in his 1876 book *L'Uchronie: l'Utopie dans l'histoire*, in which he rewrote the course of historical events in European civilization on the hypothesis that the fall of the Roman Empire had never happened.[109] In short, uchronia is fictional time, or made-up time, sometimes (but not always) with utopian overtones; and this section of the book looks at the uses fashion makes of fictional time, from revisionist to experimental accounts.

The section takes its name from Barthes's claim that fashion is always uchronic because it is predicated on 'a time which does not exist' [*Roland Barthes*].[110] From this perspective, uchronic time is the privileged time of fashion – perhaps its only possible time. Arguing that fashion consists of a permanent present, Barthes writes that 'pure Fashion, logical Fashion ... is never anything but an amnesiac substitute of the present for the past'. This claim is expanded in a footnote which, in the original French, uses the term 'uchronia' to describe 'a time which does not exist' but which the English-language translators rendered as 'achrony'. The French original states: '*En fait, la Mode postule une uchronie, un temps qui n'existe pas; le passé y est honteux et le présent sans cesse 'mangé' par la Mode qui s'annonce*.' The term 'achrony' is not in the English dictionary and perhaps the translators invented it; 'uchronia' is in the dictionary, and would therefore have been an option. The mistranslation somewhat undermines the meaning and importance of the concept for Anglophone readers and writers, which may explain why it has received so little critical attention from them. The translators' choice of 'a-chrony' does, nevertheless, suggest the 'no time' of the word 'u-chronia', which is akin to the 'no place' of 'u-topia'.

Patrizia Calefato is one of the few writers on fashion time to comment on Barthes's reference to 'uchronia', which she designates as 'a time which does not exist but which can be expressed by both verbal and non-verbal signs'.[111] To do so, she grasps at something that other writers on fashion miss: its excessive, self-devouring quality. Calefato identifies elaborate temporal exchanges in fashion

---

[108] Louis-Napoléon Geoffroy-Château, *Louis-Napoléon apocryphe. Histoire de la conquête du monde et de la monarchie universelle, 1812–1832* (2nd ed. Paris: Paulin, 1841). The first edition was published five years previously under the different title of *Napoléon et la conquête du monde, 1812–1832* (Paris: H.-L. Delloye, 1836).

[109] Charles Renouvier, *Uchronie (l'utopie dans l'histoire): esquisse historique apocryphe du développement de la civilisation européenne tel qu'il n'a pas été, tel qu'il aurait pu être* (Paris: La Critique philosophique, 1876).

[110] Roland Barthes, *The Fashion System*, trans. Matthew Ward and Richard Howard (Berkeley: University of California Press, 1990), 289, n.17.

[111] Patrizia Calefato, *The Clothed Body* (Oxford and New York: Berg, 2004), 124.

which segue between past, present and future, 'so the time of fashion is consumed in a space where it no longer makes sense to separate past and present, synchrony and diachrony' [*Patrizia Calefato*].[112]

Many scholars have written about the compelling 'presentness' of fashion [*Ulrich Lehmann*] [*Karl Lagerfeld*] [*Barbara Vinken*]. Vinken writes: 'Fashion is the moment that negates time as durée; it erases traces of time, blots out history as difference by positioning itself as an absolute, self-evident and perfect as a moment becoming eternity, the promise of eternity.'[113] Jean Baudrillard too considered fashion as an unadulterated sequence of 'the now' that exists purely by virtue of differing from what precedes it.[114] Consequently, it has no history, or, in Malcolm Barnard's words, it is 'historically ineffective'.[115] For the French philosopher Yves Michaud, fashion is 'a permanent utopia that lives from day to day, unanchored by time or place, ceaselessly renewing itself and reappearing'.[116] For Elizabeth Bye, however, fashion designers benefit from imagining the future. They are forward-thinkers by their very nature, being used to working one or two years ahead and they are comfortable 'working with ideas and concepts of things that do not exist'.[117]

Fashion is not only created by designers, though. It is a collaborative venture involving many other people: press officers, photographers, art directors, magazine editors and store buyers, to name but a few.[118] In their hands, the histories of fashion brands are continuously rewritten, with the purpose of reinventing their traditions or mythologizing them. The concept of uchronic time spans conservative and retrogressive fashion narratives on the one hand, and radical, creative and life-changing ones on the other. The first encompasses fictitious histories of the past, and this is exactly what the industry creates when it engages in heritage brand-building, marketing, promotion and trend-forecasting. Western fashion often turned its attention to vintage by emphasizing

---

[112] Calefato, *The Clothed Body*, 123.
[113] Barbara Vinken, *Fashion Zeitgeist: Trends and Cycles in the Fashion System* (Oxford and New York: Berg, 2005), 42.
[114] Jean Baudrillard, *For a Critique of the Political Economy of the Sign*, trans. Charles Levin (St. Louis, Mo: Telos Press, 1981).
[115] Malcolm Barnard, *Fashion Theory: an Introduction* (London and New York: Routledge, 2014), 63.
[116] Yves Michaud, *L'Art à l'état gazeux. Essai sur le Triomphe de l'esthétique* (Paris: Stock, 2003), 175. See also Giovanni Matteucci and Stefano Marino (eds), *Philosophical Perspectives on Fashion* (London and New York: Bloomsbury, 2016), 47–72.
[117] Elizabeth Bye, *Fashion Design* (Oxford and New York: Berg, 2010), 169.
[118] Regina Lee Blaszczyk (ed.), *Producing Fashion: Commerce, Culture, and Consumers* (Philadelphia: University of Pennsylvania Press, 2008). Lisa Skov, 'Fashion'. In *The Cultural Intermediaries Reader*, ed. Jennifer Smith Maguire and Julian Matthews (London and Los Angeles: Sage, 2014), 113–24.

the cultural value of the patina of time. In Arjun Appadurai's analysis of fashion, patina as the 'gloss of age' could be seen as the insidious logic by which late capitalism deliberately feeds people's lives with nostalgia.[119] This postmodern fetishization of the old highlights the fact that nostalgia is mediated through commodities, and for that reason – in Appadurai's and, before him, Fredric Jameson's interpretations – it creates manufactured memories instead of historical memories based on real facts.[120]

This may include the lengths a global heritage brand will go to to represent, and even fictionalize, its past; one such origin myth is the 2016 fashion film *The Tale of Thomas Burberry*, directed by the British documentary filmmaker Asif Kapadia, which combined found footage from the First World War with blockbuster fiction film techniques, to shape a film narrative 'as an exercise in brand archaeology' as Nick Rees-Roberts argued.[121] Another is Gucci's 2010 *Forever Now* advertising campaign, in which time became an eternal present through the republication of a 1953 photograph of the company's original workshop in the centre of Florence. Further examples of uchronic narratives in fashion advertising and marketing are included in the book [*Simona Segre Reinach*] [*Advertising Standards Authority*].

But, returning to the other possibility outlined above, the concept of uchronic time expands to fashions that are avant-garde or experimental, and that intentionally work outside the rhythms of the fashion industry, from modernism to postmodernism and beyond. A modernist example is the anti-haute couture dresses that the Belgian architect and artist Henry van de Velde designed for his wife Marie Louise Sèthe at the end of the nineteenth century.[122] Likewise, in 1919 the Italian futurist artist Thayaht (Ernesto Michahelles), produced a utopian, futuristic design for a *tuta*, or overall, which he felt had to be autonomous from the fashion production of his day.[123]

[119] Arjun Appadurai, *Modernity at Large: Cultural Dimensions of Globalization* (Minneapolis and London: University of Minnesota Press, 1996), 76.
[120] See Nishant Shahani, *Queer Retrosexualities: The Politics of Reparative Return* (Bethlehem: Lehigh University Press, 2012), 6–8.
[121] *The Tale of Thomas Burberry* (2016). Available at https://www.youtube.com/watch?v=6D5IZtDCS5c (accessed 30 November 2019); Nick Rees-Roberts, *Fashion Film: Art and Advertising in the Digital Age* (London and New York: Bloomsbury, 2018), 39.
[122] See Radu Stern, *Against Fashion: Clothing as Art, 1850–1930* (Cambridge, MA and London: MIT Press, 2003).
[123] See Caterina Chiarelli (ed.), *Per il sole e contro il sole: Thayat et Ram. La tuta / Modelli per tessuti* (Livorno: Sillabe, 2003).

The concept of uchronic time also connects to early twenty-first-century fashion activism and critique, such as the case of Bernadette Corporation or Serpica Naro. Bernadette Corporation is a New York and Paris based collective that invented a fictional business brand to mock corporations, and question Western identity as a 'fallacious term usurped by capital'.[124] Crossbreeding art and fashion, their activities included a line of women's wear and a 2002 film, *Get Rid of Yourself*. This claimed that 'another world is possible' but then asked, 'But I am another world. Am I possible?' against the backdrop of the Genoa G8 riots staged by anonymous Black Bloc anarchists. Their approach recalls Fredric Jameson's argument that the idea of 'absolute identity' advocated by multinational corporations matches that of the 'absolute change' pursued by fashion in search of novelty, 'in the realm of built space, "lifestyle", corporate culture, and psychic programming'.[125] Serpica Naro is a fictional designer created by a group of activists in Milan who staged a fashion show in the designer's name during 2005 Milan fashion week to denounce the precarious labour conditions of workers in the creative industries [*Ilaria Vanni*].

This section of the book also includes inventive journalism that, at its most extreme, amounts to a kind of fiction, or bluff [*Stéphane Mallarmé*]. The fashion editor Diana Vreeland's 'Why don't you?' column ran in *Harper's Bazaar* for over 25 years, providing hypothetical advice on how to be fashionable in her idiosyncratic style. 'Why don't you ... Wear a blue sapphire thistle in one ear and a ruby thistle in the other?' she asked, or 'Turn your old ermine coat into a bathrobe?'.[126] With her '*Doppie pagine*' (double-page spreads) starting in 1988 for Italian *Vogue*, the journalist Anna Piaggi constantly advocated for 'anachrony' in the way she suggested that fashion disrupts the conventional flow of events and creates its own time. She invented her own way of telling new stories by associating, in her own words, 'the fashion of the moment with the ideas of the past ... with photography, illustration, lettering. In a way that is always different. Invented'.[127] She also dealt with fashion through her neologisms, many of which entailed a uchronic notion of time: 'pack-age', 'redingothic', 'fashionmorphosis', 'rock baroque' [*Anna Piaggi*].

---

[124] Bennett Simpson, 'Techniques of Today: Bernadette Corporation', *Artforum* 43, no. 1 (2004). Available at http://www.bernadettecorporation.com/introduction.htm (accessed 20 December 2019).
[125] Fredric Jameson, *The Seeds of Time* (New York and Chichester: Columbia University Press, 1994), 17 and 18.
[126] John Esten, *Diana Vreeland Bazaar Years: Including 100 Audacious Why Don't Yous. . .?* (New York: Universe, 2001).
[127] Anna Piaggi, *Anna Piaggi's Fashion Algebra* (London: Thames and Hudson, 1998), 27.

The advent of the digital is central to the understanding of uchronic time, which in the twenty-first century manifests itself in the practices of fashion blogging, digital publishing and e-commerce. Digital fashion time can be seen as a network or mesh, rather than a linear process. Furthermore, it is not just a metaphor, but also a way to describe both commercial relations and symbolic structures. For the French theoretician and artist Edmond Couchot, the uchronic time of hypertext and of the Internet is a threat to the permanence of written history, which in the past had the function of organizing memory and, its corollary, forgetting. Digital time, instead, habituates us to think, wrote Couchot, of a 'time outside of time', in which 'events give way to eventualities'.[128] In an article on Snapchat filters as digital adornment, Jessica Barker has investigated how selfies and instant image modification could take fashion seasons and fast fashion to the extreme. She noted that: 'Encouraged by app and industry alike, individuals can easily adorn themselves with the very latest designs. Instant gratification satisfied, undesirable styles can be discarded without a second thought.'[129]

Operating as it does at a faster pace than ever, the fashion industry may find a different time dimension in the near future, for example as it increasingly embraces virtual reality. This opens up provocative questions about whether the offer of virtual clothing can replace the act of continuously buying fast fashion, with potential benefits to the environment, labour conditions and waste reduction. The same considerations may apply to the fashion models generated by AI (artificial intelligence) that by-pass the individual and social consequences of unethical labour practices in the fashion modelling industry.

Finally, the category of uchronic time in fashion has crucial implications for writing on fluid and queer identities. Writers including Lee Edelman, Judith (a.k.a. Jack) Halberstam and Elizabeth Freeman have critiqued chrono-normativity as a form of Western, mainstream and heteronormative linear time.[130]

---

[128] Edmond Couchot, 'Temps de l'histoire et temps uchronique. Penser autrement la mémoire et l'oubli', *Hybrid*, 1, 2014. http://www.hybrid.univ-paris8.fr/lodel/index.php?id=179&lang=en (accessed 6 October 2018).

[129] Jessica Barker, 'Considering Snapchat Filters as Digital Adornment', *Fashion Studies Journal*, July 2017. Available at http://www.fashionstudiesjournal.org/notes/2017/7/2/considering-snapchat-filters-as-digital-adornment (accessed 27 November 2019).

[130] Lee Edelman, *No Future: Queer Theory and the Death Drive* (Durham: Duke University Press, 2004); Judith Halberstam, 'What's That Smell? Queer Temporalities and Subcultural Lives', *The Scholar and Feminist Online* 2 (1), 2003: n.p. http://sfonline.barnard.edu/ps/printjha.htm (accessed 1 December 2019). On the concept of 'chrono-normativity' see Elizabeth Freeman, *Time Binds: Queer Temporalities, Queer Histories* (Durham: Duke University Press, 2010). See too Valerie Rohy, *Anachronism and Its Others: Sexuality, Race, Temporality* (Albany: State University of New York, 2009), xiv.

An alternative temporal model to heteronormative time is also offered by the eighteenth-century fop's and the nineteenth-century dandy's temporality [*Jules Barbey d'Aurevilly*] [*Emma Katherine Atwood*]. In this way, queer time can be seen as a 'vector for a utopian reconfiguration of life that includes a wide variety of gay, lesbian and transgender subcultures'.[131] The section on uchronic time is thus also an enquiry into fashion's potential to resist dominant codes, highlight the fictional nature of chronologies, and make the 'otherworldly' possible [*Greg French*] [*Francesca Granata*] [*Paola Colaiacomo*]. For, in the words of Roberto Filippello, 'thinking through a fashion imagination interrupts the political pessimism of the present and prioritizes instead the affective force of hope'.[132]

---

[131]   Roberto Filippello, 'Queer Asynchrony and the Fashion Imagination', seminar paper (Venice, Iuav University of Venice, 10 December 2019); Halberstam, 'What's That Smell?', n.p.
[132]   Filippello, 'Queer Asynchrony', n.p.

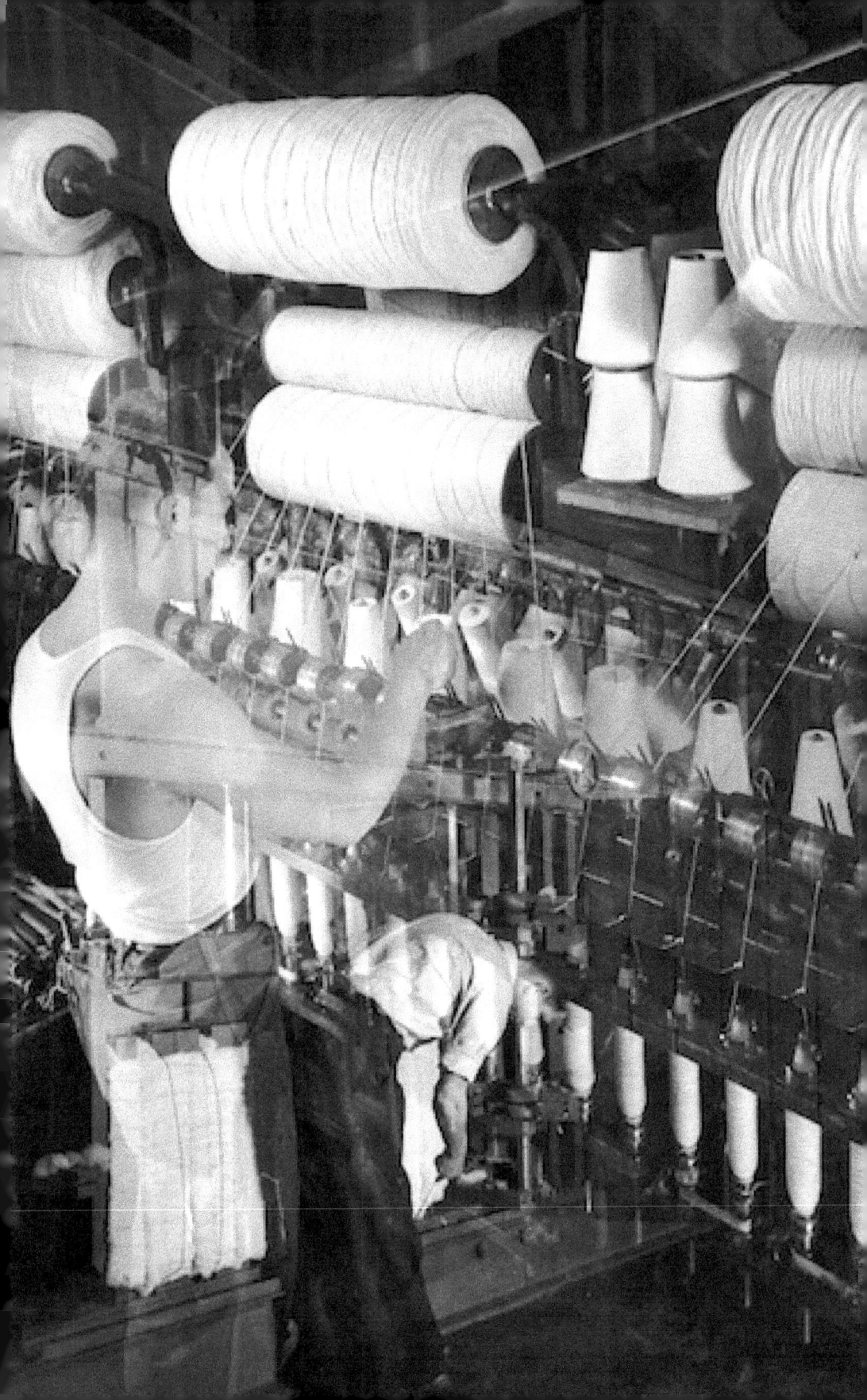

Section 1

Industrial Time

The Murderous, Meaningless Caprices of Fashion

Karl Marx

Karl Marx, *Capital Volume I* [1867] trans. Ben Fowkes
(Harmondsworth: Penguin 1976), 364–65 and 608–9.

These two passages, both from Marx's Capital *(1867), adumbrate the devastating impact of the social season on workers in the fashion and textiles industries. In the first paragraph, taken from chapter 10 on 'The Working Day', Marx describes the death in 1863 'from simple overwork' of the London milliner Mary Anne Walkley. The next two paragraphs come from chapter 15, where Marx writes at greater length about the working conditions of women and children employed in the production of 'wearing apparel' in unregulated factories. At the end of this passage, in a famous phrase, he excoriates 'the murderous, meaningless caprices of fashion'.*

The nineteenth-century social season set the pace for a biannual cycle of production that existed at all levels of the garment industry, from home dressmaking to large-scale factories. As a result of the season, Marx wrote, workers were cruelly over-worked for half the year, and equally cruelly unemployed for the other half. This biannual cycle of fashion production dominated Western, especially European, fashion for over 150 years, and still prevails today, though it has recently been challenged by the retail forms of 'fast fashion' and 'see now, buy now'.

In the last week of June 1863, all the London daily papers published a paragraph with the 'sensational' heading, 'Death from simple over-work'. It dealt with the death of the milliner, Mary Anne Walkley, 20 years old, employed in a highly respectable dressmaking establishment, exploited by a lady with the pleasant name of Elise. The old, often-told story was now revealed once again.[1] These girls work, on an average, 16½ hours without a break, during the season often 30 hours,

---

[1]   Cfr. F. Engels, *Die Lage der arbeitenden Klasse in England*, Leipzig 1845, 253–54.

and the flow of their failing 'labour-power' is maintained by occasional supplies of sherry, port or coffee. It was the height of the season. It was necessary, in the twinkling of an eye, to conjure up magnificent dresses for the noble ladies invited to the ball in honour of the newly imported Princess of Wales. Mary Anne Walkley had worked uninterruptedly for 26½ hours, with sixty other girls, thirty in each room. The rooms provided only ⅓ of the necessary quantity of air, measured in cubic feet. At night the girls slept in pairs in the stifling holes into which a bedroom was divided by wooden partitions.[2] And this was one of the better millinery establishments in London. Mary Anne Walkley fell ill on the Friday and died on Sunday, without, to the astonishment of Madame Elise, having finished off the bit of finery she was working on. The doctor, a Mr Keys, called too late to the girl's deathbed, made his deposition to the coroner's jury in plain language: 'Mary Anne Walkley died from long hours of work in an overcrowded work-room, and a too small and badly ventilated bedroom.' In order to give the doctor a lesson in good manners, the coroner's jury thereupon brought in the verdict that 'the deceased had died of apoplexy, but there was reason to fear that her death had been accelerated by over-work in an overcrowded work-room, etc.'. [...]

In factories and places of manufacture which are not yet subject to the Factory Acts, the most fearful over-work prevails periodically during what is called the season, as a result of sudden orders. In the outside departments of factory, workshop and warehouse, the so-called domestic workers, whose employment is at best irregular, are entirely dependent for their raw material and their orders on the caprice of the capitalist, who, in this industry, is not hampered by any regard for depreciation of

---

[2] Dr Letheby, Consulting Physician of the Board of Health, declared: 'The minimum of air for each adult ought to be in a sleeping room 300, and in a dwelling room 500 cubic feet.' Dr Richardson, Senior Physician at one of the London hospitals: 'With needlewomen of all kinds, including milliners, dressmakers, and ordinary sempstresses, there are three miseries – over-work, deficient air, and either deficient food or deficient digestion . . . Needlework, in the main . . . is infinitely better adapted to women than to men. But the mischiefs of the trade, in the metropolis especially, are that it is monopolised by some twenty-six capitalists, who, under the advantages that spring from capital, can bring in capital to force economy out of labour. This power tells throughout the whole class. If a dressmaker can get a little circle of customers, such is the competition that, in her home, she must work to the death to hold it together, and this same over-work she must of necessity inflict on any who may assist her. If she fail, do not try independently, she must join an establishment, where her labour is not less, but where her money is safe. Placed thus, she becomes a mere slave, tossed about with the variations of society. Now at home, in one room, starving, or near to it, then engaged 15, 16, aye, even 18 hours out of the 24, in an air that is scarcely tolerable, and on food which, even if it be good, cannot be digested in the absence of pure air. On these victims, consumption, which is purely a disease of bad air, feeds' (Dr Richardson, 'Work and Over-Work', in *Social Science Review*, 18 July 1863).

his buildings and machinery, and risks nothing by a stoppage of work but the skin of the worker himself. Here then he sets himself systematically to work to form an industrial reserve force that shall be ready at a moment's notice; during one part of the year he decimates this force by the most inhuman toil, during the other part he lets it starve for lack of work. 'Employers ... avail themselves of the habitual irregularity [in work at home] when any extra work is wanted at a push, so that work goes on till 11 and 12 p.m., or 2 a.m., or as the usual phrase is, "all hours", and in places where 'the stench is enough to knock you down; you go to the door, perhaps, and open it, but shudder to go further.'[3] 'They are curious men,' said one of the witnesses, a shoemaker, speaking of the masters, 'and think it does a boy no harm to work too hard for half the year, if he is nearly idle for the other half.'[4]

Like the technical impediments, these 'usages which have grown with the growth of trade', or business customs, were also proclaimed by interested capitalists (and still are proclaimed) to be 'natural barriers' inherent in production. This was a favourite cry of the cotton lords at the time when they were first threatened with the Factory Acts. Although their industry depends, more than any other, on the world market, and therefore on shipping, experience showed they were lying. Since then, every pretended 'obstruction to business' has been treated by the Factory Inspectors as a mere sham.[5] The thoroughly conscientious investigations of the Children's Employment Commission prove that the effect of the regulation of the hours of work, in some industries, was to spread the mass of labour previously employed more evenly over the whole year;[6] that this regulation was the first rational bridle on the murderous, meaningless caprices of fashion,[7] caprices which fit in very badly with the system under which large-scale industry operates.

---

[3] Children's Employment Commission, IV rep., nn. 235, 237, XXXV.
[4] Children's Employment Commission, n. 56, 127.
[5] With respect to the loss of trade by non-completion of shipping orders in time, I remember that this was the pet argument of the factory masters in 1832 and 1833. Nothing that can be advanced now on this subject, could have the force that it had then, before steam had halved all distances and established new regulations for transit. It quite failed at that time of proof when put to the test, and again it will certainly fail should it have to be tried.
[6] *Children's Employment Commission*, III rep., n. 118, xviii.
[7] John Bellers remarked as long ago as 1699: 'The uncertainty of fashions does increase necessitous Poor. It has two great mischiefs in it. 1st) The journeymen are miserable in winter for want of work, the mercers and master-weavers not daring to lay out their stocks to keep the journeymen employed before the spring comes, and they know what the fashion will then be. 2ndly) In the spring the journeymen are not sufficient, but the master-weavers must draw in many prentices, that they may supply the trade of the kingdom in a quarter or half a year, which robs the plough of hands, drains the country of labourers, and in a great part stocks the city with beggars, and starves some in winter that are ashamed to beg' (*Essays about the Poor, Manufactures, etc.*, 9).

The Acceleration of Fashion Change in The Eighteenth Century

Kimberly Chrisman-Campbell

Kimberly Chrisman-Campbell, *Fashion Victims: Dress at the Court of
Louis XVI and Marie-Antoinette* (New Haven and London:
Yale University Press, 2015), 10–11 and 14–17.

*The voracious appetite for fashion that Marx criticized so fiercely in the nineteenth
century was not new, however, and the phenomenon of the fashion season long
predated industrialization. The dress historian Kimberly Chrisman-Campbell
outlines the advent of seasonal fashion that began in the seventeenth century, and
describes the accelerated rate of fashion change in the late eighteenth, when 'it was
not enough for fashion to change with the seasons: it changed every day, and
sometimes several times a day, or so it was said'. Suddenly, the season required not
only new clothes, but also novelty in design. Hair arrangements like the* pouf *were
designed to change frequently, and to go out of fashion quickly. A bride's trousseau
was intended to last a season, not a lifetime. Chrisman-Campbell outlines how this
rapid style change was both created by, and reflected in, the first fashion magazines
and almanacs of the 1770s.*

During the eighteenth century there was a dramatic increase in the speed with
which fashions were emulated, and a corresponding increase in the speed with
which fashions changed. These changes were often perceived as the result of
chance or female caprice rather than deliberate (if sometimes unconscious)
emulation. For example, the *Magasin des modes nouvelles* declared:

> When you see a fashion beginning to go over the top, you will say: Its end is
> approaching, and in a little while it will be undone. As there should be constant
> variety in fabrics, in colors, in the distribution of these colors, in their
> combination, to satisfy our taste, from the instant that this variety can no longer
> be felt in comparison to some other fabric, color, or combination of colors ... it
> is indispensably necessary to change one's fabric, or color.[1]

A second and related development was the widespread perception that fashion
now signified fashion for fashion's sake: a meaningless quest for change rather

---

[1]   *Magasin des modes nouvelles*, 32ᵉ Cahier, 30 September, 1787, 251.

than a natural evolution. The death of Louis XIV marked the beginning of the breakdown of the autocratic court and the divisions between court and town, town and country. This did not (yet) bring major changes in garments, but it brought an immediate increase in the frequency with which minor changes occurred. The range of available styles expanded to meet the demand for novelty, not just among the upper echelons but across the whole social spectrum.

By the late eighteenth century, it was not enough for fashion to change with the seasons; it changed every day, and sometimes several times per day, or so it was said. The *Magasin des modes nouvelles* explained, 'It would not be enough for fashion, which we know to be so frivolous, so inconstant, not to change except after a certain time, at such an era. . . . It's why she has adopted morning clothes, dinner clothes, and evening clothes.'[2] Marie-Antoinette set an expensive example for her subjects; this may have been good for commerce, but it proved ruinous to the husbands, fathers, and, indeed, kings who financed these frivolities. By 1774, Mercier would write: 'The expense of fashion today exceeds that of the table and that of carriages. The unfortunate husband can never calculate how expensive these changeable whims will be; and he needs to have means available in order to be prepared for these unexpected caprices. He will have fingers pointed at him, if he does not pay for these trifles as faithfully as he pays the butcher and the baker.'[3]

The decade preceding the French Revolution, in particular, brought unprecedented changes in the cut and construction as well as the trimming of garments. 'What a number of changes in a short time!' marveled Goldoni in 1787. '*Polonaises, lévites, fourreaux, robes à l'anglaise, chemises, pierrots, robes à la turque*, and hats of a hundred shapes, bonnets without number, and *coiffures*! . . . *Coiffures!*'[4] Hats and hairstyles, which could be updated quickly and inexpensively, were more sensitive to the vacillations of fashion than garments, but these vacillations increasingly began to affect the whole body from head to toe.

As this happened, it became more and more difficult to keep up – and more important. 'What a puzzling Matter Dress is become within these two or three Years,' Mrs. Crewe remarked as she prepared for a ball at Versailles in 1786. 'All

[2]   *Magasin des modes nouvelles*, 10ᵉ Cahier, 20 February, 1787, 73.

[3]   Louis-Sébastien Mercier, *Tableau de Paris*, I, ed. Jean-Claude Bonnet (Paris: Mercure de France, 1994), 409.

[4]   Carlo Goldoni, *Mémoires pour servir à l'histoire de sa vie et à celle de son théâtre*, 2 (Geneva: Slatkine Reprints, 1968), 346.

the old Laws belonging to it are repealed, so that many a poor Body, who has not much Judgment or Taste, Sins more innocently, and is laughed at for an Affectation of her own, tho' her appearing so uncouthly proceeds merely from Ignorance, or Indolence and letting the Milliner decide.'[5] With the repeal of the 'old Laws' – of taste as well as etiquette – consumers were left adrift. Historian Madeleine Delpierre identified the reign of Louis XVI as the dawn of 'fashion in its current meaning of change for its own sake, without too much respect for tradition (which was by then considered the mark of a primitive society).'[6] In June 1787, the *Magasin des modes nouvelles* joked that the variable French weather was responsible for unseasonable fashions in its pages, before admitting, 'It's not the cold that is causing us to show you wool suits, it's fashion.'[7] [...]

The eighteenth century saw the birth of fashion as we know it today: that is, seasonal, international, corporate, media-driven, feminine in character, and constantly changing. Then, as now, fashion was a major domestic and export industry in France, centered in Paris but drawing clients, craftsmen, materials, and inspiration from around the world. In the second half of the century, the relaxation of the guild *(corporation)* system that regulated the French fashion trades paved the way for innovation and autonomy, and new fashions began to appear and disappear with unprecedented speed. Mass production and ready-to-wear clothing were being pioneered on a small scale, though the technology necessary to realize their full potential did not yet exist. Today's fashion industry has its roots in the reign of Louis XVI.

The advent of the fashion magazine in the 1770s ensured that these developments had a wide and immediate impact, radiating outwards from Paris to the far corners of the globe. Fashion magazines – as opposed to individual fashion plates or stand-alone costume books – first appeared in France in the 1770s, irregularly at first, then with increasing frequency until April 1793, when the Revolution put an end to such superficialities. Previously, fashions had been publicized by dolls or *poupées*, life-sized or smaller, which were sent forth fully dressed from Paris to foreign shops and customers each month.[8] Fashion

---

[5]   British Library, Add. MSS 37926, fol. 38.
[6]   Madeleine Delpierre, *Dress in France in the Eighteenth Century*, trans. Caroline Beamish (New Haven and London: Yale University Press, 1997), 151.
[7]   *Magasin des modes nouvelles*, 23ᵉ Cahier, 30 June, 1787: 179.
[8]   See Mercier, *Tableau de Paris*, 2, 409–10.

magazines were a much more effective and cost-effective form of publicity. They quickly replaced *poupées* in foreign markets, as well as finding French readers. Although these early fashion magazines targeted a small, elite audience of literate subscribers, their high frequency and rich, almost pedantic detail made them disproportionately influential. Furthermore, there is evidence that they may have reached a wider, less affluent, yet equally fashion-conscious audience above and beyond the small circle of wealthy subscribers; 1788, the editor of the *Magasin des modes nouvelles* refused to send extra copies to his subscribers, explaining, 'It is not fair that if shop assistants, porters and servants make off with copies we should have to supply them twice.'[9]

As new fashions began to appear at an unprecedented rate, commentators puzzled over how to describe and publicize them quickly and effectively. The fast pace of French fashion was a common satirical trope as early as 1721 when Montesquieu asked in his *Lettres persanes*:

> What is the use of my giving you an exact description of their dress and ornaments? A new fashion would destroy all my labor, as it does that of their dressmakers, and, before you could receive my letter, everything would be changed. A woman who leaves Paris to go and spend six months in the country returns as antiquated as if she had been gone thirty years.[10]

Fifty years later, Mercier was not entirely joking when he wrote in the *Tableau de Paris*, 'Oh! How to paint that which, by its extreme mobility, eludes the brush? I wanted to give here a little dictionary of fashions and their singularities; but as soon as I wrote, the language of the boutiques changed.'[11] And Goldoni wryly observed that the French fashions he mocked in his *Mémoires* (published in 1787) might disappear by the time the book went to press.[12] Fashion was, by definition, changeable; major advances in manufacturing, transportation, and communication over the course of the eighteenth century gradually quickened these changes to a breakneck pace.

The fashion magazine was designed to keep track of these rapid developments, though it effectively caused them as well. The *Gallerie des modes*, the first fashion

---

[9] Quoted in Daniel Roche, *The Culture of Clothing: Dress and Fashion in the 'ancien regime*, trans. Jean Birrell (Cambridge: Cambridge University Press, 1994), 7.
[10] Montesquieu, *Lettres persanes*, ed. P. Vernière (Paris: Classiques Garnier, 1992), 205.
[11] Mercier, *Tableau de Paris*, I, 398; I, 411.
[12] Goldoni, *Mémoires*, 2, 347.

magazine published with any regularity, appeared in 1778, followed in 1785 by the *Cabinet des modes* (later renamed the *Magasin des modes nouvelles, françaises et angloises*). In its inaugural issue, the *Cabinet des modes* promised 'an accurate and prompt understanding of new clothing and finery'; it was published every fifteen days in its first year, increasing to every ten days in subsequent years.[13] Improvements in the international postal system in the late eighteenth century meant that fashion magazines could travel farther and faster. These self-proclaimed 'Missionaries of Fashion' carried news and illustrations of French fashions to those 'not fortunate enough to live in Paris.'[14] But even fashion magazines found it difficult to keep up with fashion's quickening pace. In December 1786, the *Magasin des modes nouvelles* noted with some concern that it took eight days for the magazine to reach bookstores in Germany and Liège by coach, and fifteen more days for copies to reach subscribers there, by which time the contents were out of date. 'You know that in Paris, it is rare that a fashion exists beyond three weeks or a month, in a fixed and unvaried state. Who would want an outdated fashion?'[15]

The Temporal Architecture of Fashion: Its Seasons and Weeks

Aurélie Van de Peer

Aurélie Van de Peer, 'So Last Season: The Production of the Fashion Present in the Politics of Time', *Fashion Theory* 18, no 3 (2014), 328–31.

Aurélie Van de Peer provides a theoretical and historical overview of the 'temporal architecture' of Western fashion that she argues was created by the development of what today is called the fashion press. Like Chrisman-Campbell and other scholars, Van de Peer finds the origins of the fashion season in seventeenth-century France, and links it to Le Mercure Galant, *the first periodical to devote significant coverage to fashion, in the reign of Louis XIV. She highlights how Louis's motives for establishing fashion seasons were economic rather than social (he wished to expand his mercantile economy). While the first fashion seasons were poorly aligned with*

---

[13]   *Cabinet des modes*, 1ᵉʳ Cahier, 15 November, 1785, I.
[14]   *Magasin des modes nouvelle*, 19ᵉ Cahier, 20 May, 1789, 146.
[15]   *Magasin des modes nouvelles*, 4ᵉ Cahier, 20 December, 1787, 29.

the natural seasons, they were regular and biannual, following the allotted time slots reported in the periodicals that announced them, including the first fashion magazines in the 1770s. The fashion season, Van de Peer argues, allowed fashion to become anchored in society, and from there to transgress national boundaries. With the proliferation of fashion magazines in the nineteenth century came an important second stage in the development of the 'temporal architecture of fashion': the emergence of haute couture in the nineteenth century, and of fashion weeks and fashion shows in the early twentieth. Lastly, Van de Peer outlines how, throughout the twentieth century, this rigid biannual seasonal calendar affected not only designers but also the entire field of high fashion, including its customers. The very notion of the season, she argues, trains people up to think of fashion as inherently transient and changeable, and in this way the idea of change is naturalized and fashion and its institutions are able to 'order the public sphere'.

In his book *L'Ordre du Temps* (1984) the Polish philosopher of history Krzysztof Pomian developed the notion of 'temporal architecture'[1] to designate the idea that time, rather than an objective reality, is an order requiring a chronometric operation. The sociologist Eviatar Zerubavel (1982) would agree with Pomian's argument that time is a social construct.[2] He takes a more phenomenological approach, however, in understanding why we take for granted the sequential regularity of everyday life involving 'before' and 'after.' Following Harold Garfinkel's (1967) notions of 'figure' and 'ground' (themselves inspired by the work of Maurice Merleau-Ponty) in 'making sense' of 'normal' practices,[3] Zerubavel demonstrates how our everyday world, by the application of time constructs (e.g. hour, day, week, month, year, season, epoch, century), receives a temporal anchorage from which to grant free-floating figures a ground against which they can be perceived. He adds that when we encounter 'groundless figures,' we feel the strong need to establish such temporal anchorage or ground because without it the figure makes little sense. I would argue that before *la mode* received a rigid temporal anchorage it was a groundless figure.

[1] Krzysztof Pomian, *L'ordre du temps* (Paris: Gallimard, 1984).
[2] Eviatar Zerubavel, *Hidden Rhythms: Schedules and Calendars in Social Life* (Chicago: University of Chicago Press, 1981), 19–21.
[3] Harold Garfinkel, *Studies in Ethnomethodology* (Englewood Cliffs, NJ: Prentice-Hall, 1967), 43–45.

Dictionary, academic, and producers' definitions regard ephemerality and changeability as the crux of fashion, regardless of the duration of the time lapse between moments of passing. Until well into the late eighteenth century the fickle goddess of fashion was regarded with anxiety as her changes seemed beyond human control, popping up at indeterminate moments.[4] *The Mercure Galant* (1672–1724), the first periodical journal to dedicate considerable space to the topic of fashion under the auspices of Louis XIV, made the original attempt to govern its unpredictability by organizing the changes of *la mode* according to four principles: 'royal authority, social rank, the season or weather, and gender.'[5] Much earlier than Lisa Skov's observation of seasonal fashion change originating in the nineteenth century, the *Mercure* published pieces on the latest fashions in the Spring/Summer and in the Fall/Winter.[6] In doing so the periodical rendered its content into a 'timepiece' that, much like clocks and calendars, publicly displayed the new seasonal rhythm of fashion.[7] Such a seasonal ruling of fashion was primarily inspired by the wish of the Sun King and his minister of finance, Jean-Baptiste Colbert, to furnish and expand the French mercantilist economy. As Koselleck (2002: 3) reminds us, we simply cannot conceive of time without dating by naturalistic temporal divisions, although the experience of time cannot be degraded to temporal measures drawn from nature (e.g. season).[8]

Organizing fashion change by the season surely benefited the French economy because of the rhythm's propensity to be understood and accepted across borders. Yet responses were far from positive at first as the fashion seasons did not necessarily coincide with the natural seasons on which they were modeled, causing both consumers and merchants great distress.[9] It is ironic to have the most artificial phenomenon of all, as Baudelaire (1995[1863]) claimed a century later, mimic the natural changing of seasons. The budding high fashion industry thus unexpectedly turned the 'older' cyclical and eternal temporality of the 'natural season' into a

[4] Jennifer Jones, *Sexing La Mode: Gender, Fashion and Commercial Culture in Old Regime France* (Oxford and New York: Berg, 2007).
[5] Jones, *Sexing La Mode*, 28.
[6] Lisa Skov, 'Snapshot. Fashion Week'. In *Fashion Worldwide*, 230–31. Part 4 of *Global Perspectives*, vol. X, *Berg Encyclopedia of World Dress and Fashion*, eds Joanne B. Eicher and Phyllis G. Tortora. (Oxford and New York: Berg), 2007, 230–31.
[7] Hans Ulrich Gumbrecht, *In 1926: Living at the Edge of Time* (Cambridge MA: Harvard University Press, 1997), 233–40.
[8] Reinhart Koselleck, *The Practice of Conceptual History: Timing History, Spacing Concepts* (Stanford CA: Stanford University Press, 2002), 3.
[9] Jones, *Sexing La Mode*, 33.

designation that fragmented fashion time in the irrevocable time slots of the 'fashion season.'[10] Such temporal anchorage not only allowed *la mode* to transgress further national boundaries on the seeming analogy with the universal seasons of nature, it also granted the fickle changes of fashion a 'rationality' of sorts. We may not know what fashion will offer us next, but at least by the late eighteenth century we could expect major changes to occur twice a year.

A century after the *Mercure*'s initial installment of seasonal fashion change, the *Cabinet des Mode* (1785–93) entered onto the scene. At this point only the season and gender had survived from the four earlier structuring principles.[11] In the *Cabinet des Modes*, renamed *Magasin des modes nouvelles* (30 September, 1788), the fashion season worked like clockwork: 'On the seventh of this month, everyone put on their fall clothing.'[12] By the time the number of fashion publications exploded in the early and mid-nineteenth century, an important chapter in the temporal architecture of fashion had been built. In 1874 Stéphane Mallarmé had his alter ego, the fashion reporter Marguerite de Ponty, state in the fashion magazine *La Dernière Mode* that seasonal renewal was a law of fashion:

> Why do I say all this, if not that (except in the case of lingerie, which obeys other laws of fashion than those of the season) we wish, at this moment of renewal, to reclothe our lady-reader from top to toe?[13]

Other early fashion theorists followed suit. For instance, both Karl Marx (1976(1867): 608) in *Capital*[14] and Thorstein Veblen in *The Theory of the Leisure Class* (1899)[15] took for granted that fashion was temporally structured by biannual seasonal change when what was fashionable became old-fashioned.

The institutionalization of a twice-yearly *haute couture* 'fashion week' in early twentieth-century Paris marked an important second chapter in the existing temporal architecture of fashion. Gumbrecht notes that '[t]ime that is kept in the

---

10   Charles Baudelaire, 'The Painter of Modern Life'. In *The Painter of Modern Life and Other Essays*, trans. Jonathan Mayne (London: Phaidon, 1965).

11   Jones, *Sexing La Mode*, 183.

12   *Cabinet des Modes. Magasin des modes nouvelles*, 30 September 1788. Cit. in Jones, *Sexing La Mode*, 206, n. 12.

13   Stéphane Mallarmé, *La Dernière Mode*, no. 2, 20 September, 1874. Cit. in P. N. Furbank, A. M. Cain, *Mallarmé on Fashion. A Translation of the Fashion Magazine La Dernière Mode, with Commentary* (Oxford and New York: Berg, 2004), 51.

14   Karl Marx, *Das Kapital. Kritik Der Politischen Ökonomie* (Hamburg: *Otto Meissner*; New York: L. W. Schmidt, 1867).

15   Thorstein Veblen, *The Theory of the Leisure Class. An Economic Study of Institutions* (New York: Macmillan, 1899).

form of a constant rhythm needs to be publicly visible.'[16] Fashion shows grouped in 'fashion weeks' signal for a great audience of producers and consumers that the time for fashion change has yet again arrived. In 1911 *La Chambre Syndicale de la Couture Parisienne* (since 1973 *La Fédération Française de la Couture du Prêt-à-Porter des Couturiers and Créateurs de Mode*), a trade organization having its origins in the mid-nineteenth century, centralized Parisian couture into a fashion system.[17] The first institutionalized fashion shows ... further rigidified the existing temporal architecture of fashion. These trade events with ritualistic aspects expose designers' latest collections to gatekeepers, such as journalists and buyers.[18]

Presenting a new collection during the Parisian fashion week is essential for the livelihood of every aspiring high fashion designer.[19] Official inclusion on the member list of the *Fédération*, moreover, allows designers the privilege to pick the date and hour for their runway show from the calendar the *Fédération* designs every season. Like every type of calendar,[20] the show calendar of the *Fédération* strengthens in-group sentiments and exudes social control at the same time.

Moreover, the Parisian show calendar is invested with great prestige. A newly appointed designer testifies: '[a]ll my friends and staff members were surprised and excited to see my name there. You suddenly become official. People look at you differently.'[21] It is not only designers that work within this seasonal rhythm, however. The entire field of high fashion production, from fashion buyers[22] to fashion journalists, follows this rigid temporal architecture that – chronologically speaking – is always four to six months (one season) ahead of the consumers of fashion. Although the time slots between the classic two buying seasons have been shortened in recent years with pre-Fall and cruise collections,[23] the fashion weeks for the three types of high fashion (*haute couture*, prêt-à-porter, and menswear) still have the 'fashion season' as their central axis.

[16] Gumbrecht, *In 1926*, 238.
[17] Yuniya Kawamura, *The Japanese Revolution in Paris Fashion* (Oxford and New York: Berg, 2004), 38.
[18] Kawamura, *The Japanese Revolution*, 61.
[19] Kawamura, *The Japanese Revolution*, 62.
[20] Zerubavel, *Hidden Rhythms*, 111–49.
[21] Kawamura, *The Japanese Revolution*, 64.
[22] Joanne Entwistle, *The Aesthetic Economy of Fashion: Markets and Values in Clothing and Modeling*, (Oxford and New York: Berg, 2009).
[23] Ibid; Lisa Skov, 'Snapshot. Fashion Week', n.p.

In a recent contribution the sociologists Patrik Aspers and Frédéric Godart define fashion as 'the unplanned process of recurrent change against the backdrop of order in the public realm,'[24] after which they add that fashion 'can take place only given a background that is more stable than what is about to change.'[25] This section established that a public temporal order for the plentiful changes in fashionable dress was established by the investiture of the fashion season as an important chapter in the ongoing process of chronometric operations on the experience of fashion temporality. I would argue that the public display of fashion change as seasonally motivated, for instance on the pages of the fashion press and later in the time-grouped showings of the latest collections, contributed to an experience of the transience and changeability of fashion as a normal, understandable, or 'grounded' feature of everyday life. In other words, the chronological architecture of fashion as organized by the season granted its changes the required background order in the public sphere. Through a variety of public discourses and practices we have naturalized the idea that the major changes of fashion enter our day-to-day lives at least two times a year, when the buds stem on the trees or when the leaves turn brown. The now self-evident rhythm of designer fashion thus forces its *passagèreté* into a scheme of regular, entrenched moments of change in a regime of historicity[26] that largely shapes the experience of fashion change by the law of the season, although the institutionalized points of entry for the new have increased over the past decades. Admittedly, the gradual installment of the chronological anchorage of fashion over the past 300 years and the possible challenges to the chronometric operations that aimed for such irreversible order merit a more detailed account in future research. Yet I believe that it remains safe to conclude that the temporal architecture of fashion is a social convention. The next section sets out to show that the irreversible character of seasonal change has offered the high fashion industry more than a frame for global expansion: the potential to employ chronology in a politics of time.

---

[24] Patrik Aspers and Frédéric Godart, 'Sociology of Fashion: Order and Change', *Annual Review of Sociology* 39 (July 2013), 171.

[25] Aspers and Godart, 'Sociology of Fashion', 187.

[26] François Hartog, *Régimes d'historicité. Présentisme et expériences du temps* (Seuil: Paris, 2013).

Threadbare Dandy Fashion

Jules Barbey d'Aurevilly

Jules Barbey d'Aurevilly, 'On Dandyism and George Brummell'
[2nd ed. 1861] in: George Walden, *Who's a Dandy?*
(London: Gibson Square Books, 2002), 78–80.

The dandy is included here as an individual alienated from industrial time. The early nineteenth-century dandy spent hours every morning refining and perfecting his appearance before he ventured out in public. His lengthy toilette might have been designed as a challenge to the idea of standardized time as it was later to develop in the 1880s; and his perfectly tailored clothing was equally at odds with nineteenth-century ready-to-wear clothing.

In 1863, the art critic and poet Charles Baudelaire described the dandy as an aristocrat of taste in his essay 'The Painter of Modern Life'. Two years before, Jules Barbey d'Aurevilly had asserted that dandyism was far more than 'a happy and audacious dictatorship of exterior elegance and dress', in the expanded second edition of his biography of the regency dandy Beau Brummell, Du dandysme et de G. Brummell. *Dandyism was also, he wrote, an entire way of being, and, furthermore, one composed entirely of nuances. He gave an example of the dandy's flair in a footnote (itself a dandyish gesture) which is reproduced below. In it, Barbey d'Aurevilly described the extreme delicacy and lengthy time required to distress a jacket with a piece of ground glass. Roughing up an exquisite coat has its modern day parallel in the use of sand-blasting to produce distressed denim, except that the environmental consequences of the latter are far greater, and more deleterious.*

A Dandy is not just a walking, talking suit of clothes! On the contrary, what constitutes Dandyism is a particular way of wearing them. One can wear rumpled clothes and still be a Dandy. Lord Spencer managed it with an outfit that had a single coat-tail, and even that he eventually cut off, and made it into the thing that has since carried his name. At one time, believe it or not, the Dandies dreamed up a style that might be called the threadbare look. It happened under Brummell. They had reached the very limits of their impertinence, they could go no further – yet the Dandies found a way: this was the Dandyish idea (I know of no other word to express it) of having their clothes distressed before they put them on, rubbed all over till they were no more than a kind of lace – a mist of cloth. They were gods who wanted to walk in their own clouds! To do it they used a piece of sharpened glass, and the procedure was extremely delicate and time-consuming. Now that was a true act of Dandyism. The clothes themselves are nothing to do with it, since by that point they scarcely existed!

The Pace of Fashion

Georg Simmel

Georg Simmel, 'Fashion' [1904], trans. and reprinted in
The American Journal of Sociology 62, no. 6 (May, 1957): 556–57.

Industrial time impacted significantly on individual fashion consumption in the early twentieth century. In 1911 the German sociologist Georg Simmel published the extended version of his now well-known analysis of fashion, Die Mode, *in his collection of essays* Philosophische Kultur. *Simmel related rapid fashion change to economics and to industrial production, at a time when mass-produced fashion was at take-off point. In the passage leading to the one reprinted below, he differentiated the middle class, which had a vested interest in change, from the conservative upper and working classes, who resisted change. Fashion, therefore, would seem to offer more to the socially mobile middle classes. But Simmel also points out an inherent contradiction in fashion time, that transient fashion always presents the appearance of permanence. This is one of fashion's many 'antagonistic' characteristics that Simmel identifies, encapsulated in his phrase 'change itself does not change'. He also makes an argument for fashion as circular, although this obliges him temporarily to turn his back on questions of social and economic context that would suggest different meanings for the same styles when they come back round the second time. His argument anticipates one of the central concepts of this book, and the subject of its second section, antilinear time.*

Classes and individuals who demand constant change, because the rapidity of their development gives them the advantage over others, find in fashion something that keeps pace with their own soul movements. Social advance above all is favorable to the rapid change of fashion, for it capacitates lower classes so much for imitation of upper ones, and thus the process characterized above, according to which every higher set throws aside a fashion the moment a lower set adopts it, has acquired a breadth and activity never dreamed of before.

This fact has important bearing on the content of fashion. Above all else it brings in its train a reduction in the cost and extravagance of fashions. In earlier times there was a compensation for the costliness of the first acquisition or the difficulties in transforming conduct and taste in the longer duration of their sway. The more an article becomes subject to rapid changes of fashion, the greater the demand for *cheap* products of its kind, not only because the larger and therefore poorer classes nevertheless have enough purchasing power to regulate industry and demand objects, which at least bear the outward semblance of style, but also because even the higher circles of society could not afford to adopt the rapid changes in fashion forced upon them by the imitation of the lower circles, if the objects were not relatively cheap. The rapidity of the development is of such importance in actual articles of fashion that it even withdraws them from certain advances of economy gradually won in other fields. It has been noticed, especially in the older branches of modern productive industry, that the speculative element gradually ceases to play an influential *role*. The movements of the market can be better overlooked, requirements can be better foreseen and production can be more accurately regulated than before, so that the rationalization of production makes greater and greater inroads on chance conjunctures, on the aimless vacillation of supply and demand. Only pure articles of fashion seem to prove an exception. The polar oscillations, which modern economics in many instances knows how to avoid and from which it is visibly striving towards entirely new economic orders and forms, still hold sway in the field immediately subject to fashion. The element of feverish change is so essential here that fashion stands, as it were, in a logical contrast to the tendencies for development in modern economics.

In contrast to this characteristic, however, fashion possesses this peculiar quality, that every individual type to a certain extent makes its appearance as though it intended to live forever. When we furnish a house these days, intending the articles to last a quarter of a century, we invariably invest in furniture designed according to the very latest patterns and do not even consider articles in vogue two years before. Yet it is evident that the attraction of fashion will desert the present article just as it left the earlier one, and satisfaction or dissatisfaction with both forms is determined by other material criterions. A peculiar psychological process seems to be at work here in addition to the mere bias of the moment. Some fashion always exists and fashion *per se* is indeed immortal, which fact seems to affect in some manner or other each of its manifestations, although the very nature of each individual fashion stamps it as being transitory. The fact that change itself does not change, in this instance endows each of the objects which it affects with a psychological appearance of duration.

This apparent duration becomes real for the different fashion-contents within the change itself in the following special manner. Fashion, to be sure, is concerned only with change, yet like all phenomena it tends to conserve energy; it endeavors to attain its objects as completely as possible, but nevertheless with the relatively most economical means. For this very reason, fashion repeatedly returns to old forms, as is illustrated particularly in wearing-apparel; and the course of fashion has been likened to a circle. As soon as an earlier fashion has partially been forgotten there is no reason why it should not be allowed to return to favor and why the charm of difference, which constitutes its very essence, should not be permitted to exercise an influence similar to that which it exerted conversely some time before.

My Best Work Is Done Only When I Am Under Pressure

Mary Quant

Mary Quant, *Quant by Quant* (London: Cassell & Company, 1966), 147–49.

In her autobiography the British designer Mary Quant, who exemplified youth-oriented fashion in the early 1960s, describes her busy day in staccato prose that evokes the rapid-fire speed with which many fashion designers still work today. Her lack of punctuation and vernacular idiom suggest the spoken word, as if Quant were talking into a tape-recorder rather than writing (perhaps she was). 'My best work is done only when I am under pressure,' she writes, acknowledging the fact that designing a new collection was only a small part of her hectic daily schedule. In this excerpt, Quant shows how in the 1960s, just as in subsequent decades, the distinction between work and social life was blurred in London fashion, as she rushes from one appointment to another.

I have had to learn not to waste thinking time. It is not necessary to be writing or drawing all the time but you must always be thinking. If you have really thought anything out to the last detail, it can be put on paper in a matter of minutes. Any sudden demand acts like a shot of adrenalin and makes it just that much more exciting.

I give the impression that my best work is done only when I am under pressure. What is not understood is that what I produce at the last minute is the climax of all I have done before. The best work is done at the end because of all you have learned from earlier mistakes. Sudden, urgent demand brings into sharp focus all the things you have been thinking about often quite unconsciously. Everything falls into place.

But, quite apart from designing clothes, I have to do a lot of other things, too. They are all more or less important and one needs to keep one's head.

A fairly typical day in my life might go like this:

10.00 a.m. Take last night's sketches to the workroom and discuss them with the cutters.
11.00 a.m.–12.30 p.m. See the ranges from six or seven cloth merchants for a collection which will go into the shops nine months later.
12.30 p.m. Tom Wolsey to discuss the designs of labels and swing tickets for a new range for America.
1.00 p.m. Choose trimmings from a selection made by our cloth buyer.
1.15 p.m. Lunch in the restaurant round the corner with Archie, Alexander and the managing director of a hosiery firm who want to produce Quant stockings.
2.30 p.m. To Youthlines to look at the first samples of the new underwear made to my drawings.
3.15 p.m. To the Ginger Group to meet Canadian journalists doing a piece about us.
4.00 p.m. Vidal Sassoon.
5.15 p.m. Back to workroom to see latest dresses tried on by Jan de Souza or Sarah Dawson.
5.30 p.m. Austin Garrett brings some skins for the next furs.
6.30 p.m. Home. Drinks with the design director of the Butterick pattern company who publish my things from time to time.
8.00 p.m. Dinner chez Rendlesham.
10.00 p.m. The Purely Ball.

And – apart from this – I may have to talk to dozens of people on the telephone from journalists and licensees to cloth mills and scientists developing new material for us.

The thing about a day like this is that, quite apart from the maddening frustrations of trying to move from one part of London to another in a limited time, I am not stationary – physically or mentally – for any length of time in any one place.

My mind has to switch from the clothes I am itching to design at this moment to those I will be doing six, even twelve, months ahead.

In a Press interview, I have to try to turn my thoughts back six months or more to the way I was thinking when I made the dresses designed then and currently being shown to the fashion journalists and buyers before going into the shops. I have to try to cut my mind off completely from the ideas seething there for collections which will not be seen for another six months because it is obviously important that I do not disclose too soon the new colours, new shapes, new lines, beginning to come to life on the drawing board.

We're Stuck between the Old and the New Rhythm

Anja Aronowsky Cronberg and Christophe Lemaire

Christophe Lemaire. 'On Aiming for the Ideal while Rooting for Reality'. Interview by Anja Aronowsky Cronberg. *Vestoj: the Journal of Sartorial Matters*, no. 5, 'On Slowness' (Autumn 2014), 149–50.

Christophe Lemaire's many roles are typical of the early twenty-first-century designer. Artistic director of his eponymous brand, an independent Paris fashion label, he also designs the Uniqlo U Collection, and was formerly the artistic director of the luxury fashion brand Hermès. Straddling these different industry sectors, Lemaire explains in an interview with Anja Aronowsky Cronberg for the issue of Vestoj *magazine dedicated to slowness, that 'Right now, we're stuck between the old and the new rhythm.' He talks about the anxiety brought on by the accelerated pace of working in fashion today, and the discomfort of working in a globalized fashion system in the process of rapid change.*

In a business where designers often become figureheads for large corporations, to be rolled out when a perfume or handbag needs promoting, Christophe Lemaire is an unusually outspoken exception to the rule. Another exception to the unwritten fashion rules is the time that he gives to everything he does. Even interviews. Over several days, many hours and plenty of coffee Christophe talked candidly and convincingly about anxiety in the fashion industry, the ever-accelerating pace of the fashion schedule and the hypocrisy of big fashion corporations. Christophe himself, after a decade at Lacoste and four years at Hermès, is today focusing on his own company, which he runs with Sarah-Linh Tran, his girlfriend and overall sounding board in work and life. Together they are navigating the perhaps riskiest moment for a growing fashion brand – the one when all eyes are on you and those who purport themselves to be 'in the know' speak of you as the best thing since sliced bread. With fastidiousness and tenacity, while never forgetting the importance of sound design ideology and solid company ethics, they are moving forward, one step at a time.

Anja   Many people complain about the detrimental effects that the speeded up pace of contemporary fashion has on creativity. Is that something you've noticed too?

Christophe   Yes, the speed of the business now is crazy. I don't agree with it. You need time to create and to think, but today designers have to make a new collection every three months. You don't have a choice. Or I don't in any case. Pre-collections have become hugely important – if you want to increase sales, you need to offer products as early in the season as possible.

Anja   How do you think that the tempo affects those who work in the industry?

Christophe   There is so much anxiety in this business. People are anxious all the time. Every few months, you have to prove that you're still at the top of your game. The competition and the time pressure can be overwhelming at times. It's very hard to achieve something you're completely satisfied with in the limited time we have now. And at the same time, this is an industry full of sensitive, creative people who are always doubting what they do. I think this is one of the reasons why fashion people sometimes behave in ridiculous ways. We overreact and behave badly. I catch myself doing the same at times.

Anja   What do you think has prompted the industry to accelerate in this way?

Christophe   It's something that's been happening for the past ten, fifteen years. Some powerful company must have realised that the earlier they could deliver to stores, the more they would sell. If you deliver your collection in March, as we used to, you have two months to sell it before the sales start – if you deliver in January you have twice as long. Customers have become used to buying summer clothes in January now, so the smaller companies have had to follow suit to keep up. At Hermès I would be choosing fabrics for the winter collection in June/July. In September I would prepare the fashion show for spring/summer and at the same time present research, design ideas and sketches for the winter collection, which would be shown to buyers in early December. In May we would be delivering the winter collection to stores. You'd be surprised if you knew how many clients want to buy fur in May. The wealthy want to show that they're first with everything.

Anja   Has this affected the way you work at Lemaire too?

Christophe   Yes of course. Our development manager tells us that if we want to reach the next level in our own growth, we'll have to start showing the womenswear autumn/winter collection in January instead of March. The buyers all come to Paris in January with their budgets now. If you wait to show the collection until after the fashion show in March, it's too late – the big budgets have been spent. Buyers prioritise brands that they know will deliver early. So of course this shift has deep consequences for our way of working, for how our team is organised, let alone for my peace of mind. But it's just the way the industry works now; we all have to adapt to survive.

Anja   Do you think that this means that a permanent change for the fashion seasons is under way?

Christophe   Yes, I think eventually what will happen is that the fashion show schedules will shift. They'll have to happen earlier to accommodate the change in buying. Right now, we're stuck in between the old and the new rhythm. Fashion is a global business now, and there are so many brands and markets that operate on different seasons. As a designer you have to make sure that you show some wool in the summer season and lighter fabrics in the winter. It's a bit chaotic now because we have to accommodate two different timings simultaneously.

New Fashion Media and the Acceleration of Fashion Time

Agnès Rocamora

Agnès Rocamora, 'New Fashion Times: Fashion and Digital Media'.
In Sandy Black et al. (eds), *The Handbook of Fashion Studies*
(London and New York: Bloomsbury, 2013), 61, 68–71 and 73–74.

The sociologist Agnès Rocamora looks at the compression of fashion time at the turn of the millennium through new media: websites, blogs, Twitter and online magazines. In these new forms of fashion communication, as much as in fashion design, she finds evidence of accelerated speed in both work and consumption. 'Type at 80 wpm!' says the fashion blogger Susie Lau when asked her advice on fashion blogging. Rocamora notes that speed in itself is not new in fashion media which, since the eighteenth century, have contributed to 'social acceleration'. She argues, however, that the new technologies of communication that enable blogging, for example, do more than speed up the pace of fashionable consumption: they alter its structure and style, through texts and 'hypertexts' that create restless and truncated patterns of online reading, so that 'hopping on and off' a website or social media channel several times a day replaces the traditional 'daily read' of a magazine or newspaper.

On August 21, 2011, popular fashion blogger Sasha Wilkins (LibertyLondonGirl. com) posted a message apologizing for 'the unexpected hiatus in posting.' I scrolled down the page to see when she had last updated her site, expecting to see a gap of weeks or maybe even months; it turned out she had not posted for three days. Three days only. That she felt obliged to apologize struck me as an illustration of the redefinition of time the field of fashion is currently experiencing; a new time defined by the speeding up of the circulation of material and symbolic goods. It is this process of acceleration, more specifically as articulated on the Internet, that is the object of the present chapter. [. . .]

Fashion websites have become key platforms for the circulation of fashion discourse. The following section focuses on these and, more particularly, on fashion blogs. It briefly charts the rise of digital fashion platforms and discusses the ways time is embedded in them. Temporality and the idea of speed, it is shown, are part of the makeup of digital fashion both in terms of the internal organization of digital fashion pages and in terms of their structural linking, that is, the hypertextual and rhizomatic nature of digital texts. In this section, then, I approach time both as a key signifier of fashion discourse as well as an organizing, structural factor.

The first fashion websites appeared in the mid-1990s. In the United Kingdom, for instance, 1995 saw the birth of Vogue.com, with the subsequent years witnessing the launch and proliferation of more websites, including *apc.fr* (1996), *WGSN* (1998), *Net-a-porter.com* (June 2000), *SHOWstudio* (November 2000), *Dazeddigital* (November 2006), and *Nowness* (February 2010).[1]

However, a key moment in the history of digital fashion came with the creation in the early twenty-first century of fashion blogs. Among the first was *nogoodforme*, launched in 2003.[2] At first the products of nonprofessional and independent individuals, they quickly became appropriated by various fashion institutions as a way of further disseminating their visions and values. They are now central to the field of fashion and have contributed to the speeding up of its discourse, as I argue in the remainder of this section.

Blog posts appear anti-chronologically, with the most recent posts the first to appear on the screen. Their newness is signaled through the display of the date of posting but also, often, through the indication of the time at which a new entry was posted: Indeed, some bloggers update their sites many times a day. On *bryanboy.com*, for instance, the time of posting is clearly indicated above the title of the new post. The digits thereby displayed are evocative of digital clocks.

In his essay on time Norbert Elias reminds us of the symbolic and social dimension of time as captured and constructed in clocks. He asks, 'What do clocks really show when we say that they show the time?'[3] Clocks, he argues, communicate meaning. Similarly, the 'numerical symbols' shown on blogs and other digital fashion platforms to represent a specific time do not simply indicate hours and seconds.[4] Rather they function as signs: signs of rapidity, of immediacy, of the timeliness and fast pace of fashion blogs, characteristics that are also favored by most other blogs. Indeed, thanks to a web-based technology that allows for the instantaneous editing and updating of blogs, one of their defining traits resides in their ability to be in the present, to facilitate the rapid, constant

---

[1]   See also Laird Borrelli, *Net Mode: Web Fashion Now* (London: Thames and Hudson, 2002).
[2]   See Agnès Rocamora, 'Blogs Personnels de mode: Identité et Sociabilité dans la Culture des Apparences' *Sociologie et Sociétés* 43, no. 1 (2011): 19–44.
[3]   Norbert Elias, *An Essay on Time* (Dublin: University College Dublin Press [1984] 2007), 11.
[4]   Elias, *An Essay on Time*, 13.

communication of information.[5] This is particularly true of the microblogging site Twitter, which is premised on the idea of short, fast, constant news, as indicated in the reference to the time elapsed since a tweet was last sent: '2 minutes ago,' '19 minutes ago,' and '2 hours ago,' for instance.

In 2009 fashion players increasingly started to embrace the Twittersphere with the *Business of Fashion* (hereafter BOF) reporting on March 16, 2009, that tweets during the New York Fashion Week were so numerous that 'New York Fashion Week actually became the 4th biggest trend in Twitter.'[6] For the September 2009 collections they report on a new website, FashionTweek, that aggregated tweets on the New York collections, citing the platform's intention to promote 'realtime reaction to the shows, parties and people of Fashion Week NYC.'[7] This enthusiasm for the fashion 'twitterverse' (*BOF*, September 10, 2009) has gone unabated, with the 2011 collections being punctuated by the constant flow of tweets bloggers and journalists alike posted to publicize their latest encounters, mood, or impressions.

The rapid turnover of information has become a trait, more generally, of online fashion media. Not only have they responded to the popularity of the blogosphere through the launch of their own blogs, but they have also embraced speed and immediacy through the creation of sections that clearly feed into the trend for fast news.[8] *Style.com*'s 'the latest' ('The fashion feed: breaking news from across the web'), *interviewmagazine.com*'s 'most recent,' and *Vogue.com*'s 'latest trends' and 'breaking news' are but a few examples of fashion media's promotion of fast fashion news. Thus, for instance, in a 5 June, 2008, interview with *BOF*, Dolly Jones, editor of the UK site Vogue.com, notes the revamping of the site, launched in 1995:

> We have expanded the news to at least 12 stories per day, along with our daily
> Vogue.com Loves slot, we've increased the daily beauty updates. The entire site

---

[5]   Zizi Papacharissi, 'Audience as Media Producers: Content Analysis of 260 Blogs' in *Blogging, Citizenship, and the Future of the Media*, ed. Mark Tremayne (New York: Routledge), 24.

[6]   Vikram Alexei Kansara, 'Tweets and Tribes', *Business of Fashion*, 16 March 2009. Available at http://www.businessoffashion.com/2009/03/fashion-20-tweets-and-tribes.html (accessed 15 October 2012).

[7]   Vikram Alexei Kansara, 'Fashion 2.0 | New York Fashion Tweek', *Business of Fashion*, 10 September 2009. Available at http://www.businessoffashion.com/2009/09/fashion-2-0-new-yorkfashion-tweek .html (accessed 15 October 2012).

[8]   See Angela Phillips, 'Old Sources: New Bottles' in *New Media, Old News: Journalism and Democracy in the Digital Age*, ed. Natalie Fenton (London: Sage, 2010), 87–101, on the emphasis on speed in news journalism.

has a daily feel, with pods around the site updating all the time to show off the latest content – and of course we have the world's first downloadable calendar – that syncs with your own Outlook calendar.[9]

When Bonnier Magazines launched their first digital magazine, *C Mode*, by way of an iPad application in August 2011, rapidity and immediacy were also brought to the fore. The iTunes page states that readers will be able to find out 'what is new and what is hot in fashion right now', adding that the magazine, edited by popular fashion blogger Caroline Blomst, 'is a fast, fun and up-to-date review of the fashion world' and highlighting 'frequency' and 'tempo' as core values.[10]

Fashion media's embrace of the rapid passing of time is not new. The ephemeral being at the very core of fashion, the fashion media have always had to reflect, as well as support, this evanescence through the constant updating of their pages, fashion magazines being themselves fashion commodities. In the twentieth century, for instance, and still to this day perhaps, one of the most influential fashion media has been a daily newspaper, *Women's Wear Daily*, founded in 1910 and now also available online. As Rosa notes, a visible sign of social acceleration in the eighteenth century was the creation of daily newspapers.[11] However, the Internet has instilled a new pace in the media's circulation of news.[12] Blogs have disrupted 'the temporality of traditional news cycles' through their 'real-time virtual feedback loop',[13] which suggests that a daily read is no longer enough.[14] Instead, hopping on and off digital sites has become the norm. As Eriksen notes of Internet newspapers and their frequent updates, 'This kind of media instils a new rhythm and a new restlessness, and – importantly – new routines in the consumption of news'.[15]

Indeed, studies show that online readers allocate short fragments of time to each text they engage with, favoring a swift movement through web pages. Thus, Jakob Nielsen notes that 'the average page visit lasts a little less than a minute. As users rush through Web pages, they have time to read only a quarter of the text

[9] Imran Amed, 'Q&A | Dolly Jones, Editor-in-Chief of Vogue.co.uk', *Business of Fashion*, 5 June 2008. Available at http://www.businessoffashion.com/2008/06/qa-dolly-jones-editor-in-chiefof-voguecouk. html (accessed 2 September 2012).
[10] iTunes Store, available at https://itunes.apple.com/us/app/c-mode/id448580920?mt=8 (accessed 16 August 2011).
[11] Hartmut Rosa, *Accélération: Une Critique Sociale du Temps* (Paris: Découverte, 2010), 149.
[12] Rosa, *Accélération*, 149.
[13] Qason Gallo, quoted in Axel Bruns, *Gatewatching* (New York: Peter Lang, 2005), 217.
[14] Rosa, *Accélération*, 149.
[15] Thomas Hylland Eriksen, *Tyranny of the Moment* (London: Pluto, 2001), 67.

on the pages they actually visit.'[16] This rapid type of online passage has been
supported by the introduction of faster, larger broadband networks, which,
allowing customers to always be connected, have resulted in frequent short visits
to sites and e-mail inboxes.[17] By often being very short, blog posts allow for such
swift movements on- and offline and for the rapid flicking through of information.

The writing style of fashion blogs conveys this idea of a quick-paced movement
through the blogosphere, that of the bloggers. Indeed, typos, abbreviations, and
an informal tone are recurring features of fashion posts.[18] They lend the blogs an
air of immediacy, of the now that has become a key professional value.[19] When
asked for some advice on creating a blog, Susie Lau, for instance, of the popular
Stylebubble, says, 'Type at 80 wpm!' and highlights 'the beauty of the blogging
medium' as 'its ability to connect with readers quite quickly. So if writing well
researched posts are taking up too much time then perhaps you can pare it back
a bit to make it a bit more relaxed.'[20] As Tomlinson notes, contemporary media
presentation 'favours informality, direct conversational modes of address, and a
certain assumption of intimacy (sometimes even of ironic complicity) with the
audience.'[21] 'Pace' is privileged. This results in 'the removal of symbolic barriers
and conventions (the newsreader's desk) which signal the media as mediators,
rather than as, say, everyday acquaintances and interlocutors.'[22] By favoring a
casual, intimate, conversational tone of writing, bloggers have capitalized on this
valuing of immediacy, at the same time as they have reproduced it.[23]

John V. Pavlik observes that 'new technologies can transform the nature of
storytelling and media content in general.'[24] In the fashion blogosphere, they

[16] Jakob Nielson, 'How Long Do Users Stay on Web Pages?', Nielsen Norman Group, 12 September
      2011. Available at http://www.useit.com/alertbox/page-abandonment-time.html (accessed 4
      October 2011).
[17] John V. Pavlik, *Media in the Digital Age* (New York: Columbia University Press, 2008), 12.
[18] Rocamora, 'Blogs Personnels de mode'.
[19] John Tomlinson, *The Culture of Speed* (London: Sage, 2007).
[20] Imran Amed, 'Q&A: A Conversation with Susie from Style Bubble', *Business of Fashion*, 12 November
      2007. Available at http://www.businessoffashion.com/2007/11/qa-aconversation-with-susie-from-
      style-bubble.html (accessed 12 September 2011).
[21] Tomlinson, *The Culture of Speed*, 100.
[22] Ibid.
[23] Rocamora, 'Blogs Personnels de mode'.
[24] Pavlik, *Media in the Digital Age*, 4. See also Stephen Kern, *The Culture of Time and Space: 1880–1918*
      (Cambridge, MA and London: Harvard University Press, 2003), 115.

have paved the way for the frequent production of informal texts whose syntax captures and strengthens fashion and contemporary society's embrace of the ephemeral and of the rapid passing of time. Transience is also an intrinsic part of blogs' makeup by way of their textuality: a hypertextuality. Indeed, the World Wide Web and fashion websites in particular are hypertexts. These are texts whose limits exceed their immediate content, whose borders are fluid and ever-changing.[25] They are made of units that, linked to each other, are constantly on the move, shifting and brought together in endless new reconfigurations. Hypertexts are networked texts. Links, also called hyperlinks, are the arborescence through which such networks are formed.[26] They allow for a rapid movement across an infinite space of words, sounds, and images, a fluidity and rapidity that the idea of surfing through the net aptly captures.

Standard Minute Value (SMV) for a T-Shirt

Ramij Howlader, Monirul Islam (Rajib),
Tanjibul Hasan Sajib, Ripon Kumar Prasad

Ramij Howlader, Monirul Islam (Rajib), Tanjibul Hasan Sajib, Ripon Kumar Prasad, 'Practically Observation of Standard Minute Value of T-shirt', *International Journal of Engineering and Computer Science* 4, no. 3 (March 2015), 10685–89. Available at https://www.researchgate.net/publication/278030039_Practically_observation_of_standard_Minute_Value_of_T-shirt (accessed 18 December 2019).

The table below is a stark illustration of the economics of fast fashion. It comes from an article by a team of Bangladeshi researchers, including textile engineers, who explain SMV (standard minute value), a concept that underpins factory production, especially in sweatshops. SMV is used to evaluate the time, and hence the cost, of cutting out and assembling garments. Time is thereby actuarily calculated as money, and the system brings together productivity, time, workers and fashion to effect, in the authors' words from their abstract, 'a better synchronization with man, machine, materials and methods to achieve higher efficiency'.

---

[25] George P. Landow, *Hypertext 2.0* (Baltimore: Johns Hopkins University Press, 1997).
[26] Landow, *Hypertext*.

SMV is thus a form of synchronized labour created by capital, to use classical Marxist terms, that recalls E.P. Thompson's famous essay on the structuring of work by 'clock time' in the industrial age (1967). SMV follows the principles of Taylorism formulated in the early twentieth century, of the 'scientific management' of workflows; it also has something in common with the first time and motion studies pioneered in the early twentieth century by Frank and Lillian Gilbreth. It aims to increase the speed of the sewing process (the most labour-intensive part of manufacture) and to ensure a synchronized work flow in the factory assembly line. SMV is a numerical value, and the chart shows the 12 stages of sewing a T-shirt; the average time of each stage is shown in seconds in the penultimate column, which is converted into SMV in the last column. The time taken to sew a T-shirt in a Bangladeshi factory is given as 5.12 SMV, which in real time is three minutes and 43.38 seconds.

In garment production, until garment components are gathered into a finished garment, they are assembled through a sub-assembly process. The production process includes a set of workstations, at each of which a specific task is carried out in a restricted sequence, with hundreds of employees and thousands of bundles of sub-assemblies producing different styles simultaneously.[1] The joining together of components, known as the sewing process which is the most labor intensive part of garment manufacturing, makes the structure complex as to which work has priority before being assembled.[2]

Furthermore, since the sewing process is labor intensive; apart from material costs, the cost structure of the sewing process is also important. Therefore, this process is of critical importance and needs to be planned more carefully.[3] [...]

[1]   A. J. Chuter, *Introduction to Clothing Production Management* (Oxford: Blackwell Science, 1988).
[2]   Gerry Cooklin, *Introduction to Clothing Manufacturing* (Oxford: Blackwell Science, 1991).
[3]   David J. Tyler, *Materials Management in Clothing Production* (London: BSP Professional Books Press, 1991).

SMV study for a T-shirt

No.	Operation	Average Cycle time (sec)	Estimated SMV
01	Shoulder joining	13.09	0.30
02	Overlocking of lining	10.90	0.25
03	Neck piping	13.09	0.30
04	Neck joining	15.27	0.35
05	Neck overlocking	13.09	0.30
06	Sleeve hem	13.96	0.32
07	Sleeve joining	26.18	0.60
08	Side joining	34.90	0.80
09	Side top stitch	26.18	0.60
10	Side tuck cuff	26.18	0.60
11	Neck top stitch	15.27	0.35
12	Bottom hem	15.27	0.35
TOTAL SMV			5.12

Result & Calculation

SMV means standard minute value. It is a numerical value which represents the standard time of a process or operation in a standard environment for standard worker. To convert cycle time to normal or basic time we have to multiply it with operator performance rating. Here for example, if rating 100%. Now we have to add allowances for machine allowances, fatigue and personal needs etc. Add machine allowance only to those elements where machine is running and fatigue and personal needs to all elements. Now we have got standard time for each element in seconds.

Sum up all elemental time and convert seconds into minutes. This is Standard Minute Value (SMV).

Fashion, Fast and Slow

Kate Fletcher

Kate Fletcher, 'Slow Fashion', *The Ecologist*, 37, no. 5 (June 2007), 61.

An advocate of 'slow fashion' since 2003, the writer and activist Kate Fletcher argued that 'fast fashion isn't really about speed, but greed'. Her critique of fast fashion (which can get a garment from drawing board to shop floor in an astounding 12 days) is pitched in terms of both sustainability and ethics, and Fletcher makes the case for slow fashion as a more ethical system of production and consumption that does not exploit the labour force that produces it. Arguing that 'slow is not the opposite of fast', she makes a case for the decision to embrace slow fashion as a shift from quantity to quality; to consume less, but more discerningly.

Fast speed in fashion is a defining characteristic of today's textile and clothing industry. It's fast in production – tracking sales with electronic tills and just-in-time manufacturing, which can now turn a sample or design sketch into a finished product in as little as 12 days; and fast in consumption – a recent report revealed that people are buying one third more garments than four years ago, fuelled by the rise and rise of supermarkets and 'value' retailers like Primark and Matalan.

Yet the fabric in super-cheap, 'value' or fast fashion is no quicker to make or use than any other garment. The fibre takes the same length of time to grow, regardless of a product's speed to market (in the case of cotton, around a year). It takes just as long to be spun, knitted or woven, cleaned, bleached, dyed, printed, cut and sewn; and going shopping and laundering the garment takes the same amount of time no matter how speedily a design makes it from catwalk to high street retailer.

Fast fashion isn't really about speed, but greed: selling more, making more money. Time is just one factor of production, along with labour, capital and natural resources that get juggled and squeezed in the pursuit of maximum profits. But fast is not free. Short lead times and cheap clothes are only made possible by exploitation of labour and natural resources.

Yet it doesn't have to be this way. We can design a different system for ourselves that makes money while respecting the rights of workers and the environment, and produces beautiful and conscientious garments.

Slow fashion is about designing, producing, consuming and living better. Slow fashion is not time-based but quality-based (which has some time components). Slow is not the opposite of fast – there is no dualism but a different approach in which designers, buyers, retailers and consumers are more aware of the impacts of products on workers, communities and ecosystems.

The concept of slow fashion borrows heavily from the Slow Food Movement. Founded by Carlo Petrini in Italy in 1986, Slow Food links pleasure and food with awareness and responsibility. It defends biodiversity in our food supply by opposing the standardisation of taste, defends the need for consumer information and protects cultural identities tied to food. It has spawned a wealth of other slow movements. Slow Cities, for example, design with slow values but within the context of a town or city and a commitment to improve its citizens' quality of life.

In melding the ideas of the slow movement with the global clothing industry, we build a new vision for fashion in the era of sustainability: where pleasure and fashion are linked with awareness and responsibility.

Slow fashion is about choice, information, cultural diversity and identity. Yet, critically, it is also about balance. It requires a combination of rapid imaginative change and symbolic (fashion) expression as well as durability and long-term engaging, quality products. Slow fashion supports our psychological needs (to form identity, communicate and be creative through our clothes) as well as our physical needs (to cover and protect us from extremes of climate).

Fast fashion, as it exists today, strikes no such balance. Indeed, it is largely disconnected from reality, with little recognition of poverty wages, forced overtime and climate change.

Slow fashion, with the shift from quantity to quality, takes the pressure off time. It allows suppliers to plan orders, predict the numbers of workers needed and invest in the longer term. It gives companies time to build mutually beneficial relationships. No longer will suppliers have to employ temporary or subcontracted workers, or force workers to do excessive overtime to meet unpredictable orders with impossible deadlines. Instead, workers will have secure employment with regular hours and the opportunity for promotion.

Of course, quality costs more. We will buy fewer products, but higher in value. A fairer distribution of the ticket price through the supply chain is an intrinsic part of the agenda. Jobs are preserved as workers spend longer on each piece. Slow design enables a richer interaction between designer and maker; maker and garment; garment and user. A strong bond of relationships is formed, which permeates far beyond the garment manufacturing chain.

Slow fashion is a glimpse of a different – and more sustainable – future for the textile and clothing sector and an opportunity for business to be done in a way that respects workers, environment and consumers in equal measure. Such a future is but a garment away.

Slow is a different approach; a shift from quantity to quality. It links the pleasure of fashion with more awareness and fairer treatment of workers and planet.

Tips to slow down your wardrobe:

- Repair your clothes with a smile (it's easier than going shopping)
- Or ask stores about repair services . . . that may get them thinking
- Ask your friends for new ideas about how to wear the garments you already have . . . it's always good to wear things in a new way.

Subverting the Seasonal Construct

Samuel Patrick Thomas

Samuel Patrick Thomas, 'Anrealage S/S/A/W 2014–15 – Subverting the Seasonal Construct', *Tokyo Telephone* (9 April 2014). Available at http://tokyotelephone.com/anrealage-ssaw-2014-15-subverting-the-seasonal-construct/ (accessed 10 December 2018).

Writing in 2014, the Tokyo-based journalist and lecturer Samuel Patrick Thomas describes a fashion show by Japanese designer Anrealage (Kunihiko Morinaga) that transitioned in minutes from winter to summer, as a critique of the idea of the fashion season with its Eurocentric assumptions of climate-appropriate clothes. Titled 'Anseason', the collection could never go out of season because it was never in season, thus obviating the need for end-of-season discounts. It used temperature-adjustable textiles developed at NASA capable of maintaining an even temperature of 32° C all year round, in garments that could be layered or dismantled according to the time of year in any part of the world.

Taking a stand against this construct is none other than Anrealage's Kunihiko Morinaga, a fitting evolution for a designer who produces season after season of inventive fashion, but is dictated that he must come up with a brand new concept each season, rather than moving at his own, admittedly rapid, pace. He used his Tokyo Fashion Week (amusingly and pointedly held exactly one week after the official week was over) show to announce *Anseason*, a greatest hits line of sorts that would be a constant collection of his best work. In it we find a wealth of classic designs, and because they are out of 'season', they are never vulnerable to discounts and available to buyers every time they visit the showroom. It is a liberating display of confidence by Morinaga, an acknowledgment that his work is not tied to a calendar – and that was before the show even started.

The show began with sudden snowfall that panicked my camera . . . but clearly announced that we were in winter, even as it quickly became apparent that the clothes were layered for winter rather than made for it. Indeed, the first twist of the show is that every item could be worn in isolation in summer and layered as in the show, in winter.

It was a step out of Anrealage's usually conservative silhouette, and the way the clothes seemed to be escaping away from the body is a new one for this brand that seemed to divide viewers, even though the mix of shapes associated with seasonal staples was very well observed and rightly won over even the harshest critic.

Mid-show and the season became spring, and references to motifs played out year after year after year by fashion's seasons made their appearance.

Even as we entered summer, the models were layered for winter, and it is not hard to imagine how one could dismantle each ensemble to fit the temperature and humidity of the seasons.

We found out after the show that almost every garment was made of *Outlast Heat Management* textiles, a technology invented for NASA to rapidly regulate body temperature – a boon for the Japanese summer as one goes from air-conditioning to scorching heat.

Towards the end of the show some standout items began to make their appearance . . . [such as a] trypophobia inducing cool coat.

However, the last surprise was still to come as a model stood static under the runway lights [in a look that was] achieved with wires in the fabric that expand under heat allowing for not only a regulation of heat, but a change of silhouette.

While the show may have felt like the usual technical exhibition we have come to expect from Anrealage, the real provocation was a rejection of the seasonal cycle in fashion – and that is the start of something very special.

Section 2

Antilinear Time

Jetztzeit and the Tiger's Leap

Walter Benjamin

Walter Benjamin, Thesis XIV, 'Theses on the Philosophy of History',
Illuminations: Essays and Reflections, trans. Harry Zohn, ed. and introduction
by Hannah Arendt, preface by Leon Weiseltier (New York: Schocken Books,
1969), 261 [first published in *Neue Rundschau* 61, no. 3 (1950)].

*Walter Benjamin's concept of historical time is closely bound up with his analysis of
fashion and its temporality. It is the important role of fashion in Benjamin's model
of history that puts it at the beginning of this section devoted to the concept of
antilinear time.*

*'Theses on the Philosophy of History', sometimes translated as 'On the Concept
of History', is a brief but important essay he wrote in 1940 shortly before his death.
It consists of 18 short, numbered paragraphs, and 2 closing ones entitled A and B.
The whole essay is significant for Benjamin's writing on fashion and time, but Thesis
XIV is particularly important because it contains the germ of two concepts that
were central to Benjamin's thinking. These are the ideas of* Jetztzeit, *or 'now-time',
and the 'tiger's leap'. How these link to Benjamin's other writing is explained in
greater detail in the introduction.*

*Benjamin opens Thesis XIV by claiming that history consists not of 'empty time'
but of 'time filled by the presence of the now'. He thus distinguished between the idea
of 'now-time' and the present. In Thesis XV he goes on to argue against traditional
histories which follow chronological narratives and explain causes and effects. At the
end of his essay, he proposes that the past can only be accessed through brief flashes in
the present, creating a 'constellation' of moments from both the present and the past.*

*This juxtaposition is a kind of montage, and in fact Benjamin's written
metaphors were often strikingly visual, like the metaphor of the tiger's leap that he
uses here to describe fashion. As he says, fashion has a flair for the topical (which
can also be translated as a sense of the actual present) so that when it leaps over the
recent past to seize imagery from the distant past, it will inexorably find a historical*

image that is meaningful in the present. This juxtaposition, or constellation, of images of past and present is what elsewhere he called 'dialectical images', and the concept is suggested without being named as such in his final sentence, where he writes that the tiger's leap 'in the open air of history is the dialectical one'.

History is the subject of a structure whose site is not homogeneous, empty time, but time filled by, the presence of the now [*Jetztzeit*]. Thus, to Robespierre ancient Rome was a past charged with the time of the now which he blasted out of the continuum of history. The French Revolution viewed itself as Rome reincarnate. It evoked ancient Rome the way fashion evokes costumes of the past. Fashion has a flair for the topical, no matter where it stirs in the thickets of long ago; it is a tiger's leap into the past. This jump, however, takes place in an arena where the ruling class gives the commands. The same leap in the open air of history is the dialectical one, which is how Marx understood the revolution.

Illusion Tulle and *La Dernière Mode*

Stéphane Mallarmé

Stéphane Mallarmé, *La Dernière Mode*, no. 5 (1874), trans. and reprinted
in P. N. Furbank and A. M. Cain (eds), *Mallarmé on Fashion: A Translation of
the Fashion Magazine* La Dernière Mode *with Commentary*
(Oxford and New York: Berg, 2004), 126.

In 1874, the French poet Stéphane Mallarmé anonymously – and pseudonymously – edited, designed and wrote eight issues of a fortnightly women's fashion magazine,
La Dernière Mode. *A consummate bluff, the journal was written under a range of pen names including Marguerite de Ponty (who wrote on fashion), Miss Satin (an Englishwoman specializing in the fashion houses of Paris) and, the only male contributor, Ix, who wrote about theatre and books. In this short passage from the fifth issue of the magazine, Ix suggests that his own prose will be even shorter-lived than a fashionable ball dress. He compares it to both the ephemerality of delicate illusion tulle (in French,* tulle illusion*) and the longevity of silk flowers. In his article, as airy as tulle and as factitious as artificial blooms, the poet's irony lurks behind the journalist's façade, as he self-reflexively contrasts the lifespans of each*

genre. Here, fashion writing proves the perfect medium for authorial sleight of hand and ambiguously layered meanings.

At all events, what is it safe to say, given that it is almost certain that this Issue, enclosing the picture of a Ball-dress, will lie on salon tables till a fairly distant date, at least the day after tomorrow? A dress, designed according to principles meant to rule through a winter, is not so soon useless and stale as a chronicle, even a fortnightly one. To have the permanence of *tulle illusion*, or of artificial roses imitating roses and clematis: that is one's dream for every sentence one writes, not for a short story or a sonnet, but about the news of the day.

The Evaporation of Temporality

Ulrich Lehmann

Ulrich Lehmann, *Tigersprung: Fashion in Modernity*
(Cambridge, MA: MIT Press, 2002), 105–6 and 109–10.

In his book Tigersprung, *the scholar Ulrich Lehmann discusses three different iterations of Benjamin's tiger's leap in relation to different historical moments and to key writing on fashion by Baudelaire, Gaultier, Mallarmé, Simmel and Benjamin. From these modernist texts, the book turns, in a final chapter, to the emblems of the top hat, the necktie, the corset, the glove and the shoe in the work and writing of the historical avant-gardes, particularly Dada and Surrealism.*

In the passage below, Lehmann reflects on the delicate textile thread as a metaphor for time in Mallarmé's fashion writing, arguing that 'fashion appears here almost as the evaporation *of temporality'. He goes on to associate this with the nineteenth-century ballgowns by Worth and Pinguat that kept women ethereally suspended in a perpetual present. Like Ilya Parkins below, Lehmann comments on the association of fashionable women with a particular temporality at that historical juncture. While men were identified with tradition and history, he writes, women were affiliated with immediacy and novelty to a degree that amounted to an abstract value, and constituted an 'erasure of temporality' in favour of 'the instantaneous and the present'.*

For the folds to appear, cloth had first to be woven from the temporality of the *fil(s)*. The warp thread, which would later become so important in the Proustian creation of *durée*, is taken quite literally by Mallarmé. And the poetic fabric it would determine remains an element of the transhistorical potential – a recurring interplay of thread(s) as the basis of fashion's metamorphoses, creating the future while remaining rooted in 'ancient attitudes'. But this thread was also significant for the intimate and interior interpretation of fashion and finery.

Like two threads, one of silk or even wool and the other of gold, crossing each other and then entwining, we perceive the changes and the evolution of fashion during the social season. There has not been any noticeable change in the last fortnight; nothing has become manifest in the ball gowns . . . The outfits at these special occasions constitute a fantasy in themselves, sometimes a risky endeavor, bold and futuristic; this comes to light through ancient habits. Yes, do look, and you can see, in between the satins, some evidence of the secrets that already are being revealed under the gauze, under the tulle or lace.[1]

Fashion appears here almost as the *evaporation* of temporality. For the poet it marks a fantastic and irrational state that he longs to explore. But it also retains a strong social component, as the female subscribers are restricted to a 'floating world,' one of conspicuous consumption. The constant, if strictly seasonal, change in haute couture kept women in suspension – in the case of a new Worth or Pinguat creation, perhaps even in suspense. While men were expected to have a sense of epistemological tradition and historiography, women were geared only toward immediacy, the eternally new. That 'new' is not necessarily a prediction of the future, since fashion is never conceived beforehand solely as a static concept but instead reacts to and speculates about stylistics. Its shapes and forms never surprise us entirely, as everything has already existed in some other appearance. The female is thus held in the present, condemned to view the past merely as sourcebook; the coming of yet another facile change alters the surface of things but, alas, never the rules. [. . .]

The limitation of written expressions, the problem raised by Lessing, disappears within fashion's transitoriness. The visual representation of a garment is not superior to the written one, because the clothing in *La Dernière Mode* is never

---

[1]   Marguerite de Ponty, 'La Mode (On nous harangue et nous répondons . . .)', *La Dernière Mode*, no. 8 (20 December 1874): 2, in Stéphane Mallarmé, *Oeuvres complètes* (Paris: Gallimard, 1945), 830.

situated in one particular moment in time. Away from the whirl of contemporary fashion, these garments are elevated by their 'author' to an abstract value. This touch of hubris in denying his readership the latest sartorial information would cost the entrepreneur Mallarmé dearly. The concerns of the poet, however, lay elsewhere. The significance of both *fil(s)* and *pli* allowed written fashion to lose its temporal, although not historical, aspects. Furthermore, the use of words such as *vaporeux* and *nuage* renders the topoi immaterial, as we have seen. And when Mallarmé ventures into metaphysics ('*vers l'idée*'), his accounts of dresses or gowns always left them intangible, as they were fashioned into irreverent and imagined objects of the '*rêve intérieur*.' Even the close description of the lithographs managed to eschew the material and deal rather with aesthetic experience; matters of temporal succession would not affect the representation. The transitoriness and impermanence paradigmatic to fashion elevate its written form, as well as its dream potential, above any painterly account: 'What a miraculous vision, a picture one dreams about rather than painting it: for its beauty suggests certain impressions analogous to those of the poet, profound or fugitive.'[2] Ironically, this erasure of temporality occurred in the pages of a journal entirely devoted to the latest in fashion, that is, to the instantaneous and the present. But precisely because Mallarmé never forgets his artistic aspiration or lowers himself to record the emerging industry of haute couture, the representation of fashion in his magazine now floats unconstrained by any specific time and place.

Fashion, Femininity and Modernity

Ilya Parkins

Ilya Parkins, *Poiret, Dior and Schiaparelli: Fashion, Femininity and Modernity* (London: Bloomsbury, 2013), 26–27, 33–36 and 41–42.

The scholar Ilya Parkins looks at the gendered nature of time, fashion and modernity in the period 1860–1940, asking how fashion, a 'highly feminized medium', can materialize theories of modern time. She argues that fashion had the same temporal structure, or at least the same 'time consciousness', as modernity in this period.

[2] Marguerite de Ponty, 'La Mode: Toilette d'une princesse ou d'une parisienne', *La Dernière Mode*, no. 8 (20 December 1874): 3, in Mallarmé, *Oeuvres completes*, 832–33.

Her chapter fits into the category of antilinear time because she uses fashion to challenge several binaries in the historiography of late nineteenth-century and early twentieth-century modernity: linear and cyclical time, present and past, and modern and traditional. In the dominant discourses of the day, Parkins writes, women were excluded from the former, and associated with the latter. One such example is provided by Mallarmé's description of the nineteenth-century woman who is suspended in a perpetual present, as described by Lehmann above.

Parkins argues that fashion has the capacity to complicate these binaries because of its constant interplay between old and new. Here her text owes much to Benjamin's ideas about fashion and historical time, especially of 'dialectical images', which she discusses in another part of the chapter not reprinted here. 'Fashion's constellation of past and present implies movement [and] change' she writes; and she argues for an understanding of femininity not as 'singular, knowable or masterable' but as ambiguous, plural and possibly even contradictory. Concerned to break away from clichés that pit active masculinity against passive femininity, Parkins invokes the tempo of fashion as 'a kind of spectral visitation of femininity upon the masculinised world of the modern'.

[F]ashion possesses the same temporal structure as modernity itself – or, at least, as modern modes of time consciousness. Andrew Benjamin observes that fashion is 'inextricably linked to a certain conception of historical time' and suggests that, for this reason, the peculiar temporal rhythms of fashion must be seen as 'part of the construction of culture.'[1] Hence it might be fair to say that the form possesses similar political stakes or even, surprisingly enough, revolutionary capacities to modernity itself. Do the questions that critics ask of modern qualities of time – about the secret romance of the new with the old, about the failure of 'progress' in the face of eternal cycles or even regression, deterioration – do these questions then make sense in relation to sartorial fashion, that undeniably material phenomenon? Can fashion materialize theories of modern time?

If we take seriously these questions about the temporal status of fashion in modernity, we are returned to the gendered character of modernity. For fashion

---

[1] Andrew Benjamin, 'The Time of Fashion: A Commentary on Thesis XIV in Walter Benjamin's "On the Concept of History"'. In Andrew Benjamin, *Style and Time: Essays on the Politics of Appearance* (Chicago: Northeastern University Press, 2006), 25.

itself is highly gendered, its development increasingly bound up both with representations of femininity and with actual women as consumers from the early nineteenth century onward.[2] In a sense this history is useful for those of us who are interested in rethinking the figuration of femininity and modernity. By intervening in the dichotomous or oppositional positioning of past and present that characterized temporal consciousness from the Revolutionary period, fashion thus also allows us to begin to think other possibilities for women's modernity. It allows us to see our way out of the positioning of women as outside of the modern. Fashion can indeed contribute to the forging of a politics of the time of modernity, by opening up the debates on modern time to a distinct but related set of concerns in feminist theory. Thus, fashion, a medium that is highly feminized, allows us to view the time consciousness of the period from about 1860–1940 as gendered. It does so in four ways. First, it allows us to consider how ideologies that privileged newness and an orientation to the present and to the future functioned to disenfranchise women, by excluding the symbolic realm of the feminine from the possibilities for *becoming* that were seen to define the modern. Second, rather than simply admit women to the realm of the new, fashion challenges the conceptual opposition of new and traditional, present and past, upon which the exclusion of women rests. Third, fashion complicates a major feminist theoretical narrative, which tends to privilege an account of women's absolute exclusion from conceptions of the modern, by giving us a host of examples in which women were represented as quintessentially modern. Finally, fashion can show us that modern time was not only gendered, but was lived, felt, materially experienced in everyday life. This chapter examines these potentials of fashion in order to delineate where and how feminist theories of modernity and of time might be brought into a broader conversation about the structures of time in the modern age – a conversation which has largely excluded

---

[2] Though the industrialization of fashion in the early nineteenth century is generally thought to have begun with men's garments, these were military uniforms, and not fashionable clothing for sale on the commodity market. As industrialization advanced and capacity increased in the latter half of the nineteenth century, it was women's garments that came to be identified with fashion. This was due in no small part to the shift known as the Great Masculine Renunciation, in which the dark suit came to be identified as the dress standard for men, ostensibly leaving the changeability and whimsy of fashion to women's clothing. Christopher Breward, in his persuasive *The Hidden Consumer: Masculinities, Fashion, and City Life 1860–1914* (Manchester: Manchester University Press, 1999), has shown that men's garments were just as subject to fashion as women's. Nevertheless, the association of fashion overwhelmingly with femininity persisted. No doubt this was enabled by links between fashion's changeability and women's supposed fickleness and triviality.

them. In this sense, it contributes to what Emily Apter terms 'a "becoming-feminist"' of time theory itself.[3] [...]

On the face of it, what is most notable about fashion for feminist theorists is simply its dynamic, change-oriented character, which accelerated aggressively with the development of new technologies from the middle of the nineteenth century.[4] As Joanne Entwistle notes, '[f]ashion thrives in a world of social mobility, a dynamic world characterized by class and political conflict, urbanization and aesthetic innovation, so it is not surprising that fashion flourished in the nineteenth century, when social upheaval reached a new zenith with the French and the Industrial Revolutions.'[5] It is precisely this changeable character of fashion that made it so suggestive to social theorists of the late nineteenth and early twentieth centuries, who saw it as an embodiment of the fragmentary character of modernity.[6] But this equation with change deserves unpicking; the rhetoric of newness that change implies is, in fact, more complex than it first seems.

Consider first the constant interplay of past and present that is evident in fashion's tendency to 'reference' the past. The modern period gave us several important examples of this tendency, but one of the most influential and complex in the era of fashion's modernity is the revival of a modified *Directoire* dress line by Paul Poiret in 1906. Poiret borrowed the silhouette from the simple, muslin, 'Empire' waisted chemise dress popular in the *Directoire* years immediately following the French Revolution.[7] In their original incarnation, *Directoire* dresses were associated with classical Greek column dresses – this early modern fashion had itself been an 'imitation' of an earlier style. This style, then, marked the inevitability of repetition in fashion, and complicated associations of fashion with 'newness'. Indeed, Poiret's

[3] Emily Apter, '"Women's Time" in Theory', *differences* 21, no. 1 (2010): 17.
[4] Nancy L. Green, *Ready-to-Wear and Ready-to-Work: A Century of Industry and Immigrants in Paris and New York* (Durham, NC: Duke University Press, 1997).
[5] Joanne Entwistle, *The Fashioned Body: Fashion, Dress, and Modern Social Theory* (Cambridge: Polity Press, 2000), 105.
[6] Charles Baudelaire, 'The Painter of Modern Life,' in *The Painter of Modern Life and Other Essays*, trans. Jonathan Mayne (London: Phaidon, 1965).
[7] The chemise dress was the most radical of post-revolutionary styles for women. However, its simple silhouette was common for all fashionable dresses of the late 1790s and first years of the 1800s – even in formal garments such as ball gowns, which were made of more luxurious fabrics, worn with *Directoire*-styled coats and accessorized with other garments. See Laver, *Costume and Fashion*, 148–53. See Valerie Steele, *Paris Fashion: A Cultural History* (Oxford: Berg, 1998), 48–51, for a discussion of stereotypes of *Directoire* fashion.

own understanding of his *Directoire* dresses was that it was their *pastness* that guaranteed their *novelty*: by appropriating French Revolutionary styles, he was able to fashion himself and the dress line as crusaders for 'Liberty'.[8] The introduction, disappearance, and return of the bustle between about 1870–1890 offers a slightly different take on the phenomenon of historical revival – and the initial appearance of the bustle in the early 1870s was itself inspired by dress styles of the previous century.[9]

And so, Elizabeth Wilson is surely correct to declare that 'fashion *is* change'. But the *kinds* of change that modern fashion instituted – always cyclical, and so often oriented to the past – compromised associations between change and progress.[10] The nineteenth-century preoccupation with progress that characterized modern science, history, politics, and economics was countered by a secondary philosophical interest in 'eternal return' or 'eternal recurrence' as the condition of modern life. Fashion materially bore out that orientation to recurrence, and its widespread diffusion made it a powerful counter to the philosophy of progress. Thus it was a tangible and visible intervention in those philosophies of time that would disavow the relationship between past and present.[11] In Caroline Evans's elegant formulation, '[t]he traces of the past surface in the present like the return of the repressed. Fashion designers call up these ghosts of modernity and offer us a paradigm that is different from the historian's paradigm, remixing fragments of the past into something new and contemporary that will continue to resonate into the future.'[12]

Fashion's tendency to underscore the close relationship between the past and the present should engender feminist interest in this question, since fashion was

---

[8] See Poiret's description of his introduction of the line in his first and most important work of autobiography, *King of Fashion* [1931], trans. Stephen Haden Guest (London: V&A Publications, 2009), 36.

[9] Breward, *The Culture of Fashion*, 154. Breward locates the inspiration in the elaborate styles of the 1760s.

[10] As Herbert Blau notes, 'the apparent logic of fashion, its undifferentiated monomania, is something of an illusion ... [since] alterations in the significant features of dress, line, cut, contour, articulating the body, are still likely to take some time before inhabiting the fashion scene.' *Nothing in Itself: Complexions of Fashion* (Bloomington: Indiana University Press, 1999), 89.

[11] Benjamin saw fashion as a primary example of eternal recurrence as a condition of industrial capitalism; as a revolutionary historical materialist, he thus associated fashion with petrifaction and death. Benjamin was influenced by the arguments of nineteenth-century Parisian revolutionary Louis-Auguste Blanqui in *L'Eternité par les astres*.

[12] Caroline Evans, *Fashion at the Edge: Spectacle, Modernity, Deathliness* (New Haven and London: Yale University Press, 2003), 9.

so deeply feminized in the popular imagination. Recall that women were commonly figured as anterior to the modern: either as mired in the past or as altogether outside of time. This figuration was a kind of determination of their identities. Women's time was seen to relegate them to static *being*, and exclude them from the possibilities of becoming and creation, which were the qualities valued in modernity. But fashion's constellation of past and present implies movement, change, of a kind. First, if the past refuses fixity, and instead visits itself upon the present, then femininity itself can be seen to visit the time of the now, to refuse imprisonment in an inaccessible past. Second, the movement must not be seen as unidirectional, characterized by the constant thrust of the past into the present. In a cyclical structure, the present also gives way to the past; the modern gives itself over to femininity. A cleanly delineated modernity, defined against that feminized, pre-modern past, is compromised. In either case, repetition is a clear alternative to a linear temporality which presumes a definitive break with the feminized past. More importantly, in challenging the association of women with a distant past, a repetitive temporality refuses to affix women to any single time or space, or any one identity. Instead, it presumes that femininity is not singular, not knowable or masterable.[13] [...]

Foregrounding fashion as ephemeral makes it possible to think about modern women as subjects and objects of knowledge, whose location relative to modernity was neither fixed nor stable. Rather, it was the result of negotiations with a social world that was constantly changing. When we understand time as a question related to knowledge, we are able to start bringing individual gendered subjects into view, asking how they accessed and mediated modernity. Rather than straw figures of modernity – the quintessential, active bourgeois man pitted against the static, anti-modern woman – a framework of ephemerality gives us the conceptual tools to *animate* the gendered representations that we attach to the modern. Developing the potential of the ephemeral shows that thinking about time contains the potential to revitalize our understandings of the historical dimensions of everyday life in the modern period. Fashion, as an ephemeral practice that links the self to the social, is a productive ally

---

[13] For more on the question of fashion as a challenge to essentialized feminine identities, see Pamela Church Gibson, 'Redressing the Balance: Patriarchy, Postmodernism, and Feminism,' in *Fashion Cultures: Theories, Explorations, and Analysis*, ed. Pamela Church Gibson and Stella Bruzzi (London: Routledge, 2001), 349–62. Also on this point, see my 'Building a Feminist Theory of Fashion: Karen Barad's Agential Realism,' *Australian Feminist Studies* 23, no. 58 (2008): 501–15 .

in linking theoretical frameworks of time to social and cultural histories of the modern, histories that have been useful in centering women as agents of modernity.

Clothing and fashion thus show that women's figural relationship to modern time operates in several different, overlapping and sometimes conflicting registers. It is not simply about being relegated to the outside of modernity. Certainly, such representations of femininity as anti-modern are powerful and common, but they are not the only way that women's relationship with modernity has been figured. The seeds of other kinds of relationships between women and the time of the modern exist. For on one level early twentieth-century fashion depended on the positioning of women as central to the modern, thus providing an important contrast to representations of women as anti-modern. But on another level, fashion's peculiar, cyclical temporal rhythm contributed to an interrogation, even a deconstruction, of the dualistic understanding of femininity as pre-modern. Fashion's tempo, because it was materially embodied in the feminized world of garments themselves, suggested a kind of spectral visitation of femininity upon the masculinised world of the modern. Altogether, fashion helps brings into focus the ambiguity and contradictory character of representations of femininity in the modern era. Underscoring ambiguity in the relationship between women and modernity is not as straightforward as reclaiming women from historical invisibility, but it may allow us to ask questions about whether what appears to be invisibility is, in fact, a compromised, variable visibility – and to inquire into the conditions that shape such a relationship to visibility.

The Residue That History Has Discharged

Siegfried Kracauer

Siegfried Kracauer, 'Photography' [*Frankfurter Zeitung* 1927] trans. Thomas Y. Levin, *Critical Inquiry* 19, no. 3 (1993): 422–24 and 429–30.

Writing in 1927, the sociologist and cultural critic Siegfried Kracauer opens his long meditation on the nature of photography by describing a magazine cover of a contemporary actress snapped on the fashionable Venice Lido. The passage recalls an earlier one from 1863, the essay 'The Painter of Modern Life' by the art critic and poet

Charles Baudelaire, who describes himself leafing through old fashion plates in order to speculate on the nature of the eternal and the transitory. In both texts, the male writer scrutinizes images of fashionable women caught in the instant. Both highlight not only the time of the image, but also that of the spectator: the moment of looking. Both identify the tempo of fashion, and the instantaneity of the image, to some extent anticipating Roland Barthes's writing on the photograph in his book Camera Lucida.

Kracauer, however, also understood the longer trajectory of the image, including its decline, and the ways in which it could – and would – signify differently over time. He compares the image of 'the demonic diva' in 1927 with another from 1864, showing 'Grandmother' when she was a fashionable 24-year-old. Speculating on her image and its mysteries, the author establishes a dizzying historical relay between her past and present, which can only be understood as an antilinear account of time. The possibility of any continuity between past and her present is broken, he argues, by the passage of time – not only the lost memories of those who knew 'Grandmother' in her youth, but also her old-fashioned clothes that were so modern in their day, and her frozen smile. The photograph is no more than 'the residuum that history has discharged'.

For Kracauer, the photographic image is embalmed in time, and the subject's 'arrested smile' is like that of an 'archaeological mannequin'. This, he argues, is because the photograph itself is a 'representation of time' and here he draws an analogy between fashion and photography. He writes: 'If photography is a function of the flow of time, then its substantive meaning will change depending on whether it belongs to the domain of the present or to some phase of the past.' In other words, the old photograph is also a ruin. It shows no more than the spatial configuration of a moment, rather than the 'truth' of its subject, and Kracauer does not share Baudelaire's enthusiasm for the fleeting and the transitory: instead, 'The photograph becomes a ghost because the costumed mannequin was once alive.'

This is what the *film diva* looks like. She is twenty-four years old, featured on the cover of an illustrated magazine, standing in front of the Hotel Excelsior on the Lido. The date is September. If one were to look through a magnifying glass one could make out the grain, the millions of little dots that constitute the diva, the waves and the hotel. The picture, however, does not refer to the dot matrix but to the living diva on the Lido. Time: the present. The caption calls her demonic: our demonic diva. Still, she does not lack a certain look. The bangs, the seductive position of the head, and the twelve lashes right and left – all these details, diligently recorded by the camera, are in their proper place, a flawless appearance. Everyone recognizes her with delight since everyone has already seen the original on the screen. It is such a good likeness that she cannot be confused with anyone else, even if she is perhaps only one twelfth of a dozen Tiller girls.[1] Dreamily she stands in front of the Hotel Excelsior, which basks in her fame, a being of flesh and blood, our demonic diva, twenty-four years old, on the Lido. The date is September.

Is that what *Grandmother* looked like? The photograph, over sixty years old and already a photograph in the modern sense, depicts her as a young girl of twenty-four. Since photographs are likenesses, this one must have been a likeness as well. It was carefully produced in the studio of a court photographer. But were it not for the oral tradition, the image alone would not have sufficed to reconstruct the grandmother. The grandchildren know that in her later years she lived in a narrow little room with a view onto the old part of town and that, to give pleasure to the children, she would make soldiers dance on a glass plate;[2] they also know a nasty story about her life and two confirmed utterances, which change a bit from generation to generation. One has to believe the parents – who claim to have gotten it from Grandmother herself – that this photograph depicts the very same grandmother about whom one has retained these few details that may also in time be forgotten. Yet such testimonies are unreliable. It might turn out that the photograph does not depict the grandmother after all but rather a girlfriend that resembled her. None of her contemporaries are still alive – and the question of likeness? The ur-image has long since decayed. But the now-darkened appearance has so little in common with the traits still remembered that the grandchildren are amazed when urged to believe that it is the fragmentarily remembered ancestor whom they encounter in the photograph. All right, so it is Grandmother, but in reality it is any young girl in 1864. The girl smiles continuously, always the same smile, the smile is arrested yet no longer refers to the life from which it has

---

[1]   A group of militarily trained dancing girls named after the Manchester choreographer John Tiller. Introduced in the late nineteenth century by Eric Charell, the director of Berlin's Großes Schauspielhaus theater from 1924 to 1931 whose revues and operetta productions were the forerunners of the 'musicals'. See Derek and Julia Parker, *The Natural History of the Chorus Girl* (London, 1975).

[2]   In the autobiographical novel *Georg*, which Kracauer completed in 1934 during his exile in Paris, the main character at one point recalls his childhood delight at 'the glass battle fields of former times' filled with tin soldiers. 'His grandmother,' so we learn, 'had occasionally set them up on a glass plate and then tapped on the surface from underneath with her finger, in order to bring the ranks into disorder' (Siegfried Kracauer, *Georg*, in *Schriften*, 7 (Frankfurt am Main: Suhrkamp, 1973), 251.

been taken. Likeness has ceased to be any help. The smiles of plastic manikins in beauty parlors are just as rigid and perpetual. This manikin does not belong to our time; it could be standing with others of its kind in a museum, in a glass case labeled 'Traditional Costumes 1864.' There the manikins are displayed solely for the historical costumes, and the grandmother in the photograph is also an archeological manikin that serves to illustrate the costumes of the period. So that's how one dressed back then: with a chignon, the waist tightly tied, in a crinoline and a Zouave jacket.[3] The grandmother dissolves into fashionably old-fashioned details before the very eyes of the grandchildren. They are amused by the traditional costume that, following the disappearance of its bearer, remains alone on the battlefield – an external decoration that has become autonomous. They are irreverent, and today young girls dress differently. They laugh and at the same time they feel a shudder. For through the ornamentation of the costume from which the grandmother has disappeared they think they glimpse a moment of time past, a time that passes without return. While time is not part of the photograph like the smile or the chignon, the photograph itself, so it seems to them, is a representation of time. If it is only the photograph that endows these details with duration, it is not at all they who outlast mere time, but, rather, it is time that makes images of itself out of them. [...]

Once a photograph ages, the immediate reference to the original is no longer possible. The body of a deceased person appears smaller than the living figure. An old photograph also presents itself as the reduction of a contemporaneous one. The old photograph has been emptied of the life whose physical presence overlay its merely spatial configuration. In inverse proportion to photographs, memory-images enlarge themselves into monograms of the remembered life. The photograph is the sediment that has settled from the monogram, and from year to year its semiotic value decreases. The truth content of the original is left behind in its history; the photograph captures only the residuum that history has discharged.

If one can no longer encounter the grandmother in the photograph, the image taken from the family album necessarily disintegrates into its particulars. In the case of the diva, one's gaze may wander from her bangs to her demonic quality; from the nothingness of the grandmother the gaze is thrown back onto the

---

[3]   A fashionable woman's jacket from the 1860s, modelled after the uniform of the Zouave, a French colonial troop composed of Berber tribes and Europeans and recruited in Algiers in 1830–31.

chignon: it is the fashion details that hold it tight. Photography is bound to time in precisely the same way as fashion. Since the latter has no significance other than as current human garb, it is translucent when modern and abandoned when old. The tightly corsetted dress in the photograph protrudes into our time like a mansion from earlier days that has been marked for destruction because the city center has been moved to another part of town. Usually members of the lower class settle in such buildings. It is only the very old traditional dress, a dress that has lost all contact with the present, that can attain the beauty of a ruin.

The effect of an outfit that was still worn only recently is comical. The grandchildren are amused by the grandmotherly crinoline of 1864, which provokes the thought that it might hide the legs of a modern girl. The recent past that claims to be alive is more outdated than that which existed long ago and whose meaning has changed. The comic quality of the crinoline is due to the powerlessness of its claim. In the photograph, the grandmother's costume is recognized as a cast-off remnant that wants to continue to hold its ground. It is reduced to the sum of its details like a corpse yet stands tall as if full of life. Even the landscape and all other concrete objects become costumes in an old photograph. For what is retained in the image are not the features envisaged by a liberated consciousness. The representation captures contexts from which such consciousness has departed, that is, it encompasses orders of existence that have shriveled without wanting to admit it. The more consciousness withdraws from natural bonds, the more nature diminishes. In old etchings whose fidelity is photographic the hills of the Rhine look like mountains. Due to technological development they have in the meantime been reduced to tiny slopes and the grandiosity of those aged views seems a bit ridiculous.

Ghosts are simultaneously comic and terrifying. Laughter is not the only response provoked by antiquated photography. It represents what is utterly past and yet this refuse was once the present. Grandmother was once a person and to this person belonged the chignon and the corset as well as the High Renaissance chair with its turned pillars, a ballast that did not weigh her down but was just carried along as a matter of fact. Now the image wanders ghostlike through the present like the lady of the haunted castle. Spooky apparitions occur only in places where a terrible deed has been committed. The photograph becomes a ghost because the costumed mannequin was once alive.

Colonial Time

Victoria L. Rovine

Victoria L. Rovine, *African Fashion, Global Style: Histories, Innovations, and Ideas You Can Wear* (Bloomington and Indianapolis: Indiana University Press, 2015), 74–75 and 205.

The scholar Victoria Rovine theorizes 'colonial time' in relation to fashion. She draws on Homi Bhabha's concept of 'the time-lag of cultural difference' in relationship to subaltern and post-colonial agency, where he writes: 'It is the function of the lag to slow down the linear, progressive time of modernity to reveal its "gesture", its tempi, "the pauses and stresses of the whole performance".' Rovine shows how, 'during the colonial era, Africa's geographical and cultural distance from Europe was elided with chronological distance, conceptually locating the continent's cultures in a different place and time'. In her analysis of colonial time, African dress practices 'were deemed to be either "primitive" and therefore completely outside the realm of fashion, or out of date, out of touch, and therefore irrelevant to contemporary trends'. She discusses the early twentieth-century French illustrator Sem's Le Vrai et Le Faux Chic *(1914), and then takes these ideas forward to the mid-century and later, to argue that the perceived cultural distance between colonial – or postcolonial – centres and peripheries is elided with chronological distance to create colonial time. According to this model, Africa figures as 'periphery' and is therefore locked in an earlier, out-of-date time frame, imagined as 'dominated by unchanging tradition, timeless, isolated and pervasive'. Yet, as Rovine shows, this can be subverted, and twenty-first century African designers have intentionally countered the force of colonial time by stepping outside its system to challenge and resist its social order through the design strategies of recycling and reviving indigenous textiles and garments.*

In his analysis of patterns of consumption in the former British colony of Belize, Richard Wilk conceptualizes the distance between colonizer and colonized using a temporal metaphor that also illuminates our present subject: 'colonial time.'[1] For Western observers, the seat of colonial power – whether

---

[1]   Richard Wilk, 'Consumer Goods as Dialogue about Development', *Culture and History* 7 (1990): 84.

Paris, London, Brussels, or another European center – was presumed to be on the cutting edge in every aspect of cultural expression, while the colonies were deemed to be perpetually out of date, their cultures frozen in the stasis of 'tradition,' remote from the contemporary. As we have already seen, conceptualization of time is particularly germane to an analysis of fashion, arguably the art form most explicitly measured by the passage of time. Time is crucial to the economy of fashion; success in the fashion world is dependent on being up to date in the present, and on predicting the tastes of the next season. During the colonial era, Africa's geographical and cultural distance from Europe was elided with chronological distance, conceptually locating the continent's cultures in a different place and time. This distance was exemplified by dress practices across the continent, which were frequently deemed to be either 'primitive' and therefore completely outside the realm of fashion, or out of date, out of touch, and therefore irrelevant to contemporary trends. As Wilk describes: 'In colonial time the colony is described using metaphors that blend the connotative meanings of time, distance and cultural development. Primitive, backward, and underdeveloped are such blending terms.'[2] A 1914 illustrated commentary on the French fashion scene, entitled *Le Vrai et Le Faux Chic*, exemplifies the significance of fashion as a symbol of Africa's location in colonial time, temporally and spatially remote from the swiftly changing present embodied by French clothing trends.[3] The story related in the folio, which was sold in a limited edition and made more widely accessible through coverage in fashion magazines of the day, depended upon its audiences' assumption that Africa was at the opposite end of the fashion spectrum from France. Written and illustrated by the prominent cartoonist known as Sem (the pen name of Georges Goursat), *Le Vrai et Le Faux Chic* lampooned what Sem considered to be the frivolous and dangerously exotic fashions that were coming into vogue at the time. He presented a parable, introducing an unnamed Frenchman ('a Parisian man of good breeding, with delicate and sound taste')[4] who went to Africa for ten years, where he was 'completely isolated from the civilized world ... completely ignorant of the evolution of modern life.' Africa's ostensible remoteness is key to Sem's narrative; he needed a location his readers would have understood to be entirely beyond the reach of Paris fashion.

[2] Wilk, 'Consumer Goods as Dialogue about Development', 84.
[3] Sem, *Le Vrai et Le Faux Chic* (Paris: Succès, 1914).
[4] Sem, *Le Vrai*, 4.

Returning to his home ten years later, Sem's French traveler found that the elegant Parisian women he remembered were transformed; their slavish dedication to fashion trends led them to absurdities that seemed to emerge directly from 'primitive' cultures that know nothing of Parisian elegance. Sem's prancing, contorted caricatures illustrate his vivid and highly racialized descriptions of fashion's folly: 'Savage women adorned with gris-gris . . . Kanaks [an ethnic group from New Caledonia] wearing colorful mops, troglodytes covered with dangling animal skins' and, most frightful of all, 'a fuzzy-haired cannibal . . . wearing a bone through her nose.' At this last nightmarish vision, the well-bred Frenchman 'shuts his suitcases and takes the first camel bound for Timbuktu.'[5]

In her discussion of *Le Vrai et Le Faux Chic*, Troy summarizes the message of the parable: 'Paris fashions, Sem thus tells us, have become more savage, more dangerous, more threatening than anything one might encounter in deepest Africa, which, paradoxically, becomes a refuge for a sophisticated world traveler seeking to escape the irrational horrors of contemporary women's fashion in Paris.'[6] [. . .]

Here we might usefully return to Wilk's conceptualization of consumption and temporality, using his notion of 'colonial time' to further elucidate African fashion design. Wilk describes how the perceived cultural distance between colonial – or postcolonial – centers and peripheries is elided with chronological distance to create colonial time.[7] According to this model, Africa, like the Central American context Wilk addresses, figures as 'periphery' and is therefore locked in an earlier, out-of-date time frame. Fashion, as we have seen, has figured prominently in this classification of people and places, for dress practices far from Western centers are not expected to incorporate the latest styles. Instead, he notes, these places are imagined as 'dominated by unchanging tradition, timeless, isolated and pervasive.'[8] As Darkie and other African fashion designers demonstrate, clothing may also provide a means of countering the force of colonial time by stepping outside its system: 'Only when people obtain and consume objects outside the flow of colonial time, do they challenge and resist

[5]   Ibid.
[6]   Nancy J. Troy, *Couture Culture: A Study in Modern Art and Fashion* (Boston: MIT Press, 2003), 183.
[7]   Richard Wilk, 'Colonial Time and TV Time: Television and Temporality in Belize', *Visual Anthropology Review* 19, no. 1 (1990): 94–102.
[8]   Wilk, 'Colonial Time and TV Time', 96.

the social order of the colonial system.'[9] Revivals of indigenous textiles and garments offer one example of such resistance, exemplified by Gandhi's return to indigenous cotton garments. Yet, recycled clothing as fashion goes a step further, employing the products of the West itself to offer up an alternative to the flow of colonial time. Darkie, like Xuly Bet, looks not to forms associated with 'tradition,' as Gandhi did, but rather to forms that more subtly distort the temporality of colonial time. The employment of used clothing to produce fashion – a practice we have encountered in the oeuvres of several designers – has the potential to bear particularly potent associations in South Africa, where even young designers have memories of the essentially colonialist culture of apartheid.

The Historical Mode

Richard Martin and Harold Koda

Richard Martin and Harold Koda, *The Historical Mode: Fashion and Art in the 1980s* (New York, Rizzoli International, 1989), 7–9 and 11–14.

This text is from the fashion curators Richard Martin and Harold Koda's introduction to the catalogue for The Historical Mode, *an exhibition about postmodernism and historicism across fashion design, art, architecture, furniture design and other creative fields that was shown at the Fashion Institute of Technology in New York, in 1989–90. Pre-dating the development of academic analyses of antilinear time in fashion studies, the exhibition foregrounded the fashion design of the 1980s, a decade often criticized at the time for its superficiality and lack of originality.*

According to Martin and Koda, 'few clocks are more precise than those of fashion'. They identify a peculiar historical consciousness in 1980s fashion designers, with their 'learned archaisms and renewals more fundamental than merely nostalgic', as the authors describe the antilinear historical manoeuvres of specific designers. Some remain famous today: Jean-Paul Gaultier, John Galliano, Franco Moschino and Karl Lagerfeld for Chanel. Others, no less interesting, are less well remembered, such as Giorgio Sant'Angelo, Dorothée Bis, Romeo Gigli and Norma Kamali. In either case, the authors' observations, while rooted in a specific decade,

---

9   Wilk, 'Consumer Goods as Dialogue about Development', 106.

speak to a more general 'impulse to be of the past but in the present' that they
identify as quintessential to fashion: 'possessed and haunted by its acute sense of
time . . . it offers a compelling chronometer of the twentieth century'.

Charles Baudelaire, it is said, once proposed that artists 'use the past to confront
the present.' In the 1980s Baudelaire's proposition was enthusiastically embraced.
Acknowledging history as an active and abiding presence in the creation of
contemporary life, numerous artists and designers modeled works of art in the
reconstitution, re-examination, and revelation of the past. *The Historical Mode*
looks in particular at the fashion designers of the 1980s who created new art in
transfiguration of the past. [. . .]

A retreat from Modernism accompanied the rise of historicism in the 1980s.
The dauntless progressivism of the Modern movement, which posited revolution
as the model for aesthetic development, is now questioned. In its place there is an
enhanced appreciation of the step backward into history as perhaps the best
means by which to move forward.

Few clocks are more precise than those of fashion. The resurgence of vintage
clothing as a favored mode of dress for the youthful vanguard typifies the
pertinence of the historical past to the 1980s. It also acknowledges the evocative
and nostalgic power of garments. To examine – even exhume – history was a
significant motif of popular culture of the decade. If the 1984 film *Amadeus* –
which in turn inspired clothing by Jean-Paul Gaultier and other designers – was
an early 1980s indication of a popular fascination with the past, then the 1986
song 'Rock Me Amadeus' extended this reanimation of Wolfgang Amadeus
Mozart and self-consciously recalled Chuck Berry's recording of 'Roll over
Beethoven' from 1956 (every decade has its flirtations with period recreations).

The 1980s were marked by a return to France of the *ancien régime* in new
treatments on stage and screen of Choderlos Laclos's novel *Les Liaisons*
dangéreuses, of 1782. In other reenactments historical conflations occurred, as in
Franco Moschino's 1988–89 design of a Napoleonic cavalry costume, its origins
dating from the First Empire period around 1806 but in our time created to
celebrate the bicentennial of the French Revolution of 1789. A Romeo Gigli
Empire dress of 1987 could as easily have been patterned after the costume of
Liberty in Eugène Delacroix's *Liberty Leading the People*, of 1830, which
celebrated the Empire's downfall, as the period gown of Mlle Charlotte Val
d'Ognes in the 1810 painting of the same name.

In fact, the evidence of historicism in the world of fashion during the 1980s is overwhelming. British couturier John Galliano, for example, designed Empire dresses in 1986 in specific emulation of another time and place. In Paris, Karl Lagerfeld echoed eighteenth-century painting when in 1985 he created a coat for Chanel with back pleats inspired by the art of Antoine Watteau. Such journeys into the past may be prompted by specific events such as the great Watteau retrospective at the Grand Palais in Paris of 1984. They may also come about simply because designers realize that problems of apparel design may be addressed by age-old solutions. To be sure, the traditional argument against historicizing fashion is that social requirements have changed: what was appropriate to wear at Versailles, say, would be out of place in a downtown club. Bill Cunningham, fashion journalist and photographer for *The New York Times* and *Details*, has convincingly refuted these simplistic comparisons by chronicling the persistence and pertinence of traditional dress as a model for the present. [...]

Though most of the examples considered so far draw their inspiration across a great chronological distance, it has also been clear during the 1980s that the more recent past provides important historical touchstones. Henry James understood the compelling presence of such a past when in 1888 he wrote in the Preface to *The Aspern Papers*:

> I delight in a palpable imaginable *visitable* past – in the nearer distance and the clearer mysteries, the marks and signs of a world we may reach over to as by making a long arm we grasp an object at the other end of our own table. That, to my imagination, is a past fragrant of all, or of almost all, the poetry of the thing outlived and lost and gone, and yet in which the precious element of closeness, telling so of connections but tasting so of differences, remains appreciable.

In 1985, drawing on a past not strictly visitable for many of us, designer Norma Kamali extended an invitation to voyage some seven decades back in time, a time demonstrably removed from our own styles, mores, and manner of dress, though not entirely removed from our mind's eye. Kamali's solicitation is historicist in a traditional way. Perhaps this historicism seems anomalous for a designer as directional and, as one would have said some years ago, as revolutionary as Kamali. In fact, her oeuvre provides a fine illustration of the recent journey from Modernism to historicism. In the 1970s, Kamali responded to the dictates of function, fashion, radicalism, and the inherent properties of materials. These Modernist attributes were less evident in her work of the 1980s. The historically resonant designs she offered in that decade represent a fundamental change in her approach, a change that does not, as some cynics might suggest, reflect a clientele less young or a sensibility less sharp, but is rather a reflection of the past, appropriate in the context of contemporary design.

The power of Henry James's observations on the visitable past becomes even clearer as the historical object on 'our own table' becomes closer. The past just before our time, of which we are capable of recollection, and the present that is a reinterpretation and representation of that past make a fascinating juxtaposition. Marc Jacobs, Stephen Sprouse, and Thierry Mugler – three designers who celebrate themes of the 1960s and 1970s – have been attracted by this challenge. Their evocations of the immediate past illustrate how important the delicate tissue of generations became for artists and designers in the 1980s. They rightly perceive that today artists and designers visit their own remembered and barely remembered pasts with a special clarity and powerful sentiment. [. . .]

Coming on the heels of Modernist supremacy, the historicist forays in the art and design communities raise an inevitable question of some urgency. Does the present become a passive agent when we recognize, even venerate, the past with the eyes of our own time? The answer must be no. To simulate the past does not capture it. In fact, the very simulation demonstrates that the past is ever elusive. To wear or approximate the clothing of another era is not time travel in the manner of Jules Verne. [. . .]

When Romeo Gigli instills the cocoon shape of a 1920s coat and the soft chiffon of an Empire dress with an attitude distinctly 1980s, the result can only diminish our historical distance from the sources Gigli taps with the knowledge and adaptability of a virtuoso. Similarly, Christian Lacroix's prodigious historicism in his evocations of jewel-encrusted Byzantine splendor and of eighteenth century extravagance suggests both the historian's delight in knowledge and the artist's command of diverse styles.

Fashion is possessed and haunted by its acute sense of time. As it evolves from season to season, it offers a compelling chronometer of the twentieth century. The 1980s … have revealed a new measure with which to perceive a past in tandem with the present, not just in fashion but also in painting and sculpture. An unremitting modernism – a longstanding cult of the new – has seemingly come to a rapprochement with memory and an alliance with history.

Cuttings and Pastings in the Archive

Alistair O'Neill

Alistair O'Neill, 'Cuttings and Pastings', in Caroline Evans and Christopher Breward (eds), *Fashion and Modernity* (Oxford and New York: Berg, 2005), 175–79.

Reflecting on photography, the fashion magazine and the archive, this text looks at the concepts of the recently outmoded and the newly out-of-date that were briefly touched on by Martin and Koda in the previous text. The curator and fashion historian Alistair O'Neill's ruminative piece on two fashion images from the 1990s is a reminder that, amidst the brash commercialism of fashion rhetoric, there are some quieter moments. O'Neill describes Viktor & Rolf's photographs 'that claim to memorialise both a season of fashion shown and a season of fashion on the turn', so that these fashion ephemera are a melancholy elegy to time past: 'the sum of printed materials as the memory of that moment captured'. O'Neill shows the role of both collage and bricolage in constructing this aesthetic of the temporal and ephemeral in a culture of mass production and consumption.

This investigation into the uses of press cuttings by creative practitioners related to the field of fashion was inspired by a project by the fashion designers Viktor & Rolf, published in the short-lived magazine *The Fashion*. Within the spreads the designers presented photographs of press cuttings of their recent collection as origami imitating the familiar forms of historical still-life paintings. One featured a vase of paper lilies in a paper vase, in the other newspaper articles are hung like personal letters and effects on the back of a canvas stretcher.

The project was unusual enough to stop my flicking and to arrest my gaze. On reflection I realised that the photographs hadn't only disrupted the flow of the fashion magazine as it turned in my hands, but that they had also disrupted its logic. By this I mean that the published project was a form of creative expression that wasn't about recycling, it was more about the status of out-of-date magazines and the things they contain. It wasn't about the imitation of art by fashion even though it might have looked like it; it was more concerned with how the themes of still-life painting can inform the purpose of fashion magazines after their shelf life. It wasn't about looking back, or harking back, as it was just all too recent. It was the kind of 'recent' that's uncomfortable to many who work for, feature, read or even buy fashion magazines. It's the kind of 'recent' we erase in the act of assimilating what's current. The photographs force us to twist our heads back ever so slightly, to perform a rewind scan that pulls us to something we've seen in the past and asks us to reconsider its worth in the here and now. They ask us what we now make of these things, fancifully presented, torn from their original context? A witty use of worthless things? A double waste of paper?

One might suppose that Viktor & Rolf used them to memorialise their work and the manner in which they are written about: a way of visually paying tribute to the tributes. But it seemed to me that there was a lot more going on here than just artful back-slapping. As photographs in a fashion magazine they claim to memorialise both a season of fashion shown and a season of fashion on the turn. Further, they pose as visual metaphors for the condition of fashion expressed in printed form: as eternal spring and as the translation of clothing into language.[1] Yet the photographs point not only to the mutability of fashion, but also to the ephemeral quality of the material that communicates it. In this instance, the designers re-fashion the material that fashion has cast off; commemorating the moment of their own endeavour captured as printed expression.

The photographs demonstrate in visual terms the momentary fix that the fashion magazine can perform on the continuum of fashion. Yet they are rare in being able to further demonstrate a sense of loss in that moment passing, and, in their figuring of press cuttings, they present the sum of these printed materials as the memory of that moment captured. We accept that the fashion magazine is central to the articulation of fashion, even though we now accept that the fashionability it presents is often different to our own consumption of it. However, the experience of modernity remains unconcerned by this slippage, as the purpose of the fashion magazine is in only being the articulation of its continual state of transition. This denies another and equal aspect, as the fashion magazine is both the signifier and souvenir of the modern condition. It confirms the continual present whilst offering in material form a document of what is passing; an ossified sensibility of what was once felt.

What is marginalized by modernity is what is cast off and in this instance it's the simultaneous accumulation of material charting the fashion magazines rolling endeavour: it's the stack of back issues, the file of tear sheets. And it is here that we find a peculiar paradox: the practice of fashion thrives as much on the

---

[1]   Roland Barthes, *The Fashion System* (New York: Hill & Wang, 1983), x.

material that it casts off, as on what it wishes to project. Judith Clark has identified this in the monthly collages of Anna Piaggi in Italian *Vogue* noting their ability to represent in visual form the multiple histories she fuses to form the monthly variants of fashion.[2] Further, Caroline Evans has suggested that the repository that contemporary fashion designers draw upon is analogous to Benjamin's rendering of history not as narrative, but as composed of fragmented memory images, 'a labyrinthine relay between past, present and imagined future.'[3] It thus becomes apparent that the repository of fragments is essential to the articulation of fashion as a phenomenon of modernity, even though it may remain on the periphery of the vision it projects.

I wish to put forward that the pile of out-of-date fashion magazines and the collection of cuttings possessed by almost every creative practitioner related to the practice of fashion are primary to the articulation of fashion as a central tenet of modernity. While accepting *bricolage* as a practical technique of fashion design and styling informed by collage, the purpose is not to concentrate on the creativity of *cut 'n' paste* in fashion, but rather, to consider the repository of cuttings and the logic of the magazine as informing the crafting of fashion and the experience of modernity. [...]

It is widely accepted that as a medium of creative expression, collage is materially driven by mass production and, in connoting the temporal and ephemeral, it is expressive of the time, speed and duration of urban experience. In fashioning fragments from what is lost and then found, collage proposes a dislocation, supplanting a representation of reality with the materiality of reality. Yet the popular nineteenth-century pastime of the scrapbook, the multiple exposure art photographs of the 1870s and the Victorian craft of decoupage, are all recognised as precedents to what is thought of as a chiefly twentieth-century medium. In her study of collage, art historian Diane Waldman proposes that: 'Both the amateur and the professional in the nineteenth century imparted to the practitioners of collage and assemblage in our era a bittersweet quality based in sentiment and nostalgia that distinguishes collage and assemblage from their peers in twentieth-century painting and sculpture.'[4]

Yet such a bittersweet quality is not what we might readily associate with *cut 'n' paste*, a more popular term for collage, which rather than conjuring up a sense

[2] Judith Clark, 'The Judith Clark Costume Gallery', Lecture, London College of Fashion, 2002.
[3] Evans, *Fashion at the Edge*, 11.
[4] Diane Waldman, *Collage, Assemblage and the Found Object* (London: Phaidon Press, 1992), 11.

of sentimentality denotes the menace of the ransom note spelt in letterforms cut from newspapers. The abbreviation of the word *and* in the term suggests the discordant and reductive designs that characterize this particular visual language established in the mid 1970s and associated with punk as a graphic language. As a strategy of art photography also informed by the renegade nature of punk, appropriation fostered a 'take-without-asking' approach that challenged definitions of authorship and authenticity by the practice of re-photography. This was collage without the visible seams, transformation achieved through reframing and representing. And yet *cut 'n' paste* is also an abbreviation of *cuttings and pastings*, the old-fashioned pastime of filling sugar paper pages of scrapbooks with cuttings of covetable information. By titling this essay *Cuttings and Pastings* I wish to draw attention away from the creative practice of *cut 'n' paste* towards its historical predecessor, so that I am concerned not solely with the process of creativity and reconstituted meaning, but also with the process of classification and the meaning of storing printed material. [...]

[It is] the magazine's ability to be seamless, not only in how it unfolds, from start to finish, from issue to issue, from season to season, but also how it accumulates its repetitive expressions of the continual present, keeping the pages turning but remaining immutable. And it is here that the logic of the fashion magazine unveils its essential purpose to fashion and to the experience of modernity. Even though the material accumulation of its past becomes the salvaged means through which recollecting begins, it is not for its ability to remember that the fashion magazine is prized, but for its ability to continually forget. In the need to express the continual present the fashion magazine transforms multiple disparate fragments from its past into a seamless representation. In order be made to fit into the formal structure, to be made relevant or apparently contemporary, the fragments are filed down, smoothed off; their meanings reconfigured, their referents shorn. The validity and relevance of the continual present expressed by the fashion magazine can only be asserted by disregarding, or momentarily forgetting, the continual present it replaces.

Therefore, the repetition of replacement without recall practiced by the fashion magazine can only function by the equal repetition of re-collecting and recollecting. As the fashion magazine loses a sense of what has just passed, so the repository gains a remembrance of something more recent. As the popularity of the exhibition *Unseen Vogue* (2002) at the Design Museum in London would seem to suggest, we now appear to be far more interested in the process of the fashion magazine and its archive, rather than its end result. However, it remains to be seen as to whether this will remain a dominant trend in promoting the logic of the fashion magazine.

Martin Margiela's Carnivalized Time: Margiela's Theatrical Costume Collection

Francesca Granata

Francesca Granata, 'Fitting Sources – Tailoring Methods: A Case Study of Martin Margiela and the Temporalities of Fashion', in Heike Jenss (ed.), *Fashion Studies: Research Methods, Sites and Practices* (London and New York: Bloomsbury 2016), 148–51 and 154–57.

Reviewing various theories of fashion time, the fashion scholar Francesca Granata analyses designer Martin Margiela's production of 'carnivalized time'. Carnival involves the suspension of ordinary time and daily dress, as in masked balls, carnival costumes and role-playing, all of which depend on invention and fantasy. In this sense carnivalized time is a good metaphor for the no-time of uchronia, and her text spans the categories of uchronic and antilinear time.

In particular, the notion of antilinear time is suggested by her description of carnival as 'an inverted and topsy turvy time when temporalities of past, present and future are revered and/or thoroughly confused'. Here she draws on the Russian cultural historian and literary theorist Mikhail Bakhtin's (1895–1975) concepts of the carnivalesque and of the grotesque, and follows up a footnote in which he speculated that it would be interesting to develop these ideas in relation to the history of fashion and dress. And to the analysis of Bakhtin she adds a discussion of Julia Kristeva's essay on 'women's time'.

In the first part of her text, Granata expounds this theoretically, before going on to analyse two of Margiela's outputs: the Spring/Summer 1993 Theatre Costumes collection, and his retrospective exhibition in Rotterdam in 1997. In both she explores what she calls 'Margiela's penchant for carnivalizing time and playing with the order of temporalities'. From there, she develops a theoretical and methodological discussion of the field of fashion history in general, arguing that Margiela's designs amount to 'visual and material theorizations of "new history" and its attendant historiographical methods ... [that] debunk ... the traditional paradigm of history'.

Bakhtin's conception of time, expounded in relation to the carnival and the everbecoming nature of the grotesque, brings to mind the constantly changing nature of 'fashion time', characterized by ephemerality as opposed to the stability and immortality traditionally claimed by other cultural forms. Thus, one could argue that, to some extent, all fashion partakes of the carnival and the grotesque in its relation to time, yet Margiela's work makes this argument most convincingly: by recycling his own collections, as well as old clothes from various past decades, he highlights the cyclical nature of fashion, which is sometimes denied by the linear and progressive teleological narrative of Western history, and fashion history in particular. The latter often follows traditional art history and art historical survey texts in their dependence on strict chronology and suggestions of progress.[1] Margiela's interest in transience and in the recycling of old garments, however, is shared by a great number of artists and designers of this period, and can be partially read as a response to anxieties surrounding ever-accelerating times of production and consumption, as well as a rejection of the aesthetic of excess characterizing the preceding decade. These anxieties over progressively faster temporalities occurred concomitantly across design and art disciplines – including fashion – and Margiela's work can be seen as part of this larger debate occurring simultaneously across theory and practice.[2]

As the literary and psychoanalytical theorist Julia Kristeva points out, cyclical time stands in opposition to 'time as project, teleology, linear and prospective unfolding time; time as departure, progression and arrival – in other words the time of history'.[3] Kristeva adds that cyclical time is 'traditionally linked to female subjectivity'; a point which reveals a continuum between fashion, the feminine, and the grotesque. The concept of cyclical time, in fact, dovetails with Kristeva's

---

[1] On these debates within art history, see, for instance, responses in relation to the substantial and somewhat radical updating of the canonical survey text from 1962 by H. W. Janson 'History of Art' which was recently (in 2006) revised and republished by a number of authors under the title *Janson's History of Art: The Western Tradition*. For a range of responses to the substantial revision, see Randy Kennedy, 'Revising Art History's Big Book: Who's In and Who Comes Out', *New York Times*, 7 March 2006.

[2] Linda Sandino, 'Oral Histories and Design: Objects and Subjects', *Journal of Design History* 19, no. 4 (2006): 283–93; Evans, *Fashion at the Edge*, 36–39 and 249–60.

[3] Julia Kristeva, 'Women's Time'. In *Feminism: Critical Concepts in Literary Cultural Studies*, vol. II, ed. Mary Evans (London: Routledge, 2001), 30.

discussions of the subject-in-process, which presupposes constant and endless change. This temporal modality is also central to the 'ever-becoming' grotesque body of carnival. The cyclical nature of fashion history, which contradicts popular understandings of fashion as a chronological progression in search of the *new*, can be observed in Barbara Burman Baines's account of fashion's endless revivals, which she explored within the context of the English dress in her book *Fashion Revivals from the Elizabethan Age to the Present Day*.[4] This concept has also been theorized in three-dimensional form by Judith Clark's exhibition *Malign Muses: When Fashion Turns Back*; which was dialogically developed with theorist Caroline Evans. The exhibition employed a system of interlocking cogs on which garments from different periods were placed to explore the cyclicality and nonlinearity of fashion time.[5]

Margiela, however, takes this process a step further and produces what could be described as a carnivalized time. I use the expression 'carnivalized time' as a further elaboration of Bakhtin's theories of the carnival to mean not only the cyclical time of carnival festivities but, more specifically, an inverted and topsy-turvy time when temporalities of past, present, and future are reversed and/or thoroughly confused.[6] Through a close material and visual analysis of his work and, in particular, his *Theatre Costumes* and *Trompe l'oeil* collections, I observed how Margiela's work denies the ineluctable linearity of Western industrial time, and literally inverts past and future, thus carnivalizing time. Margiela's garments and performances invert and accelerate time, as well as confound both the aging process of the garments and the historical time of fashion history. He inverts and refutes teleological and progressive notions of time and history, by making the old anew and rendering the new as old. These tendencies, however present in the majority of his work, can be best observed in his Spring/Summer 1993 and Spring/ Summer 1996 collections – two collections that have been largely ignored

4 Barbara Burman Baines, *Fashion Revivals from the Elizabethan Age to the Present Day* (London: B. T. Batsford, 1981).
5 Judith Clark, *Spectres: When Fashion Turns Back* (London: Victoria & Albert Museum, 2004).
6 The expression 'carnivalized time' is surprisingly seldom used within Bakhtinian literature. The few times it surfaces, it is generally synonymous with carnival time: it retains the more expansive meaning of the cyclical and renewable time of carnival festivities. Bakhtin uses the term to refer to time in Dostoyevsky's novels, as pointed out by Richard Peace, 1993, 'On Rereading Bakhtin'. *Modern Language Review* 88 (1), 137–46. The only other recurrence of the term in the literature can be found in an article on Seneca's *Apocolocyntosis* to refer to the monstrous body of Claudius: see Susanna Morton Braund and Paula James. 1998. 'Quasi Homo: Distortion and Contortion in Seneca's Apocolocyntosis', *Arethusa* 31 (3), 285–311.

within the literature on the designer – captured in the designer's ten-year retrospective at the Museum Boijmans Van Beuningen in Rotterdam in 1997.

Theater costumes collection: Spring/Summer 1993

The designer's Spring/Summer 1993 collection presented 'historically inspired underwear and skirts' alongside 'reworked and over-dyed jackets of Renaissance and eighteenth century style theater costumes in velvet and brocade worn on bare torsos, closed with safety pins or belted with Scotch tape.'[7] Besides the obvious irony of using Scotch tape and safety pins to 'style' historical theater costumes, their inclusion adds another layer to Margiela's play with temporalities. These costumes, which were transformed and further aged through an over-dying process, in fact, already carry a reference to historical time. Not unlike historical film costumes, they approximate a historical past by often resorting to established conventions of how the past has come to be represented (i.e., puffed sleeves and velvets become a shorthand for the Renaissance, neck ruffs for the Elizabethan era). In the case of this collection, very scant examples of clothing were available and, with the exception of two pieces from the aforementioned private collection, I had to base my analysis on photographic documentations of the clothes comprising the collection. These were examined alongside the Costume Institute's curatorial notes for the deconstruction section of the exhibition *Infra-Apparel* from 1993, which included material analysis of some of Margiela's Theatre Collection pieces. The analysis was also further informed by the Maison's own detailed press release, which I was able to access in the museum collections.

Theater costumes present a simplified and emphasized version of 'history': even more so than cinematic ones, distilled in a few immediately readable signs, which need to be recognizable by an audience at a distance. As a result, they often shed more light on contemporary rather than past fashions, and on the way the conventions, according to which we represent and imagine various historical periods, are, in fact, rooted in the present. This is particularly evident in the theater costumes that Margiela included in his 1993 collection, whose historical

---

[7]   Martin Margiela et al., *Martin Margiela (914/1615)* (Rotterdam: Museum Boijmans Van Beuningen, 1977).

approximation and vagueness are furthered by the reworking of the garments, which ultimately look rather contemporary and vaguely pan-historical. The reworked theater costumes, having been taken out of the context of an entire ensemble and undergoing photographic close-up, give away their lack of historical accuracy: snap buttons, which are often used in theater costume to allow for quick changes, are visible on 'Renaissance' jackets worn open and on a vaguely military eighteenth century jacket. A waistcoat, once taken out of context, conveys a nineteenth century riding habit, such as a Redingote à la Hussarde. Stomachers and corsets paired with exposed belly buttons underscore contemporary mores rather than whatever period they were originally meant to represent.

Margiela's Spring/Summer 1993 collection brings to mind the complex filmic time of historical movies, where the past is imagined via the present. Historical films, such as the 1967 gangster/romance film *Bonnie and Clyde*'s portrayal of 1930s America, merge fashion from different decades and convey how a decade, be it our own or, in the case of *Bonnie and Clyde*, the 1960s, represented a particular past. This process is in great part achieved via costumes and mise-en-scène. Similarly, Margiela's reconstructed theater costumes highlight the ways in which history is constructed and make visible how the past is mediated and available only through the present. His designs reinforce an understanding of history – or better, histories – as reflexive, interpretative, and thus necessarily mediated and culturally constructed, rather than a stable and unmediated reconstruction of the past, which could be fully disinterested or objective.

It is through my material and visual analysis of the collection that I build my argument that the Belgian designer's garments constitute visual and material theorizations of 'new history', and its attendant historiographical methods, which developed with particular force from the 1970s onward to debunk the so-called 'Master Narratives' and the traditional paradigm of history.[8] Written from a Western vantage point, this paradigm was highly dependent on official documents in its quest for causality and objectivity, and was characterized by an interest in the chronological unfolding of national and international political events (needless to say, this mode of history had very little space for fashion).

---

[8] The literature on new history and historiography is, of course, vast, but for an exhaustive summary of these debates, see Keith Jenkins (ed.), *The Postmodern History Reader* (London: Routledge, 1997). For a nuanced discussion, see also Peter Burke (ed.), *New Perspectives on Historical Writing* (University Park, PA: The Pennsylvania State University Press, 2001).

Margiela's reconstructed theater pieces instead forcefully point to the ways in which reality is socially and culturally constructed, and expose how one 'cannot avoid looking at the past from a particular point of view.'[9] Such a reading of Margiela's work opens up the field of inquiry and suggests new theoretical models for the study of fashion histories, which, as with Kristeva's conceptualization of temporalities, understand histories as nonlinear, as well as inevitably mediated. Thus, ultimately, Margiela's reworking of theater costumes provides further evidence that fashion has a theoretical dimension.

Under closer scrutiny, and as the suspension of disbelief afforded by the stage is removed, Margiela's garments reveal themselves for what they are: obviously 'fake' replicas and approximations of a historical past often achieved by quoting more recent pasts; such is the case with his eighteenth-century-like, small fur jacket, which seems to be adapted from a 1940s garment, and a Renaissance-like blouse whose laced sleeves seem to be quoting the nineteenth century, and were possibly made of textiles of that period. [...]

Rendering the conflation of various historical periods explicit, Margiela's pieces dismantle the illusion of a stable and 'authentic' past that the theater costumes are meant to represent. The reconstructed theater costumes deny fixed and stable origins. They carnivalize linear history and, in their obvious fakeness and inverted complex time, question a historical past that is stable and unmediated. These clothes show the complex temporalities of dress history where, at closer scrutiny, one finds a palimpsest of historical periods within a single garment. [...]

Performing garments: Martin Margiela's Rotterdam exhibition

Margiela's ironization of processes of nostalgia became, perhaps, even more evident in the designer's retrospective at the Museum Boijmans Van Beuningen, a museum of art and design in Rotterdam, which was organized by the Maison Martin Margiela itself in 1997. The exhibition was painstakingly documented in the accompanying catalog, which was also authored by the Maison, remaining as the rare documentation of this time-based work.[10] As a result, the catalog became

---

[9] Burke, *New Perspectives on Historical Writing*, 6.
[10] La Maison Martin Margiela 1997; for a review of the exhibition, see Caroline Evans, 'The Golden Dustman: Martin Margiela', *Fashion Theory* 2, no. 1 (1998): 73–93.

an object of study in its own right and the basis for my analysis of the exhibition – a temporal event that no longer exists. (Its transformation into an artifact is made further evident by its retailing for over $1000 in the secondhand book market.) In fact, it would be more precise to call the exhibition a performance, as it was composed of an event, which unfolded over time, and where (rather uncharacteristically) the main subjects were garments as opposed to the people wearing them. The Rotterdam retrospective entered the realm of performance art as the garments became performing 'subjects'; the clothes came alive or, rather, their organic life and lifespan was made manifest. Pink yeast, red or yellow bacteria, and green mold were applied onto clothes from Margiela's past collection, which had been treated with the growing medium agar. Their application accelerated processes of aging and decomposition, particularly as the clothes were placed 'in incubating structures' in the museum's garden. The use of bacteria is also reminiscent of disease and contagion – a reference, however, subverted by the beautiful pattern obtained through their applications. This reference to disease and medicalized spaces constitutes an undercurrent to experimental fashion produced in the late 1980s and 1990s, and can be observed in experimental fashion's challenge to the clean facade of the body and its boundaries, which can, in part, be read as meditating anxieties and obsessions with bodily borders surrounding the AIDS crisis.[11]

The application of molds and bacteria allowed for the fabrication of signs of aging and of patina onto the clothes across a relatively short span of time. Once the bacteria had grown on the garments' fabric and achieved the desired effect, the clothes were exhibited on dress forms alongside the perimeter of the museum's garden, presumably to further age. They were visible to the museum goers both from inside the exhibition hall and in rear view from the museum garden in which the visitors could walk. The mannequins were placed on a plinth outside, but facing in as if looking through the glass walls of the exhibition space at the visitors on the empty space inside. This initiated the first of a series of inversions by switching the traditional placement of mannequins vis-a-vis viewers and playing with categories of inside and outside. Thus, what appeared at first sight as a dismal and abandoned site (especially once the garments were taken out of the enclosures and exposed to the elements) was in actuality

[11] See Francesca Granata 'The Bakhtinian Grotesque in Fashion at the Turn of the Twenty First Century', PhD thesis (London: University of the Arts, 2010).

painstakingly produced and documented in the book accompanying the exhibition. The garments were aged according to a scientific process in a controlled environment so that the process of fabricating imagined histories and a sense of nostalgia was literally deconstructed and put on display.

In the exhibition, one encounters, once again, Margiela's penchant for carnivalizing time and playing with the order of temporalities. He ages garments that had withstood the passage of time and almost overnight tatters them to pieces. Moreover, he does so in the context of the museum, a place traditionally engaged with the conservation rather than the destruction of objects. Margiela inverts the temporality of the retrospective, which is supposed to anoint a designer's or most often an artist's oeuvre into the 'eternal' and stable time of the museum. The designer converts the relation of the museum to permanence to transience. As design historian Linda Sandino points out, in her discussion of contemporary art works, by incorporating ephemeral elements, museums are 'complicit in the transition of transient to durable,' as they are 'dedicated to preserve the fiction that works of arts are fixed and immortal.' As a result, 'transience [which well-describes Margiela's entire retrospective] subverts the presumed timeless significance and value of the museum collection.'[12]

The Maison initiated another central inversion during the Rotterdam exhibition, in which its clothes become animated via the application of bacteria, yeast, and mold to the fabric. To this end, Margiela employed a scientific method, which is fully documented in the catalog accompanying the exhibition. The designer's 'animated' garments are also intent on fully exploring fashion's potential for problematizing fixed categories of inside/outside, animate/inanimate, body/clothing, and its potential for continual change and transformation. They are not only animated but also generative as is underlined by the Maison's description of the first stage of the exhibition as 'the gestation period.' Margiela's 'fecund' dresses go against the understanding of fashion (and the woman of fashion) as 'profoundly inorganic and anti-maternal'[13] and reiterate experimental fashion's exploration of the generative potential of the body and of different models of subjectivities and cyclical temporalities, as articulated by Bakhtin and Kristeva. [...]

---

[12] Linda Sandino, 'Here Today, Gone Tomorrow: Transient Materiality in Contemporary Cultural Artefacts', *Journal of Design History* 17, no. 3 (2004): 289.
[13] Evans, 1998, 91.

As argued in this chapter, a close analysis of Margiela's work highlights fashion's cyclical nature, and points to the way that history is unstable and constructed. A study of his work suggests new theoretical models for the study of fashion design and its histories, models that are more fluid in their approach to temporalities and provide an understanding of history as inevitably mediated. Thus, my work underscores the need for scholars and students of fashion to allow theory and practice to enter, in a Bakhtinian 'spirit' into dialogical exchanges with each other.

Quotations: The Past and Future of Fashion

Angelo Flaccavento

Angelo Flaccavento, 'Alessandro Michele: Quotations, the Past and Future of Fashion. Here's My Vision', *Vogue Italia*, September 2017, no. 805, p. 191, trans. Antony Bowden. Available at http://www.vogue.it/en/fashion/ news/2017/09/01/alessandro-michele-quotations-past-future-fashion- interview-vogue-italia/ (accessed 3 January 2020).

In this article for Italian Vogue, *the fashion journalist and author Angelo Flaccavento looks at the design aesthetic and methods of Alessandro Michele, creative director of Gucci. Michele's rampant eclecticism is very different from the historicism of 1980s' fashion outlined above by Martin and Koda, which they describe as a form of 'hybrid historicism'. Michele's modus operandi, by contrast, is a lavish yet literal form of quotation that borders on copying. As he says in this interview, 'I do find things, but many things find me, because chance is also imaginative.'*

The colossal ambition of Michele's eclecticism rearranges time and historical narrative in his collections. A Gucci show is like an exercise in the visualization of antilinear time. In the online publication Anothermagazine.com (3 March 2016) the British journalist Alex Fury described Michele's 'non-linear, non-narrative approach that scrambles notions of chronology and causality' in his Gucci autumn/ winter 2016 show Rhizomatic Scores, *a title inspired by the philosophical concept developed by Gilles Deleuze and Félix Guattari in their* Capitalism and Schizophrenia *project (1972–1980).*

In his Vogue *article, Flaccavento argues that Michele's hyperactive elaborations of the past arrest time, or try to. He analyses Michele's multi-temporalism, and discusses whether his collapsing of time is also a form of cultural appropriation. The article invites the question of what types of time can be encompassed in the idea of antilinearity, and at what point historical bricolage strays into cultural appropriation.*

In fashion, the new originates from an incessant, cathartic, superstitious elaboration of the past that stops time, or at least it tries to, through remaking, endlessly. What would the '80s have been without the '40s, and the '70s without the '20s? Even the modernism of the '60s, so inebriated with the future, clearly owes more than a little bit to the brisk lines of the jazz era. Not to mention the creators, who are always amazingly indebted. What would Yves Saint Laurent have invented had he not looked at the *Rive Gauche* of the protesters or at Mondrian; or Gianni Versace had he not laid his eyes on Greek vases and on Beppe Spadacini's prints; or Walter Albini had he not been intrigued by Benito's drawings and by the sophistications of the *Gazette du Bon Ton*? 'I am brazen. For me, creating means regurgitating, distorting and assembling everything that has passed through me and continues to do so,' says Alessandro Michele, tireless appropriator and Gucci's creative director. [. . .]

For sure, Alessandro Michele is not the first appropriationist in fashion history and will not be the last. But he is probably the most archaeological and accurate and surely the most derisive, because he plays it hard and risky with pseudo copies that unsettle the moralists while he keeps on elaborating new juxtapositions. 'I am almost pornographic in the way I pay homage to what I like and what has influenced me,' he explains, referring to the deliberate literalness of his own citations. The assemblage, instead, is always idiosyncratic, hectic and Dionysian. 'I find things, but many things find me, because chance is also imaginative,' he adds, describing his *modus operandi* made of both chaos and order. 'Quoting means rehabilitating, transforming. Denying this means nullifying the very act of creation.'

Such crystal clarity leaves no room for doubts, but despite it Alessandro Michele has often been questioned for the very same zest for appropriation which is his own creative trademark, and ended up being the victim par excellence of the anti-appropriation police. 'My sources are so evident that, perhaps wrongly, I don't consider captions necessary,' he explains. 'For me, reworking the past over and over again is a way not to trivialise the garments and not to obsess over hem lengths. What I am interested in, as a matter of fact, is telling a story and, if someone sees fragments of other stories in it, be my guest. I don't have to justify myself. What is urgent for me is what I want to say.' Michele especially refers to the controversy that spread on Instagram at the end of May for a look in the cruise 2018 collection which refers quite literally to the work of Daniel Day, the tailor who in the '80s in Harlem created a magnificent idea of appropriationist ghetto tailoring with the Dapper Dan atelier, defining the image of the first hip-hop stars from scratch, through the illicit theft of luxury labels' logos. 'Maybe I should have said it openly, but to me it was far too obvious,' he explains. Theorising the neo-mannerist wave of the '80s, art critic Achille Bonito Oliva forged the formula 'the traitor's ideology', which is a perfect way to define appropriation as creative practice. It is exactly the way Michele works: he respects his sources by betraying them at will to compose overwhelming symphonies. This includes Cranach's paintings, Walter Albini's and Botticelli's beauties, which, however, don't trigger the politically correct rage of social media censors. 'I believe the problem springs from a widespread cultural attitude. Citations have always been a fundamental part of everyone's cultural journey. Today, however, citations are confused with paralysing nostalgia. On the contrary, I believe obsessing over the future is the best way not to live the present.' Here we get to the vital point. Seeing the past as a lively mine full of references and possibilities is a way to bring the present into the limelight. What is fascinating in Alessandro Michele's work is his rewriting of time, akin to a psychedelic trip that frees cognition and knowledge, and that finds the value of today exactly in archaeology. 'I grew up with a father who didn't wear a watch and this has permanently marked my relationship with time,' he concludes. 'All that inspires me and all that I quote, whether it is one day or four hundred years old, occurs at the same time before my eyes, so it becomes the present. It's my present, my time and it's the only thing that I can and want to describe.'

Vintage Fashion and Memory

Heike Jenss

Heike Jenss, *Fashioning Memory: Vintage Style and Youth Culture* (London: Bloomsbury, 2015), 139–40.

In her book on vintage, Jenss traces the relationship of memory to fashion time. Her chapter on 'Untimely Fashion' opens by situating fashion within the rhythms of modern, capitalist time: the time of 'modernity'. It is against this backdrop, as she writes, that fashion is 'a material mode of making time', and a 'temporal anchor' in the experience of the 'multiple temporalities' of modern life. Jenss captures the push and pull between fashion's fast pace and the slower, more varied times in which we accumulate our wardrobes; she uses this to describe how fashion is part of memory, and memory of fashion. It is in this context that she locates the growing importance of vintage, as a desire to recall the past, but with a certain distance in time, one that dissociates it from fashion's seasonal pattern.

Fashion, here as fashioning body and self, can be understood as a material mode of 'making time,' perhaps as an effort of making time and present materially graspable, of inscribing oneself into the moment. In this way, the wearing of fashion, as a 'moment of temporary closure,' could then further be seen as a kind of temporal anchorage, of manifesting a moment. As has been shown, the temporality of fashion is not absolute or universal as its narration of newness and ephemerality suggests, rather in everyday life fashion is part of the creating, coexistence and experience of multiple temporalities.[1] Despite the proclamation of seasonal change and even weekly promotions of 'new arrivals,' the space and content of most wardrobes accumulates things from varied times, that are used and re-worn over stretches of time.[2] And as has been noted here before, despite all attempts to work against memory and stimulate forgetting with the proposal of the new, memory is constitutive to the workings of the temporal dynamics of fashion – not least because it is through our ability to remember that we come to

---

[1] See also Elizabeth Shove, Frank Trentmann and Richard Wilk, *Time, Consumption and Everyday Life: Practice, Materiality and Culture* (London: Bloomsbury, 2009), 3.

[2] See Sophie Woodward, *Why Women Wear What They Wear* (London: Bloomsbury, 2007).

recognize and identify what is 'new' or 'old'. In that sense again, fashion is effectively part of 'memory' – or 'fashioning memory'.

The growing interest in old clothes as vintage, as recognizably 'old', shows not only the tendency in fashion to refuse the past, but also the desire to recall – though usually with a temporal twist – through a certain distance in time. This distance is perhaps the one needed in order to blur any immediate personal or sartorial remembrance with the dynamics of cultural memory – incorporating other people's memories. Vintage gives old clothes a new name, and connotes with that a meaning that comes to evolve through passing a temporal (and commercial) threshold: from passé to 'past' – from outmoded to ripe to be 'old-fashioned'. Vintage means, at least currently, not the clothes from last season – in the way the term was used by *Vogue* in 1913. While vintage works with memory, it does not do so with the 'short-term' memory of just a few seasons; on the contrary.

Section 3

Uchronic Time

Fashion, A Time Which Does Not Exist

Roland Barthes

Roland Barthes, *The Fashion System* [1967], trans. Matthew Ward and
Richard Howard (London: Jonathan Cape, 1985), 288–89.

*Here, the semiologist and cultural critic Roland Barthes argues that fashion both
kills the past and, in its constant reinvention, consumes the present. He thus
characterizes fashion as a 'vengeful present'. In the original French the writer uses
the term 'uchronia' (*uchronie*) in a footnote to identify the way in which fashion
creates a kind of non-time:*

> In fact, Fashion postulates an achrony, a time which does not exist: here the past
> is shameful and the present constantly 'eaten up' by the Fashion being heralded.

*That footnote was rendered as 'achrony' by the English-language translators, a point
which is discussed at greater length in the Introduction to this book, and that is how
it appears below. The footnote follows Barthes's claim that fashion abolishes long-
term memory, and is 'never anything but an amnesiac substitution of the present for
the past'. In a text that is characterized by density, paradoxes abound. In consciously
destroying the past, 'Fashion' acknowledges the past's existence. And in waging war
against time itself, fashion becomes the only entity that is able to mark time.*

The Fashion present tense

The formal purity and closure of B ensembles is sustained by the very special
temporality of Fashion. Of course, in A ensembles, the equivalence between
garment and world is also subject to Fashion, i.e., to a vengeful present which each
year sacrifices the signs of the preceding year: it is only *today* that prints stand for
the Races; yet, by opening its signs to the world in the form of functions and
reasons, Fashion seems to subject time to a more natural order: in it the present

becomes mute and somewhat shameful, carried within connotation along with Fashion itself. All naturalistic alibis disappearing from B ensembles, the Fashion present tense thereby guarantees the declared arbitrariness of the system: this system is all the more closed over its synchrony in that each year it reverses entirely and at a single stroke collapses into the nothingness of the past: reason or nature no longer supervising the signs, everything is granted to the system, beginning with the declared murder of the past. B ensembles, or, one might say, logical Fashion, thus sanction an exemplary confusion of present and structure; on the one hand, the Fashion's *today* is pure, it destroys everything around it, disavows the past with violence, censures the future, as soon as this future exceeds the season; and on the other hand, each of these *todays* is a triumphant structure, whose order is extensive with (or alien to) time,[1] in such a way that Fashion tames the new even before producing it and achieves that paradox of an unforeseeable and yet legislated 'new': in short, we can say that Fashion domesticates the unforeseen without, however, stripping it of its unforeseen character: each Fashion is simultaneously inexplicable and regular. Long-term memory thus abolished, time reduced to the couple of what is driven out and what is inaugurated, pure Fashion, logical Fashion (that of B ensembles) is never anything but an amnesiac substitution of the present for the past.[2] We could almost speak of a Fashion neurosis, but this neurosis is incorporated into a gradual passion, the fabrication of meaning; Fashion is unfaithful only insofar as it *acts out* meaning, *plays* meaning.

Sovereign Time

Patrizia Calefato

Patrizia Calefato, 'Time', Chapter 12 of *The Clothed Body*
(Oxford and New York: Berg, 2004), 123–24.

The fashion scholar Patrizia Calefato posits a different model again of time as 'sovereign' or 'wasted', drawing on George Bataille's notion of 'general economy', and thereby

---

[1]   As we have said, Fashion is systematically unfaithful. Now fidelity (like paralysis within the past) and infidelity (like the destruction of this same past) are equally neurotic, once they assume a form, the former of a legal or religious duty (of the Erinys type), the latter of a natural right to 'life.'

[2]   In fact, Fashion postulates an achrony, a time which does not exist: here the past is shameful and the present constantly 'eaten up' by the Fashion being heralded.

grasps something that other writers on fashion miss: its excessive, self-devouring quality, something like potlach, *as Roland Barthes writes. Calefato identifies complex temporal relays in fashion as it segues between past, present and future, 'so the time of fashion is consumed in a space where it no longer makes sense to separate past and present, synchrony and diachrony'.*

Uchronia is perhaps the most speculative and experimental concept of fashion time covered in this book. Calefato identifies fashion as the author of its own uchronias: a self-referential meta-discourse that includes paradoxes, masks and ambitions. If all this sounds unduly abstract, most of the excerpts that follow Calefato's are very concrete and down-to-earth examples of fashion uchronias, or alternate histories: they span fashion marketing, journalists' hyperbole, activism and the avant-garde.

Barthes writes that fashion substitutes 'for the slow time of wear, a sovereign time free to destroy itself by an act of annual potlach'.[1] The expression 'sovereign time' shows that the time of fashion is not cumulative, chronological or historical, but a 'wasted' time that exceeds the ordered signs of 'useful' consumption.

Senseless destruction is celebrated by fashion. It is everything that goes beyond the waste predicted by the economic laws of value; even though the 'general economy', as Bataille calls it, always takes into account that there is refuse, or waste, to be destroyed every time energy is produced. Bataille writes that only laughter, parody, irrational consumption and sacrifice escape this economy. They are all part of sovereign time, a time which mocks itself, and ridicules accumulation:

> Above all, the general economy shows that excess energy is produced which, by definition, cannot be used. This excess energy can only be wasted without any purpose, and, consequently, it is senseless waste. Such useless, senseless waste is sovereignty.[2]

The speed of the fashion system renders its mechanisms of production and destruction inaccessible. Potlach imitates consumption as caricature, since it plays at raising the stakes, and does not limit itself to an equal exchange. In this way fashion is part of Bataille's 'sacrifice'; that is, 'not only the rite itself, but every representation or narrative in which the destruction (or threat of destruction) of a hero or, more generally, a being, has an important role'.[3]

[1]   Roland Barthes, *The Fashion System* (Berkeley: University of California Press, 1990), xii.
[2]   Georges Bataille, *Inner Experience* [1954], trans. Stuart Kendall (Albany, NY: State University of New York, 2014), 191.
[3]   Bataille, *Inner Experience*, 195.

Everything would be part of the general economy if the destruction were 'real', if the experience of death were a direct experience without mediation. The fashion experience, however, plays on spectacle, on the distance offered by images. Fashion exhibits its production mechanisms in its physiognomy: in this 'ostensive' sense, it is text *and* body, text *as* body, a body where every single sign tells a story. So the time of fashion is consumed in a space where it no longer makes sense to separate past and present, synchrony and diachrony. Both directions, towards the past and towards the present, coexist in what Barthes calls (in a linguistic cast of the term 'utopia') 'uchronia', a time which does not exist, but which can be expressed by both verbal and non-verbal signs. Everything that can be said *about* fashion is said *by* fashion: the meta-discourse of fashion shares with the system it discusses paradoxes and ambitions, masks and transgressions.

The Art of the Perfect Moment

Barbara Vinken

Barbara Vinken, *Fashion Zeitgeist* (Oxford and New York: Berg, 2005), 42.

The literary and fashion scholar Barbara Vinken reminds us that fashion ('the empire of the ephemeral') consists of the art of capturing the moment. And this is reflected in the words of Pierre Bergé, former CEO of Yves Saint Laurent, in the New York Times *(28 October 2015): 'Fashion is so very fragile, you see. Really, what it is is a moment between the past and future, and it has to encapsulate the present.'*

The time of fashion is not eternity, but the moment. Coco Chanel defines the art of the designer as 'l'art de capter l'air du temps.' Paul Morand, her ghostwriter and friend, compared it for that reason to Nemesis, the goddess of destruction: it lives from destruction, not only that of the preceding fashion, but also from its own extinction: 'The more ephemeral fashion is, the more perfect it is. You can't protect what is already dead.'[1] Fashion is defined as the art of the perfect moment, of the sudden, surprising and yet obscurely expected harmonious apparition – the Now at the threshold of an immediate future. But its realization is, at the

[1]   Paul Morand, *L'allure de Chanel* (Paris: Hermann, 1976), 140.

same time, its destruction. By appearing, and giving definitive form to the moment, fashion is almost already part of yesterday. Courreges's immaculate very young girl, a modern, minimalist virgin, lean, clad in white, and waiting for things to come, is a perfect allegory of fashion. For the same reason, perhaps, fashion shows traditionally end with the veiled bride, a figure of great expectations. Fashion is the moment that negates time as durée; it erases the traces of time, blots out history as difference by positioning itself as absolute, self-evident and perfect as a moment becoming eternity, the promise of eternity. The veil of melancholy only heightens the poignant beauty of the fleeting moment, its ephemerality and frailness.

Fashion Is Now and Tomorrow

Karl Lagerfeld

Karl Lagerfeld, 'Karlism 25', www.karl.com/karlism/2013/karlism-25/#karlism-1 (accessed 12 November 2013); 'Karl Lagerfeld on Fur (Yea), Selfies (Nay) and Keeping Busy', interview with Matthew Schneier, *New York Times* (3 March 2015).

The Utopian resistance of fashion to time often underpins the stories that designers tell about themselves. In the first statement below, made by Karl Lagerfeld in 2013, the experienced artistic director and designer explains how he feels disconnected from both his era and his personal history. In this 'Karlism of the Day', as he called the numbered aphorist statements he regularly posted on his website, he describes himself as 'floating' in time, suggesting that he inhabits the uchronic realm of 'pure Fashion' identified by Roland Barthes.

In the second passage, an interview from 2015, Lagerfeld pays brief homage to the present, which he sees as the antidote to the sickness of our times: that of paying too much attention to the past. Unlike many creative directors who work for historic haute couture houses and who are continually required to reference the brand's heritage, Lagerfeld claimed not to be interested in the archive, and to save nothing from the past.

I don't want to be my own souvenir or a typical symbol of the '60s. I'm from no generation, I'm part of no group, I'm totally floating and this is the whole story and why I can survive.

This is one of the sicknesses of our period, to look back. No, forget about it. Fashion is now and tomorrow. Who cares about the past? ... I don't take ideas from my own past. Sometimes I see things [and say] 'Oh, it's not that bad'. And people tell me, 'You did that 20 or 30 years ago'. Maybe – I forgot. As long as you're in the business, you must not think about your own work. In Germany, they made a huge exhibition of everything I did, Fendi, Chanel, Lagerfeld, Chloé and all that. I'm not even going to the show. I don't care.

There's no history. I don't even have archives, myself. I keep nothing. What I like is to do – not the fact that I *did*. It doesn't excite me at all. When people start to think that what they did in the past is perhaps even better than what they do now, they should stop. Lots of my colleagues, they have archives, they look at their dresses like they were Rembrandts! Please, forget about it.

Made in Italy and Double Vintage

Simona Segre Reinach

Translated from: Simona Segre Reinach, 'Antropologia e studio della moda', Maria Giuseppina Muzzarelli, Giorgio Riello and Elisa Tosi Brandi (eds), *Moda. Storia e storie* (Milan and Turin: Bruno Mondadori, 2010), 111–13.

The fashion scholar Simona Segre Reinach takes an anthropological look at the marketing term 'Made in Italy' and comes up with the concept of 'double vintage'. She explains how Italian luxury fashion firms have re-written recent history and altered the initial idea behind Made in Italy. Instead of dwelling on the particular history of innovation in industrialized fashion, they have exploited sham associations with craftsmanship and heritage. Periods of Italian art history as varied as the Renaissance and Futurism are fair game for plundering in this process of mythologizing. It both distorts the actual history of fashion production and disguises the fact that much current Italian production takes place elsewhere. The concept of vintage, which usually describes second-hand clothes, is here applied to a nation. Segre Reinach's analysis has some similarities with Arjun Appadurai's ideas about patina and nostalgia in a postcolonial context, where the dominant culture strives to bring the imagined glories of a lost world back into the present. The re-writing of history for marketing purposes is a common form of uchronic narrative in fashion.

History for an anthropologist is not so much the passive acceptance of what has been written about the past, primarily concerned with understanding how the history of the subject of enquiry might influence one's current analysis. It is a process of mutual exchange rather than a matter of one serving the other. My study on the relationship between Italians and Chinese in fashion has inevitably meant revising some assumptions about the history and meanings of 'Made in Italy'.

While I was working on how China was establishing its own fashion identity,[1] I realised that the identity of Italian fashion had also been undergoing rapid transformation since the second half of 2000. An analysis of recent press confirmed an increase in products that highlighted the *historical* prestige of Italian production, of the so-called Made in Italy phenomenon, and which an anthropologist is called upon to interpret. Some of these projects and concepts appear no less strange and distant than the social practices of the tribes that are commonly analysed by anthropologists. On Palazzo Pitti's catwalks in January 2009, for example, men's socks imprinted with the Italian national anthem, the history of Garibaldi and other cornerstones of the history of the Italian national unity were presented. The Lavazza Coffee calendar for 2009 depicted Roman scenes, ranging from the Wolf suckling the two twins to the *dolce vita* and, of course, allusions to the Renaissance, still the most commonly invoked reference to Italian creativity. From the Renaissance there is a direct leap to Futurism, whose centenary in 2009 was also immediately reflected in fashion communication. Laura Biagiotti made this link between the past and the present explicit at the Pitti 2008 show, when she stated that 'Since art and culture are in my DNA and in my country's, I have dedicated the collection that I will present in Pitti on Tuesday to the centenary of Futurism and of Marinetti's Manifesto.'[2] A few months later, in April 2009, at the Salone del Mobile in Milan, the artist Gaetano Pesce proposed a new Futurist Manifesto entitled *Avanti Tutta*, published in the *Corriere della Sera* on 22 April 2009: 'Italian designers and industrialists have turned "Made in Italy" into a value which is envied throughout the world. "Avanti Tutta" (full speed ahead) means investing more in creativity – the only great natural resource in Italy. And on innovation, in order to ensure we overcome the crisis as soon as possible.'[3]

---

[1] Juanjuan Wu, *Chinese Fashion: From Mao to Now* (Oxford and New York: Berg, 2009).
[2] Statement by Laura Biagiotti at the Salone Pitti of January 2009. Cit. in Paola Pollo, 'E la Biagiotti punta su Pitti dopo 20 anni', in *Corriere della Sera*, 10 January 2009: 25.
[3] Gaetano Pesce, *Avanti tutta*, supplement to *Corriere della Sera*, on the occasion of the Salone del Mobile, 22 April 2009.

The issue, however, is not so much one about the endless recycling myths, nor do I mean to assert Made in Italy's veracity. As Caroline Evans writes 'history as a labyrinth allows the juxtaposition of historical images with contemporary ones; as the labyrinth doubles back on itself what is most modern is revealed as also having a relation to what is most old.'[4] There are so many initiatives and examples of the revamping of Italian identity, however, that it is hard to consider them merely as a practice common to many companies, a simple commercial or communication issue. It is more probable that they are signs of a problem, and a critical area that it may be of interest to analyse. What we take from the past may also be a key for interpreting the contradictions of the present. I am particularly interested, from an anthropological point of view, in dwelling on one aspect, that of the creativity and craftsmanship associated with Made in Italy. This is a significant fabrication, since Made in Italy was born precisely from the desire to replace craftsmanship with a new model of industrial fashion. Indeed the 1980s model, from which the Made in Italy concept emerged, is the first Italian model of creative industrial fashion. After an initial first attack on French hegemony by the Florentine *prêt-à-porter de luxe* – comprising fashion creators such as Emilio Pucci and Donna Simonetta Colonna di Cesarò – Italian fashion left the aristocratic city of the arts, Florence, and moved its fashion shows to Milan, the city of commerce. Thus was born *prêt-à-porter*, characterised by the so-called 'industrial aesthetics' of the future stylist-businessmen, the creators of Made in Italy. 'Putting It Together', as the American periodical *Womens Wear Daily* describes the *total look* proposed in 1978 by Walter Albini,[5] with its coordinated garments and accessories, is a good metaphor for Italian *prêt-à-porter*. What is 'put together' is, on the one hand, an emphasis on design creativity and, on the other, a reinforcement of mass production and standardised sizing systems.[6] This twofold model became the Italian way for modern fashion.

The re-launch of Made in Italy thus makes use of history as an epic and highly imaginative tale, but omits the real history of fashion, which is the fact that Made in Italy is a recent phenomenon, situated and modern. And, especially, that it is no longer what it was in the 1980s. Italian fashion evokes not just the myths of

---

[4]   Caroline Evans, *Fashion at the Edge* (New Haven and London: Yale University Press, 2003), 9.
[5]   Maria Luisa Frisa and Stefano Tonchi, *Walter Albini and His Times: All Power to the Imagination* (Venice: Marsilio, 2010).
[6]   Marco Ricchetti and Enrico Cietta, *Il valore della moda. Industria e servizi in un settore guidato dall'innovazione* (Milan: Mondadori Bruno, 2006), 25.

ancient history, but also those of its more recent history. This operation may well be defined as 'double vintage'. The idealisation of a glorious, remote past gives rise to the idea of craftsmanship and of creative workshops, which may then be married at pleasure with a sense of political supremacy as in the Roman Empire, artistic primacy as in the Renaissance, and of the avant-garde as in Futurism.

The emphasis on craftsmanship, which by now has become ubiquitous, has the further, and not unimportant, aim of highlighting the difference between those who have the ideas and those who execute them materially. Made in Italy propaganda disguises the 'secrets', partly or entirely, of delocalised production in China. Such separation, however, also facilitates the classification of all that is exported from Italy under the polysemous and very general label of 'Italian brands', as the work of skilled craftsmen, with no acknowledgement of globalisation, as if stilled in a time bubble.

Final Adjudication on Two National Press Advertisements for Louis Vuitton

Advertising Standards Authority

Advertising Standards Authority (UK) Adjudication on two national press advertisements for Louis Vuitton, 2010.

The Advertising Standards Authority (ASA) is an independent government organization that regulates the advertising industry in the United Kingdom. In 2010, it received three objections to a Louis Vuitton advertising campaign, complaining that the photographs in two magazine advertisements had misleadingly implied that Louis Vuitton leather goods were made by hand. As it is bound to do, the ASA investigated the complaint, and found in favour of the complainants. Like all ASA findings, the judgement, which is reprinted below in full, is in the public domain, and can be supplied on request.

The ASA adjudication is a meticulous deconstruction of the two advertising photographs. It reveals semiotic methods usually occluded in the fashion industry, namely how a company builds its own myths, and that is one aspect of uchronic thinking. The adjudication carefully describes how the photographs depict fashion models holding nineteenth-century tools in poses similar to those of traditional craftsmen, and questions their veracity. In so doing, it reveals one of the many ways in which a twenty-first-century luxury brand builds its narrative, through romantic images of craft and hand-making in its advertising campaigns.

This emphasis on the handmade is not unusual in the marketing narratives of luxury goods companies. In Italy in 2010, Gucci promoted an initiative, Artisan Corner, *which sent artisans from Gucci's Florence workshops to demonstrate their techniques in shops across the world: Tokyo, Osaka, Rome, Paris, San Francisco, Chicago, Beverly Hills and New York. Similarly, in the UK, Burberry's* Makers' House, *held in London in September 2016 and 2017, gathered together small scale makers and artisans to demonstrate their techniques in an exhibition space to suggest, by association, a connection with heritage and the hand-made. And the Valentino haute couture press release for Spring/Summer 2016 listed in lascivious detail how many hours of specialist hand sewing went into each creation: '"Isadorable", powdered mauve plissé chiffon winged dress, burnished gold impressions. 2,000 hours of work to complete', and '"Mnémosyne", mineral green chiffon plissé and antiquated velvet cape dress with burnished gold impressions. 1,800 hours of work to complete'. Here, indeed, fashion's memory is selective, in its exclusive focus on the work of the hand.*

Louis Vuitton UK Ltd	Case number:	A09-113306/RM
Churchill House	Media:	National press
160 New Bond Street	Sector:	Retail
London	Agency:	Ogilvy & Mather Ltd
W1S 2UE		

Number of complaints: 3

Ad

Two national press ads for Louis Vuitton:

a. The first ad featured a photograph of a woman stitching the handle of a handbag. Text underneath stated 'THE SEAMSTRESS WITH LINEN THREAD AND BEESWAX. A needle, linen thread, beeswax and infinite patience protect each overstitch from humidity and the passage of time. One could say that a Louis Vuitton bag is a collection of details. But with so much attention lavished on every one, should we only call them details?'

b. The second ad featured a photograph of a woman creating the folds of a wallet. Text underneath stated 'THE YOUNG WOMAN AND THE TINY FOLDS. In everything from Louis Vuitton, there are elements that cannot be fully explained. What secret little gestures do our craftsmen discreetly pass on? How do we blend innate skill and inherent prowess? Or how can five tiny folds lengthen the life of a wallet? Let's allow these mysteries to hang in the air. Time will provide the answers'.

Issue

Three complainants challenged whether the ads misleadingly implied that Louis Vuitton products were made by hand.

Response

Louis Vuitton UK Ltd (Louis Vuitton) said the images in the ads were a homage to the craftsmanship which was carried out every day by Louis Vuitton's artisans. They explained that their artisans were trained over many years to be able to carry out the various activities involved in the creation of one of their accessories.

They said the images were posed by models in order not to show favouritism to any particular employee and the images were coloured, lit and styled to make them pleasing to the reader. They also said that the pince device featured in ad (a) was an older version and the real ones were now made of metal, but ultimately they believed the images accurately reflected what took place in their workshops. They said the models in the ads were instructed on technique and posture by Louis Vuitton artisans during the photo shoots to ensure accuracy.

Louis Vuitton said they had 200 employees working on different aspects of their products in each workshop; there were over 100 stages of production for each individual leather bag and wallet and their manufacture was not automated. They said that the ads did not seek to show all the tools which were used in their workshops and that hand sewing machines were also used in the making of both the products featured in the ad.

Louis Vuitton submitted training documents which showed some of the processes involved in making handbags and purses. They also submitted step-by-step guides for the manufacture of two other products which also showed the amount of time that was spent on each stage. They said those documents illustrated that their employees were not assembling pre-packed pieces, but were taking individual handcrafted and hand-sewn parts through a range of hand-made stages to reach a final item. Louis Vuitton said that, as a successful international business many of their processes were documented, however because traditional skills remained a feature that was largely passed on within the atelier they were unable to provide more documentation.

They said that hand sewing machines were used for some aspects of items because they were more secure and necessary for strength, accuracy and durability. They believed that the use of hand sewing machines and the associated tasks were part and parcel of what would be expected to amount to 'hand made' in the 21st century. They said it would not be against public expectation for a hand-made product to be produced within an industrial setting, although they did not regard their workshops as industrial in nature. They provided photographs of their workshops to illustrate this.

Assessment

Upheld

The ASA noted that the images were stylised interpretations of real stages of the production process of both of the items featured. However, we considered that consumers would interpret the image of a woman using a needle and thread to stitch the handle of a bag in ad (a), alongside the claim '... infinite patience protects each overstitch ... One could say that a Louis Vuitton bag is a collection of fine details. But with so much attention lavished on every one, should we only call them details?' to mean that Louis Vuitton bags were hand stitched.

We also considered that the image of a woman hand-crafting a wallet using a basic manual tool in ad (b), alongside the claim 'In everything from Louis Vuitton, there are elements that cannot be fully explained. What secret little gestures do our craftsmen discreetly pass on? How do we blend innate skill and inherent prowess' would be understood by consumers to mean that Louis Vuitton products were hand crafted, throughout most or all of the entire production process.

We noted that Louis Vuitton had provided training materials and tables which outlined the manufacturing processes for some items. We noted from that documentation that various hand crafting techniques were used as were sewing machines. However, we also noted that we had not seen documentation that detailed the entire production process for Louis Vuitton products or that showed the proportion of their manufacture that was carried out by hand or by machine. Because we had not seen evidence that demonstrated the extent to which Louis Vuitton products were made by hand, we concluded that the ads were misleading.

The ads breached CAP Code clauses 7.1 and 7.2 (Truthfulness).

Action

The ads must not appear again in their current form.

I Have Seen Her in the Mirror

Elsa Schiaparelli

Elsa Schiaparelli, 'Foreword', *Shocking Life* (London, J. M. Dent, 1954), vii–viii.

In her autobiography (1954), the fashion designer Elsa Schiaparelli alternates between first and third person narratives, constructing herself as a madcap, fictional persona. In these two opening pages she paints a vivid, impressionistic picture of herself as an observer of herself: 'I have seen her in the mirror.' To reinforce the idea of the image reflected or multiplied in the mirror, Schiaparelli defines herself as a 'fifth dimension', something presumably beyond the three conventional dimensions of space, and the fourth, time, in as much as time can be called a fourth dimension. Although Schiaparelli does not explain what she means by the 'fifth dimension', it is possible to imagine it as a dimension in which spacetime coordinates collapse, and is therefore potentially both utopian and uchronic at once.

I merely know Schiap by hearsay. I have only seen her in a mirror. She is, for me, some kind of fifth dimension.

She is unpredictable but, in reality, disarmingly simple. She is profoundly lazy but works furiously and rapidly. Her laughter and tears collide; on a job of work she is fun, soaring from despair to heavenly delight. She is generous and mean, for there are occasions when she would rather give away half her possessions than the handkerchief in her hand-bag.

Intensely human, she both despises and loves human beings: those whom she dislikes find themselves looked right through as if they were transparent.

Sorrow and loss she readily accepts, but she does not know how to deal with happiness.

Her life has been a means to something else – an everlasting question-mark. Truly mystic, she believes in IT, but has not yet found out what IT is.

She is now of concrete age, but in reality has never grown up. Believing tremendously in friendship, she expects too much of her friends: sheer disappointment in their capacity to respond has often made her enemies. Flattery and small talk bore her, and she has never understood how anybody can consider life an achievement in itself.

If she is charming she can also be the most hateful person in the world. She is aware of this but cannot help it.

People believe that she is a good business woman and not, perhaps, very tender in love. In fact, she is a very poor business woman, continually taken in – exploited – and few people have been so deeply hurt in their feelings or so cruelly wounded in their pride. I have seen her in the mirror.

Then again there is a famous painting by Picasso. Her friends (oh, yes, she has many!) say that this picture is a portrait of her.

There is a cage. Below it are some playing-cards on a green carpet. Inside the cage a poor, half-smothered white dove looks dejectedly at a brilliantly polished pink apple; outside the cage an angry black bird with flapping wings challenges the sky.

She would not part with this painting for a fortune even if she were, through her supreme indifference to material values, reduced one day, as her mother predicted, to a crust of bread and some straw to sleep on in an empty room. The room would not be empty. The Picasso would be hanging on the wall!

But let us hope that her mother's prediction will not come true.

And if it does, she will know that in spite of success, glamour, and despair, the only escape is in oneself, and nobody can take that away – it is stronger than jealousy, hardship, or oppression.

Elsa Schiaparelli
1954

Elsa Schiaparelli and Miuccia Prada: Impossible Conversations

Miuccia Prada

Schiaparelli and Prada: Impossible Conversations – Introduction with Baz Luhrmann. Film dir. Baz Luhrmann, 2012, with dialogue by Miuccia Prada. Additional dialogue (adapted from the writings of Elsa Schiaparelli) by Andrew Bolton, Sam Bromell, Baz Luhrmann, Schuyler Weiss. Transcript. Available at https://www.youtube.com/watch?v=c55tCFU2Oho (accessed 5 January 2020).

This dialogue is from the first of eight short films that director Baz Luhrmann made to accompany the Metropolitan Museum of Art's fashion exhibition Impossible Conversations *(2012), which staged a fictional conversation between two Italian designers from different eras, Elsa Schiaparelli (d. 1973) and the contemporary Miuccia Prada. In the film, Prada plays herself, while Schiaparelli is played by the actress Judy Davies. While the video and the dialogue are freely available online, the identity of the fictional Schiaparelli is more elusive. The film's credits are limited to one: 'starring Miuccia Prada'. A dialogue across decades, the film puts into question who is the actress and who is the 'real' designer.*

Elsa Schiaparelli   You know, Miuccia, I hate talking to designers. It's the worst.

(**Miuccia Prada** laughs)

ES   So this impossible conversation between us is something like an exception for me.

MP   Yes, yes I can talk about fashion with so few people because they really are the ones that know what I'm talking about.

ES   Yes.

MP   Otherwise, it's kind of ridiculous or super technical.

ES   You know, I never even intended to be a dress maker.

MP   But what I'm really interested in is about your life, and that is all about, also about my work. I'm always interested in the life of people.

ES   Ah! That we can talk about. About life and maybe dresses a bit? You know, I was the most impossible, super impetuous child.

MP   I tried to obey.

ES   Too wild an imagination . . . always into trouble.

MP   Not right for a good girl.

ES   No no, not at all. Maybe you too were cut from this troublesome cloth when you were younger, yes?

MP   Yes. At those time I was searching what was the strangest, the most silly things to do. And mime, at those times . . .

ES   Mime?

MP   Yes, the most crazy thing I could do, in Milano, still living with my family.

ES   But Miuccia, you could not have been as troublesome as me.

MP   Completely. The theatre was a world of sins.

ES   Okay. Did you run away?

MP   No, no.

ES   I think it's no secret that I met a man.

MP   Yes, yes.

ES   And I had a daughter, Gogo, and then my husband . . . he ran away, so. But eventually, by chance, my salvation was stumbling into fashion.

MP   Yes, of course.

ES   Finding beauty in my own way.

MP   You had a much more difficult life than mine and that's why one of the reasons why I like your life, and I like your job, because . . .

ES   Ah, no.

MP   I see all the pain of it.

ES   So, I'm curious now, Miuccia. How did you go from the mime back to fashion?

MP   Yes, I liked fashion. I found myself in fashion, hating it and doing what it was the most horrible thing I could do with the people I was living with. To be a woman, a fashion designer, in the sixties and seventies, was the worst. But I liked it so much that I did it anyway.

ES   Yes, I think now, I realized why we are here. It's not just the fashion.

MP   Yes.

ES   But maybe it's the way we live.

MP   In the end, there are many similarities.

ES   Yes, many similarities, yes. *Salute!*

Doppie Pagine

Anna Piaggi

Anna Piaggi, *Anna Piaggi's Fashion Algebra* (London and New York, Thames & Hudson, 1998), 26, 42, 92, 184 and 290.

In these five examples from the fashion journalist Anna Piaggi's 'doppie pagine' or 'double page spreads' for Italian Vogue, *Piaggi displays her inimitable graphic style and idiosyncratic fashion imagination. 'Synthetically Yours' reads like a personal*

*manifesto: 'to associate the fashion of the moment with the ideas of the past ...
with photography, illustration, lettering. In a way that is always different. Invented.'
'Fashion Algebra' fuses the formats of autobiography and manifesto in
mathematical similes. 'On the surface' continues the autobiography while 'Double
pages' explains the concept: 'double pages as a non-system, a free association' and a
vision that spills over the edges of the page as Piaggi composed them on a wall, she
explains. She signs off with her typical fashion rhetoric in 'In pieces'.*

Synthetically Yours

Over the years, I have chosen to express myself synthetically. To associate the
fashion of the moment with the ideas of the past ... with photography, illustration,
lettering. In a way that is always different. Invented.

Fashion Algebra

From the beginning the pages took me by the hand as if in an imaginary algebraic
equation, where fashion did all the calculations, adding the stimuli together,
multiplying the coincidences; fashion was the root matrix and coefficient of the
imaginary. It was the parabola, the paradox, the number, the notation. Above all,
it was not a system, a schema: it was an unconscious operation that could never
have happened without Italian *Vogue*. Italian *Vogue* is a special theorem both a
filter and a document of fashion, which, on its pages, becomes truly unique and
inimitable. Unaffected artifice. An equation of style and at the same time a dis-
equation of canonical rules. Mathematical chic that can afford elegant errors and
the play of beautiful-sounding words.

On the surface

Alfa had an intellectual training and I had a very frivolous disposition. But we
met. With Alfa I breathed in a world of high culture, of passionate research. To
me these were amazing particles, extraordinary molecules, but I would never
allow them to affect my superficiality.

  For me it was important never to lose the thread of my instinct – my instinctive
reaction against deep thought. I was refusing to think deeply, to swerve from the
sharp tickle of intuition, the antechamber of visual thought, of illogical logic, of
the paradox of contrasts.

  In the summer of 1988, when Alfa was spending his time in the Paris metro in
the city's outskirts documenting graffiti – that disquieting cryptic sign of a

transgressive occupation of public spaces . . . one of the fashionable icons in Italian *Vogue* was the white shirt: pure, unsullied, minimal.

Double Pages

The Double Pages as a non-system, a free association, a sequence, a vision that transcends the fold of a binding (since I am used to seeing them spread out on a wall). Over these past years the Double Pages have been for me like a dress taking shape, yet a different entity as well, at the hands of the art director in charge. Fabien Baron. Juan Gatti. Luca.

In pieces

Pages in pieces. Ready to be reassembled. Disassembled. To continue. Not a retrospective.

A geometry. The end.

The Otherworldly

Greg French

Greg French, 'The Otherworldly' in Theo-Mass Lexileictous, Robert Klanten, Sven Ehmann (eds), *Otherworldly: Avant-garde Fashion and Style* (Berlin, Gestalten, 2016), 2–8.

Greg French investigates fashion as 'otherworldly' and immersive, through its mesmerizing visual games and its appeal to fantasy, but he is particularly interested in how these effects are created by 'this-worldly' processes, from the possibilities afforded by the Internet to 3D printing. Yet, as he observes, fashion has always produced iterations of the otherworldly, and he looks at a range of twentieth-century individuals who reinvented themselves as fabulous, artificial creatures through prosthetics, makeup and sheer nerve. He moves from Elsa Schiaparelli, to Grace Jones, to Cypriot artist Alexis Themistocleous and his alter ego Theo-Mass Lexileictous, and then on to the rich potential of fashion photography and film today to create 'fictitious sets, computer-generated anthropomorphic aliens, and impossible narratives'. It is these 'impossible narratives', made possible by digital fashion image-making, that make uchronic time such a rich concept with which to explore at a moment when, as French writes, 'the rendered pixel has become the new home of the otherworldly, able to change its form and function within a split second'.

What is the otherworldly? It seems only appropriate to begin with that question, even if we may not be able to conclude with an answer. After all, the concept is informed by the unknown or the unexplainable. For something to be otherworldly, its content or context must be unbound by earthly constraints. It is a space for fantasy and a space for dreams.

Fashion, with its propensity for playing with fantasy and making dreams into reality, is a sort of gateway for immersing ourselves in the idea of the otherworldly. From the repetitive weaving of the designer's needle to the acute precision of a 3D printer, and from the flash of the photographer's bulb to the pixel rendered on a digital display, fashion transforms our naked bodies, pages and screens into something other than their most basic forms. These transformations are the otherworldly results of this-worldly processes. This book examines moments in which such an approach is placed center stage in an attempt to demystify this often hazy yet pioneering area of dress.

This moment in the twenty-first century is an appropriate time for such scrutiny – particularly because of the way our era has played with concepts of the postmodern. Fashion has finally been handed capabilities, thanks to the rise of new digital technologies, with which to bring to life the often dreamlike and seemingly unattainable musings of its creators. The internet provides an arena in which designers can realize whatever creation their 3D printers and alternative materials are still incapable of materializing. It offers an opportunity to play the role of Dr. Frankenstein – or even the role of Frankenstein's monster itself. Ultimately, we as a civilization are entering a time that can be classified as post-human, where the very fabric of our DNA is changing. Gender has become little more than a social construct, robotics can replace or enhance our own weakening limbs, and drones now fly side-by-side with birds in our skies.

And yet, the moment in which we currently find ourselves is not a point of departure from the general course that we have traveled thus far. Fashion has interacted with the idea of the otherworldly throughout history. There have always been icons who lived their lives dressed like apparitions from another world, like Marchesa Luisa Casati of the Belle Epoque era, who would roam the canals of Venice on a gondola with whitened skin, kohl black eyes, and fiery red hair alongside her bejewelled pet cheetahs and white peacocks. This interaction between fashion and the otherworldly can be seen most clearly in times of great subcultural revolution. The desire to change that which is, is an inherent part of the human psyche. Acting on that desire is a necessary step in the evolution of our species.

The individual, the outsider, the pioneer, and the mutant: these are the characters who so frequently lead that mutiny. And because of the visual nature of the fashion industry, their contributions are especially visible. As Elsa Schiaparelli once said, 'In difficult times, fashion is always outrageous.'

Indeed, Schiaparelli herself was considered an 'outrageous' designer on the basis of her much-replicated skeleton dress and her use of optical illusions. Her simple introduction of shocking pink to the palette of a world where women so often favored monotonous clothes was enough to lift fashion out of the drudgery of a war-torn world. This is just one example of fashion's power to alter the reality in which we live.

The musician Grace Jones may be one of the best examples of the application of that reality-altering power. Her constant reinvention of herself is a testament to the metamorphic nature inherent to fashion. Her androgynous features, most notably her shaved head, were to garner attention among the international fashion community. Jones exemplifies the use of fashion to forge a look in total rebellion against those around you — her hair itself was a revolt against the strict religious atmosphere of her family life. 'One creates oneself,' as she said. 'Art and illusion are supposed to be fantasy.'

From Mugler to McQueen, and from Bowie to Bowery, we have seen milestone figures champion this notion of advancing or transforming society through design in their own explosive ways. Yet, more importantly, these pioneers have also set in motion a ripple effect that has seen artists and designers at varying levels produce some astonishing bodies of work while providing subject matter for some of our most idiosyncratic imagemakers. Olivier Theyskens' early work in the late 1990s employed plumes of dismembered bird wings swarmed around masked models to give the appearance of fantasy through *mise-en-scène*. Aitor Throup Studio has generated clothing from concept drawings, cloaked models beneath skeletal headgear, and deployed tech-spec trousers to create a utilitarian army of the future. Vetements and Craig Green play with distortions of the human body through proportion or abstract adornment, spawning a look that recodes the human silhouette. Often these designs toe a fine line between clothing and costume, sometimes poised so ambiguously between the two that it becomes difficult to distinguish the act of wearing them from performance art.

A costume, by its nature, is designed to change or enhance the identity of its wearer. In stepping into a costume, you commit yourself to being something other than the character you play each day. It is a transformation capable of changing the mannerisms of the wearer, granting them access to an entirely different life. This may be why extreme fashion choices, which often play with the characteristics of costume, are so frequently adapted by radical individuals in their attempts to challenge the establishment of everyday life.

This approach was perhaps most notably seen in the 1980s and 1990s, when club-kid culture catalyzed a scene where these creative practices merged together, becoming a melting pot for anarchistic schools of thought. In the cities of London and New York, which at the time were beset by economic depression and political unrest, creatives sought to forge their own worlds as a form of escapism. Avant-garde dress was every bit as important as music, drugs, and alcohol in enabling them to escape from this world and create another.

The subculture's dependence on fantasy can be seen in the theatre, film, and art of that time. Due to fashion's ability to convey the otherworldly, it became the current that would run through them all. For instance, the last decade of the twentieth century saw the release of Matthew Barney's *The Cremaster Cycle* – a series of five feature-length films that explored concepts of embryonic gender development. The films play out across a series of transcendental worlds and feature mythical characters who control the progression of the plot. Their costumes frequently borrow from the land of club-kid dress, with assistance from iconic designers like Isaac Mizrahi, Manolo Blahnik, and Prada, and input from MAC Cosmetics and Vidal Sassoon. The same can be said for dystopian movies like *The Fifth Element*, whose costume designer was Jean Paul Gaultier, or Tarsem Singh's *The Cell*, which saw designer Eiko Ishioka produce spectacular clothing that relayed the fantastical musings of a serial killer's mind.

Why and how, then, have these extremities of otherworldly fashion come about? What explains this cultural phenomenon and the steps leading up to it? The work of Cypriot artist Alexis Themistocleous may help us find the answer. Daubed in black face paint, diamond-encrusted ski masks, or restrictive suiting, Themistocleous was able to mask his true identity and forge an entirely new creature altogether. This character was then captured through film, photography, and 3D scanning. The glitchy nature of these mediums was used to heighten the enigmatic nature of the strange new being. Out of this imagery he created an online profile, achieving a kind of existence for his alter ego that takes Grace Jones's notion of creating oneself to an entirely new dimension.

Themistocleous further developed this idea in 2012 when he took the character he had created out of the realm of the internet and began living it in real life. Fashion equipped him with the ability to do so by his use of props, headpieces, and garments to alter his appearance. But the exercise did not stop there: Themistocleous created not only costumes but also his own currency, all while creatively hijacking galleries and wall spaces around the world. He even graced the cover of the fashion magazine *Dazed & Confused*, a nod to how easy it has become to completely mutate oneself. He christened his new identity Theo-Mass Lexileictous, an anagram of his own name that roughly translates to 'god of the masses'. It is this character who is the editor of this book.

The ability to realize such otherworldly ambitions on such a scale may be new, but the impulse is not. The writings of the Situationist Guy Debord may help make sense of the phenomenon. His work, especially his 1967 text *Society of the Spectacle*, examines a world that has become mediated by the imagery of the spectacular. He argues, 'everything that was directly lived has moved away into a representation'. This is true for the otherworldly in fashion – when the world has become so dehumanized, as in Theo-Mass's case, an entirely new fantasy world can be created. This, in essence, is why fashion is so important as a revolutionary tool and why it has the ability to challenge societal conventions. Debord says, 'Images detached from every aspect of life fuse in a common stream in which the unity of this life can no longer be re-established. Reality considered partially unfolds ...' Ultimately, Debord's writing suggests that the more spectacular the image, the further it is from reality itself and the more otherworldly it becomes.

Clothing complicates this idea though, for no matter how extravagantly we dress, beneath the layers of garments lies the essence of the terrestrial: our bodies.

The imagery created for fashion – particularly photography of which you will find many examples in this book – creates a space where the otherworldly can be most clearly explored. A selection of fashion photographers and image-makers have delved deep into the realm of the otherworldly, creating fictitious sets, computer-generated anthropomorphic aliens, and impossible narratives. This approach can be traced back to some of the earliest fashion photographers, like Erwin Blumenfeld, who used smoke and mirrors to create the illusion of celestial beings bound not to reality, but rather to the black ether on which they were shot. Likewise, Guy Bourdin used the Polaroid, an artistic form known for instantly capturing that which can be seen, to present unearthly stills, which were often devoid of complete bodily forms or obscured in ways that created a sinister presence. Mert & Marcus, Tim Walker, and Steven Klein also explored these techniques, conjuring up mythical landscapes in which their macabre and inhuman figures found solace.

The rendered pixel has become the new home of the otherworldly, able to change its form and function within a split second. Technology has given us new ways of creating as well as new ways of seeing, and the work of Nick Knight is a testament to that. 'Now we have a number of wonderful apps and the ability to do whatever we want with an image,' he once told me. 'Now it's different processes, different chemicals – based on phosphorous on a screen. I can make a 3D object out of anything with the press of a button.'

For Tokyo retail giant Lane Crawford's spring/summer 2013 campaign, Knight used 3D scanning software to record four of the season's looks on model Ming Xi. The resulting render was then combined with animation and digitally manipulated so that the walking model would shatter into a thousand fragmented pixels, reducing the mutated human body to nothing less than a swirling geometric dust cloud. The effect elevated the character, distancing it from the truth-capturing capabilities of the conventional video camera. The resulting figures were transported out of the confines of reality by fashion.

But it is not just within fashion imagery that we have seen the effects of the digital revolution. Technology has equipped us with the ability to live out of some of our fictitious fantasies in the real world, morphing the capabilities of the human body into something superhuman. Military research, which often has the end game of producing soldiers who are stronger, faster, and less susceptible to fatigue and health risks, has seen the production of third-generation robotic suits capable of doing just that. We also now have living fabrics that react to weather conditions or perspiration, mechanical dogs whose piston legs are capable of jumping to inhuman heights, and even prosthetic limbs that enable Paralympic athletes to compete in their disciplines once again.

Aimee Mullins is one such athlete – at once otherworldly and yet very, very real. The double-amputee also starred in the aforementioned *The Cremaster Cycle*, portraying six different fantastical characters, and appeared on the cover of *Dazed & Confused*. Her appearances question the role and responsibility of fashion within the wider world. Mullins's disability was celebrated in Alexander McQueen's spring/summer 1999 show, for which the designer and his team carved an exquisitely detailed prosthetic leg out of elm wood for Mullins. In doing so, Mullins passed unnoticed amongst the other models around her, subverting expectations about her condition. 'I made a point of not putting her in sprinting legs. We did try them on, but I thought no, that's not the point of this exercise,' commented McQueen after the show. 'The point is that she would mold in with the rest of the girls.'

The idea of the otherworldly in fashion provides us with a passage through which we can transport ourselves into partial or even complete fantasy. At one end of the spectrum, that may mean immersing ourselves in a spectacular runway show; at the other, it could mean using fashion's transformative power to forge an entirely new character altogether. Once we are there, we can subvert the socio-political hierarchies of the everyday and the reality in which they are grounded. As Debord and the Situationists suggested, we are now able to live our lives almost entirely within an alternate reality that is constructed solely by the individual. That is why, in the spirit of Schiaparelli, we can be sure that fashion itself will thrive and help us to evolve as terrestrial beings, even, or especially, in times of great instability. That is what makes the otherworldly so very important: it helps us make a version of the world that we can have an impact on.

And now, at the end, we return to the beginning. What is the otherworldly? It is a tool – a powerful tool for radically altering the world we see around us. The pages of this book will show you how it can be used to create new ways to see and live – and the fantastic people responsible for remaking our realities.

Fashion Fabulation: Serpica Naro at Milan Fashion Week 2005

Ilaria Vanni

Ilaria Vanni writes about the fictional fashion designer Serpica Naro, an anagram of the name for San Precario, *the fictitious patron saint of precarious workers. Vanni describes the shenanigans got up to by Serpica Naro (in reality the activist group Chainworkers assisted by sundry precarious workers in the fashion industry), including having the designer admitted to Milan Fashion week, and then getting as much publicity as possible through the various stunts they engineered throughout the city.*

Vanni brings academic research based in design activism to bear on the concept of fabulation. Drawing on the work of design theorist Daniela K. Rosner, she argues that critical fabulation is a speculative proposal for a better way to live (and work) in the present and the future: it involves 'the imagination of fashion practices to come that might still be otherwise'. Serpica Naro's intervention, then, is an alternate history of Milan fashion week achieved through activism and intervention rather than writing or other forms of polemic. In this sense, the group's activities represent the future anterior tense of activism. As Vanni demonstrates, Serpica Naro's uchronic temporality gave a voice to Milanese activists, showing how the actions of a fictional character can have real impact through collective action.

Serpica Naro, *Milano Moda Donna*, Milan Fashion Week 2005

On 26 February 2005 *Milano Moda Donna*, one of the most celebrated events in the Milan Fashion Week calendar, closed with the show of an unknown Anglo-Japanese designer: Serpica Naro. In the grammar of Fashion Week, the closing show has relevance as an unique feature, acknowledgement and celebration. The *Milano Moda Donna's* program included more than 100 designers and involved popular Italian brands such as Armani, Prada, Versace and Ferragamo. For an unknown, unconventional designer closing Fashion Week was no small credit. Serpica Naro was a remarkable remix of sleek and street style: her look book, website and press releases showed a designer able to interpret urban trends, such as protests, or the distinctive style of the gay community in Tokyo, and remix them with high tech and innovative textiles. The scant details about the designer herself revealed that she was of Anglo-Japanese background, which gave her a cosmopolitan outlook on life and design, and that she spent her time between London and Tokyo, scouting for whatever was new in urban cultural trends. Her logo, an outline of her face with a scar, brought these biographical details together in a distinctive graphic form.[1]

Once in Milan, Serpica Naro became embroiled in a series of media spats with local queer activists, who accused her of having exploited the gay community in Japan, and with anti-precarity activists, who at the time were contesting with direct actions some of Fashion Week's major shows. For instance the fictitious patron saint of precarious workers, San Precario, was mobilized during the Prada and Laura Biagiotti shows to draw attention to precarious work in the fashion industry, and activists announced direct actions against Serpica Naro.[2] The designer responded through her media manager, complaining about the difficulty of working in Milan, a city blocked by bureaucracy and communists.[3]

Tone-deaf to the media spats and the activists' protests, Serpica Naro, to stress her closeness to street cultures, decided to hold her show on an anonymous overpass near a *centro sociale* (a self-managed cultural and social centre home of the anti-precarity activist group Chainworkers), which she had previously and unsuccessfully tried to hire. Journalists and police gathered on the date of the show, imagining newsworthy protests. However, a surprise was waiting. It turned out in fact that Serpica Naro, the cosmopolitan and controversial Anglo-Japanese designer, did not exist as such. The media campaign, the protests, the look-book and website were all part of an elaborate hoax, orchestrated by the activist group Chainworkers in close collaboration with precarious workers along the supply chain of the fashion industry, and Serpica Naro was their imaginary collective creation.[4]

The show itself, of course, went on, as per agreement between Serpica Naro and the National Chamber of Italian Fashion, which had screened Serpica Naro's

[1] Serpica Naro, 'Serpica Naro, Il Media Sociale', *Serpica Naro*, 27 January, 2013. Available at https://www.serpicanaro.com/serpica-story/serpica-naro-il-media-sociale (accessed 4 January 2020).
[2] Ilaria Vanni and Marcello Tarì, 'On the Life and Deeds of San Precario, Patron Saint of Precarious Workers and Lives,' *Fibreculture*, no. 5 (2005). Available at http://five.fibreculturejournal.org/fcj-023-on-the-life-and-deeds-of-san-precario-patron-saint-of-precarious-workers-and-lives/ (accessed 4 January 2020).
[3] Serpica Naro, 'Serpica Naro, Il Media Sociale'.
[4] Ibid.

application (including her look-book, press clips and list of buyers) and registered her to show her collection as part of Milan Fashion Week. The show included three independent labels working through remixing and bricolage: the British Sailors Mars, with a collection made with waste from London's East End; the Milanese Industrial Couture, with aerographed outfits; and the Catalan Yomango, which advocates 'social disobedience and direct action against multinational corporations, as total lifestyle'.[5] The other part of the show consisted of eight 'allegoric' designs, capturing and distilling shared experiences of precarity. For instance, the outfit 'Se 60 giorni vi sembrano pochi' (If you think 60 days are not many) was made of trousers and several numbered t-shirts worn in layers. Each t-shirt could be taken off at the end of each working day to count how many days elapsed between the completion of a job and its payment. As a comment on the demands for flexibility Serpica Naro presented 'Tutta T Job On Call,' a reversible outfit that can be worn as pyjamas at night and as working overalls during the day, and 'Call Donald/Mac Center,' a garment that could be worn both to work in a fast-food restaurant and in a call-centre. Three outfits commented upon gender and harassment. They included 'Mobbing Style' (an outfit with soft squishy toys to help de-stress), 'Bisex Tenderness' (a coat with fur trimmings that could be used as a moustache or long hair, depending on the gender demanded by the job), 'Pregnant Lady' (an abdominal binder to hide pregnancies) and 'Mouse Traps' (a skirt covered in mouse traps to deter common forms of sexual assault). The final outfit was a 'Bridal Gown,' a comment on the impossibility for migrant women to become Italian citizens and be allowed to work in Italy unless they married an Italian man.[6]

Fabulation: making an alternate history

Serpica Naro, as an activist intervention, fashion event, communicative action, and the creation of material and digital artefacts, worked from within the dynamics of Milan Fashion Week, borrowed its language, and followed its

5   Yomango, '¿Qué Fue de Yomango?,' Yomango, 2011. Available at http://yomango.info/2011/07/¿que-fue-de-yomango/ (accessed 4 January 2020).
6   Serpica Naro, 'Serpica Naro, Il Media Sociale'; Silvia Gherardi and Annalisa Murgia, 'Staging Precariousness: The Serpica Naro Catwalk during the Milan Fashion Week', *Culture and Organization* 21, no. 2 (2015): 174–96. Available at https://www.tandfonline.com/doi/abs/10.1080/14759551.2013.837051 (accessed 4 January 2020); Ilaria Vanni, '"Why Save the World When You Can Design It?" Precarity and Fashion in Milan', *Fashion Theory* 20, no. 4 (2016): 441–60. Available at https://doi.org/10.1080/1362704X.2015.1088738 (accessed 4 January 2020).

temporality. At the same time, Serpica Naro also critiqued the system underlying Fashion Week, and offered a different model 'to create alternative constellations of people and artefacts and rearrange channels between them.'[7] While the inventions and actions described above tackled the political issue of precarity in the fashion and creative industries, they also dealt with the practicalities of material and immaterial aspects of fashion events. To analyze this political and material entanglement, it is useful to outline some elements of design scholar Guy Julier's work on design activism.

Julier discusses themes that connect design culture and design activism. These themes include intensification, intended as density of designerly intervention, and temporality, understood as the way in which speed, slowness, or even open-endedness may be dealt with.[8] Julier argues that the tactic of intensification is used in design culture to mobilize affects, engage bodily dispositions and emotions, and in the process engender and exploit enthusiasm for its own end.[9] As an example, Fashion Week is conceived as a complete designerly experience. In design activism, intensification produces new forms of cognition, in Serpica Naro's case, for instance, the understanding of the precarious conditions of work in the fashion system. Design activism also brings to the world new practices, like the collective and collaborative processes enacted by Serpica Naro. Finally, it generates new political subjectivities.[10]

Serpica Naro used the tactic of intensification by appropriating elements of the prank and the hoax in the tradition of cultural activism and guerrilla communication. However, the fabrication of artefacts required to enter Fashion Week, as well as the media campaign, designs, and show, meant producing objects that in addition to mobilizing the politics of precarity through communication practices also proposed materially different ways of making fashion. The organization of a network of workers and activists along the entire supply chain of Fashion Week created a distinct set of practices that confronted existing working and creative conditions and galvanized a wealth of knowledge and skills traditionally elided in narratives of fashion weeks.

[7] Guy Julier, 'Introduction: Material Preference and Design Activism', *Design and Culture* 5, no. 2 (2013): 145. 145–50. Available at https://doi.org/10.2752/175470813X13638640370652 (accessed 4 January 2020).

[8] Guy Julier, 'From Design Culture to Design Activism', *Design and Culture* 5, no. 2 (1 July, 2013): 227, 215–36. Available at https://www.tandfonline.com/doi/abs/10.2752/175470813X13638640370814 (accessed 4 January 2020).

[9] Julier, 'From Design Culture', 229.

[10] Ibid.

In this regard, the intervention of Serpica Naro at Milan Fashion Week 2005 is a fashion fabulation. Although fabulation as a critical concept to narrate counter-histories has an established tradition in cultural, literary and feminist studies and in philosophy, here I lean on Daniela Rosner's definition of fabulation in relation to design.[11] Rosner proposes critical fabulations as a mode of storytelling that blends the real and the plausible and engages with how designed objects enter and operate in the world. To do this, she challenges the dominant understanding of design methods and reworks them in a feminist paradigm offering an alternate genealogy of critical design and technoscience studies that 'open up different understandings of the past that reconfigure the present, creating new opportunities for a just future.'[12] Critical fabulations, therefore, work across multiple temporalities to 'make way to live differently in the present.'[13] In this sense, they also offer a key to understand how an intervention such as the one described above can be read as a way to make an alternate history of Milan Fashion Week. Rosner introduces four orienting tactics to imagine 'times and places where what is yet to come might still be otherwise.' The four tools to generate critical fabulations and alternate versions of a given setting are: alliances, which are composite of relations greater than the sum of its parts; interferences, understood as disruptions of equalising narratives that reveal uneven conditions in a design setting; recuperations, or recovery of narratives forgotten or omitted; and extensions, defined as the creation of new circulation of content through translations in different forms and media.[14]

More specifically, alliances are collaborative relations that create contaminations and opportunities among multiple and heterogeneous people.[15] In the case of Serpica Naro, these collaborations had their roots in existing relations, but also brought about new ones arising from the present need to imagine in detail an alternate development to Fashion Week. Serpica Naro's intervention, for instance, both mobilized, and was the result of, the collaborations of precarious workers in industries along the whole fashion supply chain, from fashion design and clothing production to modelling, to graphic design, to

---

[11]   Daniela K. Rosner, *Critical Fabulations. Reworking the Methods and Margins of Design* (Cambridge, MA: MIT Press, 2018).
[12]   Rosner, *Critical Fabulations,* 25.
[13]   Ibid.
[14]   Rosner, *Critical Fabulations,* 81–83.
[15]   Rosner, *Critical Fabulations,* 83–87.

logistics, and media. As Alice Mattoni writes, Serpica Naro's intervention in Fashion Week was planned as a media event, and its realization relied on the grasp of the fashion system and its timing, but also on the knowledge of the news-making practices and news cycles of mainstream media organizations.[16]

Drawing on the heterogeneous knowledge of both fashion and media systems, Serpica Naro disturbed the prevailing narrative of coolness, creativity and glamour of Fashion Week. For this reason, Serpica Naro can be considered an interference that first took apart and then recoded the prevailing representation of Fashion Week. In this process, it exposed the event's inner workings and inherent power structures, but it also demonstrated that fashion events 'might still be otherwise.'[17]

As a recuperation, defined as a technique to 'revive stories enmeshed within a current design setting but suppressed by prevailing design narratives,' Serpica Naro recognized and made visible precarious workers' histories omitted in the glamorous hype of Fashion Week. It is important to stress that the importance of Serpica Naro in the Italian fashion landscape exceeds the value of the hoax reported in the media and described above. Serpica Naro, with the detournement of Fashion Week, aimed at bringing attention to the central role of precarious work in the fashion industry. It also clearly demonstrated the creative and productive power of precarious workers' networks.

One of the ways in which the temporality of Serpica Naro's intervention was tweaked was through the creation of extensions, or transitions of the initial idea into multiple and still-evolving practices. Julier suggests that in design culture objects are not singular and completed, but instead they evolve from sketches to prototypes, to products, and then are upgraded, repackaged and repositioned.[18] Soon after the interference in Fashion Week the open-endedness described by Julier and the ability to think and make alternatives was captured in the theory and practice of the 'metabrand,' or liberated trademark. Liberating the trademark overturned the perception and representation of designers as individual creative forces behind a brand. Instead, it emphasized how Serpica Naro was the outcome of a collective social process, based on the sharing of knowledge, experience and skills. The collective voice of Serpica Naro explains how:

---

[16] Alice Mattoni, *Media Practices and Protest Politics. How Precarious Workers Mobilise* (Farnham, Surrey: Ashgate Publishing Company, 2012).

[17] Rosner, *Critical Fabulations*, 81, 90–92.

[18] Julier, 'From Design Culture', 230.

After the show, many people approached us to know where to buy Serpica Naro's clothes. Clearly, it was part of a fascination with the glamour of the operation that led to the creation of the designer, but also a desire to evade serial fashion and the anxiety of being universally branded, and a desire to reclaim a cleaner and more ethical personal style without necessarily being wrapped up in solidarity hessian bags. People were looking for a place where they could find clothes free from exploitation produced by small artisanal firms not enmeshed in the fashion industry. A place where free and non-profit exchanges of clothing and ideas could be promoted and encouraged.[19]

The liberated trademark was regularly licensed, drawing inspiration from hacker culture, free software, open source and existing Creative Commons licenses. Unlike other forms of creative outputs such as software, music, writing or images, Serpica Naro's creators had to develop a license that would work not only with ideas, code, and reproducible creative output, but also with the material making of items that could be reproduced and serialized freely.[20] With a few restrictions this new, liberated, trademark can be used by anyone who recognizes the value and imaginary produced by Serpica Naro, under a Creative Common Share Alike license.

To sum up, Serpica Naro produced an opportunity to envision and fabricate an alternate history to the Italian fashion system. Since 2005 Serpica Naro has become a site of social, creative and political experimentation, a laboratory that remixes theory with practices, functions as public pedagogy organising workshops, classes, and events to share knowledge, skills, and empower others.[21]

Conclusion

Serpica Naro reclaimed the creative, cultural and social capital of precarious workers to imagine and generate an alternate history. This alternate history exposed how precarity is central to the way the Italian fashion system operates. Serpica Naro drew upon the knowledge and skills of workers along the whole fashion supply chain, from drivers, event organisers, make-up artists, models,

[19] Serpica Naro, 'Serpica Naro, Il Media Sociale'.
[20] Serpica Naro, 'Il Metabrand', Serpica Naro, 30 July 2012. Available at https://www.serpicanaro.com/metabrand-license (accessed 4 January 2020).
[21] Serpica Naro, 'La Licenza', *Serpica Naro*, 6 January 2013. Available at https://www.serpicanaro.com/la-licenza-del-marchio (accessed 4 January 2020).

media workers, to designers and so on to produce an entirely plausible, if unheard of, designer. By doing so, it revealed two facets of Fashion Week, and of the fashion industry at large. First, that events like Fashion Week depend on the exploitation of the wealth of knowledge, networks and skills of precarious workers. Second, that fashion events are about the production of imaginary and aspirational lifestyles, more than about the manufacturing of fashion items. The organization and aims of the hoax were explained in an interview with a fictitious journalist of the fictitious website www.settimanadellamoda.it, another fake created as part of Serpica Naro's mediascape:

> The operation was articulated in several levels of action, which involved different groups of people: the creation of the digital persona and her release in the media, the production of the fashion show, the engagement with people involved in autonomous experiments in fashion production, the logistic management of the space and the necessary paperwork, the relationship with workers in the fashion circuits ... After we revealed Serpica Naro as a fictitious designer all these levels became visible, and more significantly it became evident that to be accepted to be part of the Fashion Week's official calendar was not the main aim of the intervention. Rather the most important things were the establishment of relationships between precarious workers in the creative industries and precarious workers and their own creativity, and the values that were shared within the framework of the contestation.[22]

Serpica Naro, as the quotation above explains, was primarily a means to connect and empower precarious workers in the creative industries. As a hoax, it also deconstructed Fashion Week and made visible how the event is produced, highlighting how fashion events are about the production of social imagination. This insight was made possible by the activists' self-reflexive practice on the dynamics of Fashion Week and its repercussions on the cultural, social and work organization in Milan.[23] In this sense Serpica Naro can be considered a fashion

[22] Chainworkers, 'Yvonne Brenta Intervista Serpica Naro', Reader – uno schema per leggere quello che si è scritto, 2005. Available at https://web.archive.org/web/20180612154056/http://www.precaria. org/wp-content/plugins/downloads-manager/upload/chainworkers_reader.pdf (accessed 4 January 2020).
[23] Chainworkers Crew, 'Chainworkers Reader. Uno Schema per Leggere Quello Che Si è Scritto', Precaria.org, 2006. Available at https://web.archive.org/web/20180612154056/http://www.precaria. org/wp-content/plugins/downloads-manager/upload/chainworkers_reader.pdf (accessed 4 January 2020).

fabulation, an example of prefigurative politics and of the imagination of fashion practices to come that might still be otherwise.

Ilaria Vanni, University of Technology Sydney

Queer Time

Emma Katherine Atwood

Emma Katherine Atwood, 'Fashionably Late: Queer Temporality and the Restoration Fop', *Comparative Drama* 47, no. 1 (2013): 85–87.

Writers on 'women's time' such as Julia Kristeva and Ilya Parkins have used the concept to critique the normativity of male-dominated clock time. Yet the only example of 'men's time' included so far in this anthology – though not foregrounded as such – is the dandy, who appears in the section on 'industrial time' as a challenge to nineteenth-century ideals of productive time, because of the extremes to which he went to perfect his daily appearance before his late-morning sortie.

Atwood looks at one of his antecedents, the fop of the English Restoration (the period from 1660 to the early 1700s) and his 'fashionable lateness'. She argues that this was 'an aggressive performance of nonchalance' which challenged the social conventions of the day, and thus proposed other possibilities for living. Lateness is seen here as an act of social imagination. The fop's refusal of clock time, long before it was identified by E.P. Thompson as an industrial construct, constituted 'important cultural work', in Atwood's words, that highlighted the normativity of clock (or straight) time. Queer theorists like Lee Edelman have shown the link between linear time and heteronormativity, as opposed to queer time, which critiques it. Queer time undermines the distinction between women's time and men's time, in favour of a more fluid model of both time and gender.

Rather than queering gender, the fop actually queers time. In this way, fops need not be gendered by definition, nor do they have to be men. As Judith Halberstam (a.k.a. Jack Halberstam) suggests in a rubric for theorizing queer time: 'much of the contemporary theory seeking to disconnect queerness from an essential definition of homosexuality has focused upon queer space and queer sexual practices, but such theories depend, implicitly, upon a rarely articulated notion of queer time.'[1] She continues to separate queer time from sexual identity: 'By articulating and elaborating a concept of queer time, I suggest new ways of understanding the nonnormative behaviors that have clear but not essential relations to gay and lesbian subjects.'[2]

These 'clear but not essential' connections provide an opportunity for the Restoration and early eighteenth-century fop to move beyond readings that depend on gender without discrediting these approaches. If the fop's queerness is located in his or her engagement with time, then the fop can speak to important cultural issues beyond gender alone, including but not limited to a variety of temporally dictated constructs such as social participation, evolving economic systems, family obligations, and the interplay between work and leisure.

By saying that the Restoration fop queers time, and not gender, I mean to define the fop in a new way, distinct from definitions that champion his gender play, his flamboyance, his ego, his Frenchification, or his role as a comic figure.[3] I argue instead that the Restoration fop can be more comprehensively defined by his queer engagement with time, and specifically what I call his fashionable lateness. Although the phrase 'fashionably late' became popular to the point of cliché in the nineteenth century, I find it useful in the way it playfully merges fashionability and temporality, thus mirroring the behavior of the fop. As I define it, to be fashionably late is to arrive notably after an agreed upon time, but to do so with such éclat that the social faux pas is forgiven, even celebrated. Fashionable lateness is a habitual mode of social entrance. By arriving late, the fop purchases social exception, excusing the tardy individual from obligations to which his prompt acquaintances are held. The Restoration fop's fashionable lateness is an aggressive performance of nonchalance that allows an individual to manipulate the very social contracts otherwise central to Restoration and early eighteenth-century culture. In theory, queer time always communes with alternative social behavior and contracts. Elizabeth Freeman asserts that 'queer temporalities,

---

[1] Judith Halberstam, '"What's That Smell?": Queer Temporalities and Subcultural Lives', *The Scholar and Feminist Online* 2 (2003): n.p. Available at http://sfonline.barnard.edu/ps/printjha.htm (accessed 5 January 2020).

[2] Judith Halberstam, *In a Queer Time and Place: Transgender Bodies, Subcultural Lives* (New York: New York University Press, 2005), 6.

[3] For a reading of the fop as a critique of manners, see Andrew P. Williams, *The Restoration Fop: Gender Boundaries and Comic Characterization in Later Seventeenth Century Drama* (Lewiston, NY: Edwin Mellen Press, 1995), 2.

visible of interruption ... are points of resistance to this temporal order that, in turn, propose other possibilities for living in relation to indeterminately past, present, and future others.'[4] The fop's habitually late arrival is just this sort of interruption; his performance on the popular professional stage made 'resistance to this temporal order' accessible to the culture at large.

The Restoration fop's temporal disengagement is queer in the sense that it throws otherwise normative attitudes toward clock time, which regulates social interaction, into question. This queer temporality affects both the play the fop inhabits as well as Restoration and early eighteenth-century culture at large. Amy Witherbee, for example, has shown how 'Britain's eighteenth-century financial and political expansion was made possible only by the introduction of a new articulation of what time was and what it could do.'[5] These changes are especially obvious in literary representations. As Stuart Sherman argues, 'during the Restoration and after, the temporality of Tick, Tick, Tick recognizably presides over remarkable developments in both chronometry and narrative ... [thus] textual practices developed along parallel lines.'[6] Intersections between technology, temporality, culture, and literature make Restoration drama – drama being at heart a temporal art – an especially rich object of study. In her theory of queer time, Valerie Rohy suggests that queer time and its opposite 'straight time' are conceptually at odds with one another, aligning 'straight time' with 'clock time'. She states, 'The 'obviousness' of straight time masks its contingency: every child knows that the clock runs steadily in one direction. In literature, however, the artificial temporality of narrative form alerts us to the fictional dimension of chronology as such: after all, time is a trope and anachronism a figure.'[7] The fact that the Restoration fop is a dramatic and thus fictional trope, then, makes his queering of time especially salient. The fop's socially subversive queer time performs important cultural work in that he 'alerts us to the fictional dimension of chronology' and asks his audience self-consciously to reconsider the 'obviousness' of clock, or 'straight', time.

[4]   Elizabeth Freeman, *Time Binds: Queer Temporalities, Queer Histories* (Durham, NC: Duke University Press, 2010), xxii.
[5]   Amy Witherbee, 'New Conceptions of Time and the Making of a Political-Economic Public in Eighteenth-Century Britain' (PhD diss., Boston College, 2009) (ProQuest/UMI Publication no. 3349581): 2.
[6]   Stuart Sherman, *Telling Time: Clocks, Diaries, and English Diurnal Form, 1660–1785* (Chicago: University of Chicago Press, 1997), 8.
[7]   Valerie Rohy, *Anachronism and Its Others: Sexuality, Race, Temporality* (Albany: State University of New York Press), 2009.

Miss Havisham

Charles Dickens

Charles Dickens, *Great Expectations* [1861]
(London: Chapman and Hall, 1867), 31–33.

This is the moment in Charles Dickens's novel Great Expectations *when the reader first encounters Miss Havisham, an old lady who as a girl was jilted on her wedding day. Ever since, she has worn the wedding dress and one shoe that she had on at the very moment she heard the news. At that moment, she stopped the clocks and preserved the room exactly as it was at the moment of her heartbreak. In this description, Dickens shows her many years later, in the now decayed wedding dress and silk stockings, wearing the single shoe. The unworn shoe remains on her dressing table.*

As Emma Katherine Atwood writes in the preceding excerpt, the artificial temporality of narrative form alerts us to the fact that chronology has a fictional dimension. This passage from Dickens reveals the flip side of uchronia, dyschronia, which has affinities with dystopia. And just as there are dystopian fictions, so too are there dyschronic ones, like this image of Miss Havisham surrounded by the decayed traces of her tragic past.

In an arm-chair, with an elbow resting on the table and her head leaning on that hand, sat the strangest lady I have ever seen, or shall ever see.

She was dressed in rich materials – satins, and lace, and silks – all of white. Her shoes were white. And she had a long white veil dependent from her hair, and she had bridal flowers in her hair, but her hair was white. Some bright jewels sparkled on her neck and on her hands, and some other jewels lay sparkling on the table. Dresses, less splendid than the dress she wore, and half-packed trunks, were scattered about. She had not quite finished dressing, for she had but one shoe on – the other was on the table near her hand – her veil was but half arranged, her watch and chain were not put on, and some lace for her bosom lay with those trinkets, and with her handkerchief, and gloves, and some flowers, and a prayer-book, all confusedly heaped about the looking-glass.

It was not in the first few moments that I saw all these things, though I saw more of them in the first moments than might be supposed. But, I saw that everything within my view which ought to be white, had been white long ago, and had lost its lustre, and was faded and yellow. I saw that the bride within the bridal dress had withered like the dress, and like the flowers, and had no brightness left but the brightness of her sunken eyes. I saw that the dress had been put upon the rounded figure of a young woman, and that the figure upon which it now hung loose, had shrunk to skin and bone. . . .

It was then I began to understand that everything in the room had stopped, like the watch and the clock, a long time ago. I noticed that Miss Havisham put down the jewel exactly on the spot from which she had taken it up. As Estella dealt the cards, I glanced at the dressing-table again, and saw that the shoe upon it, once white, now yellow, had never been worn. I glanced down at the foot from which the shoe was absent, and saw that the silk stocking on it, once white, now yellow, had been trodden ragged. Without this arrest of everything, this standing still of all the pale decayed objects, not even the withered bridal dress on the collapsed form could have looked so like grave-clothes, or the long veil so like a shroud.

So she sat, corpse-like, as we played at cards; the frillings and trimmings on her bridal dress, looking like earthy paper. I knew nothing then, of the discoveries that are occasionally made of bodies buried in ancient times, which fall to powder in the moment of being distinctly seen; but, I have often thought since, that she must have looked as if the admission of the natural light of day would have struck her to dust.

The Simultaneous Dress

Paola Colaiacomo

Paola Colaiacomo, *Natasha's Dress: Language of Literature, Language of Fashion* (Oxford and Bern: Peter Lang, 2018), 262–64.

By contrast to Dickens's darkly dyschronic literary portrait of Miss Havisham, Paola Colaiacomo paints a uchronic word-picture in her critical text that encapsulates the future as a hypothetical and imagined time. She juxtaposes Virginia Woolf's novel Orlando *(1928) with the artist Sonia Delaunay's* Simultaneous Dress *(1913), navigating the complex temporalities of both. In* Orlando, *which ranges from the Elizabethan age to the twentieth century, Woolf merged gender, identity and time in revolutionary ways. In Colaiacomo's words, 'Orlando was simultaneously wearing her new female body and a dress.' In* The Simultaneous Dress, *Delaunay opened the idea of the 'now' (perhaps akin to Benjamin's now-time) to the possibility of multiple time through the idea of simultaneity.*

Quoting Virginia Woolf, Colaiacomo argues that Elizabethan dramatists seemed able 'to move their limbs more freely'. Taking the idea forward into the twentieth century, she conjoins this mental fluidity from the first Elizabethan age with the New Woman's physicality in the 1920s. Colaiacomo thus makes a tiger's leap forwards (as opposed to Benjamin's backwards leap) to open up the modernist subject's possibilities of 'a life and a lover' – and, of course, the promise of a dress, one day in the future.

There is no reflexive interval between body and dress for Orlando, in the sense that she is simultaneous with her dress. For Sonia Delaunay, in 1913, the experimentation with the simultaneous dress had been the highest point of a series of pictorial studies on the simultaneity of perceptions. By presenting herself at the famous Bal Bullier wearing the dress she had created, the naturalized French artist, born in Ukraine, had meant to reconceptualize her own body as the most proper location for the artwork she herself had produced. 'We might then term the *robe simultanée* a "biograph" in the sense that it is a writing (*graphé*) of oneself as a subject, as the producer of reality through embodied phenomenal experience (*bios*).'[1] Thus, the dress's simultaneity was literally autobiographical. By wearing it, the subject wrote itself on itself. And as it wrote – and not narrated – itself, the subject could not but be simultaneous with its own experiences. Vreeland's words on Delaunay's work could just as easily apply to Orlando's thoughts while sailing back to England:

> collage, the quintessentially modern visual language, was the soul of Sonia's work. Her favorite word, *simultanée*, could mean seeing several things at once or seeing several aspects in one thing. [...] the clarity and power of the hues still reverberate in fashion and style to this day.[2]

The famous *robe simultanée* was both a collage of different pieces of fabric and a collage of thoughts. That is why Blaise Cendrars entitled the poem inspired by the vision of Sonia in that dress, '*Sur La Robe Elle a un Corps*' (1913), 'On her

---

[1]   Man Ray, *The Age of Light; in Photographs by Man Ray: IOS Works 1920–34* (New York: Dover Publications, 1979), n.p.

[2]   Diana Vreeland, 'Foreword' to *Sonia Delaunay: Art into Fashion* (New York: George Brazilier, 1986), 9.

dress she has a body', and not the other way round – which might seem more rational – because that dress was flesh and writing together – a work of self-knowledge always in progress.

Orlando was simultaneously wearing her new female body and a dress on *The Enamoured Lady*. Like the model running towards the photographer, that kicking at her skirts liberated a sexual energy of a new type. Of the Elizabethan age, when she had first seen the light three and a half centuries earlier, Orlando still preserved – as the most cherished of her legacies – an 'undissociated sensibility' – that is to say, a sensibility which had taken shape this side of that 'dissociation' of which Virginia had first heard from her friend Tom – the poet T. S. Eliot – who had used that expression in 1921, in his essay on 'The Metaphysical Poets'. 'Dissociation' meant that, by the second half of the seventeenth century, thought went one way and feeling another. A thought was no longer an experience: instead of 'constantly amalgamating disparate experience', poets 'reflected'. They thought and felt by fits. This she had read in Tom's essay. With Orlando, though, things were to be different: with her, a thought – as well as a gesture, a kick – was to be a feeling – an autobiographical experience, in the profoundest sense. 'Elizabethan dramatists,' Woolf had written just before putting pen to paper and creating *Orlando*, 'seem to have an attitude toward life, a position which allows them to move their limbs freely.'[3] As an Elizabethan, Orlando had to move her limbs freely. Like her future contemporary of the 1920s, when she had just discarded the narrow skirts obliging her – like all fashionable women of that time – to hobble along, taking small mincing steps, what Orlando longs for – two centuries ahead of fashion's schedule – is a Vionnet dress. She longs for what a Vionnet dress could do for a woman like her: life, and a lover.

> By discarding the corset and quite literally stripping away the superfluities of fashion and contemporary notions of respectability, Vionnet became part of the revolution in fashion, evoking a new form of femininity that spoke of freedom, independence and experimentation.[4]

But for this dress, she will have to wait.

---

[3] Virginia Woolf, 'The Narrow Bridge of Art', *The Collected Essays of Virginia Woolf*, vol. II, ed. Leonard Woolf (London: Chatto & Windus, 1966–69), 220.

[4] Rebecca Arnold, 'Vionnet & Classicism'. In Judith Clark (ed.), *Vionnet: 15 Dresses from the Collection of Martin Kamer* (London: Judith Clark Costume Gallery, 2001), 3–8.

Figure 5 Flaming Clothes. Controlled test on a mannequin of flammable clothing from *Picture Post*, 31 January 1953. Photo by John Chillingworth/Picture Post/Hulton Archive/Getty Images.

Bibliography

Advertising Standards Authority. 'Final Adjudication'. *Advertising Standards Authority Archives*, no. A09-113306/RM. 12 May 2010.

Agamben, Giorgio. 'What is the Contemporary?'. In *What is an Apparatus? and Other Essays*, translated by David Kishik, and Stefan Pedatella, 39–54. Stanford: Stanford University Press, 2009.

Amed, Imran. 'Q&A: A Conversation with Susie from Style Bubble'. *The Business of Fashion*, 12 November, 2007. Available at https://www.businessoffashion.com/articles/fashion-tech/qa-a-conversation-with-susie-from-style-bubble (accessed 12 September 2011).

Amed, Imran. 'Q&A: Dolly Jones, Editor-in-Chief of Vogue.co.uk'. *The Business of Fashion*, 5 June, 2008. Available at https://www.businessoffashion.com/articles/fashion-tech/qa-dolly-jones-editor-in-chief-of-voguecouk (accessed 2 September 2012).

Amed, Imran, and Kate Abnett. 'Burberry Aligns Runway and Retail Calendar in Game-Changing Shift'. *The Business of Fashion*, 5 February, 2016. Available at https://www.businessoffashion.com/articles/news-analysis/burberry-aligns-runway-and-retail-calendar-in-game-changing-shift (accessed 21 June 2018).

Appadurai, Arjun. *Modernity at Large: Cultural Dimensions of Globalization*. 1996. Minneapolis: University of Minnesota Press, 2003.

Apter, Emily. '"Women's Time" in Theory'. *differences* 21, no. 1 (2010): 1–18.

Arnold, Rebecca. 'Vionnet & Classicism'. In *Vionnet: 15 Dresses from the Collection of Martin Kamer*, edited by Judith Clark, 3–8. London: Judith Clark Costume Gallery, 2001.

Ash, Juliet, and Elizabeth Wilson, eds. *Chic Thrills*. London: Pandora, 1992.

Aspers, Patrick, and Frédéric Godart. 'Sociology of Fashion: Order and Change'. *Annual Review of Sociology*, 39 (July 2013): 171–92.

Atwood, Emma Katherine. 'Fashionably Late: Queer Temporality and the Restoration Fop'. *Comparative Drama* 47, no. 1 (Spring 2013): 85–111.

Baines, Barbara Burman. *Fashion Revivals from the Elizabethan Age to the Present Day*. London: B.T. Batsford, 1981.

Barbey d'Aurevilly, Jules. *Du dandysme et de G. Brummell*. 2nd ed. Paris: Poulet-Malassis, 1861.

Barker, Jessica. 'Considering Snapchat Filters as Digital Adornment'. *Fashion Studies Journal*, July, 2017. Available at http://www.fashionstudiesjournal.org/notes/2017/7/2/considering-snapchat-filters-as-digital-adornment (accessed 27 November 2019).

Barnard, Malcolm. *Fashion Theory: An Introduction*. London and New York: Routledge, 2014.

Barnes, Liz, and Gaynor Lea-Greenwood. 'Fast Fashioning the Supply Chain: Shaping the Research Agenda'. *Journal of Fashion Marketing and Management* 10, no. 3 (2006): 259–71.

Barthes, Roland. *The Fashion System*. 1967. Translated by Matthew Ward, and Richard Howard. London: Jonathan Cape, 1985.

Bataille, Georges. *Inner Experience*. Translated by Stuart Kendall. Albany, NY: State University of New York, 2014.

Baudelaire, Charles. 'The Painter of Modern Life'. In *The Painter of Modern Life and Other Essays*. Translated by Jonathan Mayne. London: Phaidon, 1965.

Baudrillard, Jean. *For a Critique of the Political Economy of the Sign*. Translated by Charles Levin. St. Louis, MO: Telos Press, 1981.

Baudrillard, Jean. *Seduction*. Translated by Brian Singer. New York: St. Martin's Press, 1990.

Baudrillard, Jean. *Symbolic Exchange and Death*. Translated by Iain Hamilton Grant. Thousand Oaks, CA: Sage Publications, 1993.

Bauman, Zygmunt. 'Perpetuum Mobile'. *Critical Studies in Fashion and Beauty* 1, no. 1 (2010): 55–63.

Bauman, Zygmunt. *Legislators and Interpreters: On Modernity, Post-Modernity, Intellectuals*. Ithaca, NY: Cornell University Press, 1987.

Benjamin, Andrew. *Style and Time: Essays on the Politics of Appearance*. Evanston, IL: Northeastern University Press, 2006.

Benjamin, Walter. 'Some Motifs in Baudelaire'. In *Charles Baudelaire: A Lyric Poet in the Era of High Capitalism*. 107–54. London: Verso, 1983.

Benjamin, Walter. 'Theses on the Philosophy of History'. In *Illuminations: Essays and Reflections*. Translated by Harry Zohn, edited and introduction by Hannah Arendt, preface Leon Weiseltier, 253–64. New York: Schocken Books, 1969.

Benjamin, Walter. *The Arcades Project*. Translated by Howard Eiland and Kevin McLaughlin. Cambridge, MA and London: The Belknap Press of Harvard University Press, 1999.

Bergé, Pierre. 'Pierre Bergé on Luxury, Morocco and Hedi Slimane', interview by Elizabeth Paton. *New York Times*, 28 October 2015.

Bhabha, Homi K. *The Location of Culture*. London and New York: Routledge, 1994.

Blaszczyk, Regina Lee, ed. *Producing Fashion: Commerce, Culture, and Consumers*. Philadelphia: University of Pennsylvania Press, 2008.

Blau, Herbert. *Nothing in Itself: Complexions of Fashion*. Bloomington: Indiana University Press, 1999.

Borrelli, Laird. *Net Mode: Web Fashion Now*. London: Thames and Hudson, 2002.

Brand, Jan, and José Teunissen, eds. *Fashion and Imagination: About Clothes and Art*. Arnhem: ArtEZ Press, 2009.

Braund, Susanna Morton, and Paula James. 'Quasi Homo: Distortion and Contortion in Seneca's Apocolocyntosis'. *Arethusa* 31, no. 3 (1998): 285–311.

Breward, Christopher. *The Culture of Fashion: A New History of Fashionable Dress*. Manchester and New York: Manchester University Press, 1995.

Breward, Christopher. *The Hidden Consumer: Masculinities, Fashion, and City Life, 1860–1914*. Manchester: Manchester University Press, 1999.

British Library, Add. MSS 37926, fol. 38.

Bruns, Axel. *Gatewatching*. New York: Peter Lang, 2005.

Burke, Peter, ed. *New Perspectives on Historical Writing*. University Park: The Pennsylvania State University Press, 2001.

Bye, Elizabeth. *Fashion Design*. Oxford and New York: Berg, 2010.

Cabinet des modes, 1ᵉʳ Cahier, 15 November, 1785.

Cabinet des modes, 30 September, 1788.

Calefato, Patrizia. *The Clothed Body*. Oxford and New York: Berg, 2004.

Calefato, Patrizia. *Gli intramontabili. Mode, persone, oggetti che restano*. Rome: Meltemi, 2009.

Campbell, Timothy. *Historical Style: Fashion and the New Mode of History, 1740–1830*. Philadelphia: University of Pennsylvania Press, 2016.

Chainworkers. 'Yvonne Brenta intervista Serpica Naro. Reader – uno schema per leggere quello che si è scritto'. *Precaria.org*, 2005. Available at http://www.precaria.org/ wp-content/plugins/downloads-manager/upload/chainworkers_reader.pdf. (accessed 4 January 2020).

Chainworkers Crew. 'Chainworkers Reader. Uno schema per leggere quello che si è scritto'. *Precaria.org*, 2006. Available at http://www.precaria.org/wp-content/plugins/ downloads-manager/upload/chainworkers_reader.pdf. (accessed 4 January 2020).

Chiarelli, Caterina, ed. *Per il sole e contro il sole: Thayaht & Ram. La tuta / Modelli per tessuti*. Livorno: Sillabe, 2003.

Chrisman-Campbell, Kimberly. *Fashion Victims: Dress at the Court of Louis XVI and Marie-Antoinette*. New Haven and London: Yale University Press, 2015.

Chuter, A. J. *Introduction to Clothing Production Management*. Oxford: Blackwell Science, 1988.

Clark, Hazel. 'Slow + Fashion – an Oxymoron – or a Promise for the Future ...?'. *Fashion Theory. The Journal of Dress, Body & Culture* 12, no. 4 (2008): 427–46.

Clark, Judith. 'The Judith Clark Costume Gallery'. Lecture, London College of Fashion, London, 2002.

Clark, Judith. *Spectres: When Fashion Turns Back*. London: Victoria & Albert Museum, 2004.

Clayton, Kevin. 'Time Folded and Crumpled: Time, History, Self-Organization and the Methodology of Michel Serres'. In *Time and History in Deleuze and Serres*, edited by Bernd Herzogenrath, 31–50. New York and London: Continuum, 2012.

Colaiacomo, Paola. *Natasha's Dress: Language of Literature, Language of Fashion*. Oxford and Bern: Peter Lang, 2018.

Colaiacomo, Paola, and Vittoria Caterina Caratozzolo. *Cartamodello: antologia di scrittori e scritture sulla moda*. Rome: Sossella, 2000.

Cooklin, Gerry. *Introduction to Clothing Manufacturing*. Oxford: Blackwell Science, 1991.

Couchot, Edmond. 'Temps de l'histoire et temps uchronique. Penser autrement la mémoire et l'oubli'. *Hybrid*, no. 1 (2014). Available at http://www.hybrid.univ-paris8.fr/lodel/index.php?id=179&lang=en (accessed 6 October 2018).

Craik, Jennifer. *The Face of Fashion: Cultural Studies in Fashion*. London and New York: Routledge, 1993.

Crary, Jonathan. *24/7: Late Capitalism and the Ends of Sleep*. London and New York: Verso, 2013.

Cronberg, Anja Aronowsky. 'Editor's Letter'. *Vestoj. The Journal of Sartorial Matters*, no. 5 On Slowness (Autumn 2014): 9–12. Available at http://vestoj.com/issues/issue-five-on-slowness/ (accessed 24 June 2018).

Cvoro, Uros. 'Dialectical Image Today'. *Continuum: Journal of Media & Cultural Studies* 22, no. 1 (2008): 89–98.

Deeny, Godfrey. 'Fast Forward to Slow Fashion'. *Financial Times*, 2 February, 2007: 7.

Deleuze, Gilles. *The Fold, Leibniz and the Baroque*. Translated by Tom Conley. London: Athlone Press, 1993.

Deleuze, Gilles, and Félix Guattari. *A Thousand Plateaus: Capitalism and Schizophrenia*. 1980. Translated by Brian Massumi. London: Athlone Press, 1987.

Delpierre, Madeleine. *Dress in France in the Eighteenth Century*. Translated by Caroline Beamish. New Haven and London: Yale University Press, 1997.

Derrida, Jacques. *Specters of Marx: The State of the Debt, the Work of Mourning, and the New International*. Translated by Peggy Kamuf. New York and London: Routledge, 1994.

Dery, Mark. 'Black to the Future'. In *Flame Wars: The Discourse of Cyberculture*, edited by Mark Dery, 179–222. London and Durham: Duke University Press, 1994.

Dickens, Charles. *Great Expectations*. 1861. London: Chapman and Hall, 1867.

Eco, Umberto. *The Book of Legendary Lands*. 2013. Translated by Alistair McEwen. London: MacLehose Press, 2013.

Edelman, Lee. *No Future: Queer Theory and the Death Drive*. Durham: Duke University Press, 2004.

Eismann, Sonja. 'Afrofuturism as a Strategy for Decolonising the Global Fashion Archive'. In *Fashion and Postcolonial Critique*, edited by Elke Gaugele and Monica Titton, 64–73. Berlin: Sternberg Press, 2019.

Elias, Norbert. *An Essay on Time*. 1984. Dublin: University College Dublin Press, 2007.

Ekardt, Philipp. *Benjamin on Fashion*. London and New York: Bloomsbury Academic, 2020.

Entwistle, Joanne. *The Fashioned Body: Fashion, Dress, and Modern Social Theory*. Cambridge: Policy Press, 2000.

Entwistle, Joanne. *The Aesthetic Economy of Fashion: Markets and Values in Clothing and Modeling*. Oxford and New York: Berg, 2009.

Eriksen, Thomas Hylland. *Tyranny of the Moment*. London: Pluto, 2001.

Esten, John, and Diana Vreeland. *Why Don't You . . . ? Audacious Advice for Fashionable Living: Diana Vreeland, "Bazaar" Years*. New York: Universe, 2001.

Evans, Caroline. 'The Golden Dustman: A Critical Evaluation of the Work of Martin Margiela and a Review of Martin Margiela Exhibition (9/4/1615)'. *Fashion Theory. The Journal of Dress, Body & Culture* 2, no. 1 (1998): 73–93.

Evans, Caroline. *Fashion at the Edge: Spectacle, Modernity and Deathliness*. New Haven and London: Yale University Press, 2003.

Evans, Caroline. *The Mechanical Smile: Modernism and the First Fashion Shows in France and America, 1900–1929*. New Haven and London: Yale University Press, 2013.

Evans, Caroline. 'Yesterday's Emblems and Tomorrow's Commodities: The Return of the Repressed in Fashion Imagery Today'. In *Fashion Cultures Revisited: Theories, Explorations and Analysis*, edited by Stella Bruzzi, and Pamela Church Gibson, 77–102. 2nd ed. London and New York: Routledge, 2013.

Evans, Caroline. 'Materiality, Memory and History: Adventures in the Archive'. In *Isabella Blow: Fashion Galore!*, edited by Alistair O'Neill, 137–41. Milan: Rizzoli, 2013.

Evans, Caroline and Alessandra Vaccari. *Il tempo della moda*. Milan and Udine: Mimesis, 2019.

Evans, Caroline and Alessandra Vaccari. 'Il tempo della moda. A Dialogue on Fashion and Time'. *ZoneModa Journal* 9, no. 2 (2019): 169–72.

Filippello, Roberto. 'Queer Asynchrony and the Fashion Imagination'. Seminar paper, Iuav University of Venice, Venice, 10 December, 2019.

Fisher, Mark. *Capitalist Realism: Is There No Alternative?* Winchester (UK): Zero Books, 2009.

Flaccavento, Angelo. 'Alessandro Michele: Quotations, the Past and Future of Fashion. Here's My Vision'. Translated by Antony Bowden. Online version of 'Sono spudorato'. *Vogue Italia*, no. 805 (September 2017): 191–94. Available at http://www.vogue.it/en/fashion/news/2017/09/01/alessandro-michele-quotations-past-future-fashion-interview-vogue-italia/ (accessed 3 January 2020).

Fletcher, Kate. 'Slow Fashion'. *The Ecologist* 37, no. 5 (June 2007), 61.

Fletcher, Kate. 'Slow Fashion: An Invitation for Systems Change'. *Fashion Practice* 2, no. 2 (2010): 259–65.

Fletcher, Kate, and Mathilda Tham. 'Clothing Rhythms'. In *Eternally Yours: Time in Design*, edited by Ed van Hinte, 254–74. Rotterdam: 010 Publishers, 2003.

Ford, Tom. 'Press Release autumn/winter 2016'. Available at https://www.tomford.com/TFBrand_AW16_Presentation_2.html?fdid=brand (accessed 27 June 2018).

Fortunati, Leopoldina, and Elda Danese. *Manuale di comunicazione, sociologia e cultura della moda*. Vol. III, *Made in Italy*. Rome: Meltemi, 2005.

Foster, Hal, ed. *The Anti-Aesthetic: Essays on Postmodern Culture*. Port Townsend (Washington): Bay Press, 1983.

Freeman, Elizabeth. *Time Binds: Queer Temporalities, Queer Histories*. Durham: Duke University Press, 2010.

Freeman, Elizabeth. 'Synchronic / Anachronic'. In *Time: A Vocabulary of the Present*, edited by Joel Burges and Amy J. Elias, 129–43. New York: New York University Press, 2016.

French, Greg. 'Foreword'. In *Otherworldly: Avant-garde Fashion and Style*, edited by Theo-Mass Lexileictous, Robert Klanten, and Sven Ehmann, 2–8. Berlin: Gestalten, 2016.

Frisa, Maria Luisa, and Stefano Tonchi. *Walter Albini and His Times: All Power to the Imagination*. Venice: Marsilio, 2010.

Frisa, Maria Luisa, Anna Mattirolo, and Stefano Tonchi, eds. *Bellissima: l'Italia dell'alta moda, 1945–1968*. Milan: Electa, 2014.

Frisa, Maria Luisa. *Le forme della moda. Cultura, industria, mercato: dal sarto al direttore creativo*. Bologna: Il Mulino, 2015.

Furbank, Philip Nicholas, and Alex M. Cain. *Mallarmé on Fashion: A Translation of the Fashion Magazine La Dernière Mode, with Commentary*. Oxford and New York: Berg, 2004.

Fury, Alexander. 'The Rhizomatic Style and Influence of Gucci'. *Another Magazine*, 3 March, 2016. Available at http://www.anothermag.com/fashion-beauty/8435/the-rhizomatic-style-and-influence-of-gucci (accessed 5 October 2018).

Gann, Jack. 'Stitching Pleats in Time: Multi-temporality in Alexander McQueen's "Savage Beauty" Exhibition'. *Leeds Centre for Victorian Studies*, 27 August, 2015. Available at http://www.leedstrinity.ac.uk/blogs/leeds-centre-for-victorian-studies/stitching-pleats-in-time-multi-temporality-in-alexander-mcqueens-savage-beauty-exhibition (accessed 27 November 2019).

Garfinkel, Harold. *Studies in Ethnomethodology*. Englewood Cliffs: Prentice-Hall, 1967.

Geoffroy-Château, Louis-Napoléon. *Napoléon et la conquête du monde, 1812–1832. Histoire de la monarchie universelle*. Paris: H.-L. Delloye, 1836. Reprint, *Napoléon apocryphe. Histoire de la conquête du monde et de la monarchie universelle, 1812–1832*. Paris: Paulin, 1841.

Gherardi, Silvia, and Annalisa Murgia. 'Staging Precariousness: The Serpica Naro Catwalk during the Milan Fashion Week'. *Culture and Organization* 21, no. 2 (2015): 174–96. Available at https://www.tandfonline.com/doi/abs/10.1080/14759551.2013.8 37051 (accessed 4 January 2020).

Gibson, Pamela Church. 'Redressing the Balance: Patriarchy, Postmodernism, and Feminism'. In *Fashion Cultures: Theories, Explorations, and Analysis*, edited by Pamela Church Gibson and Stella Bruzzi, 349–62. London: Routledge, 2001.

Goldoni, Carlo. *Mémoires pour servir à l'histoire de sa vie et à celle de son théâtre*. Geneva: Slatkine Reprints, 1968.

Granata, Francesca. 'The Bakhtinian Grotesque in Fashion at the Turn of the Twenty-First Century'. PhD diss., University of the Arts, London, 2010.

Granata, Francesca. 'Fitting Sources – Tailoring Methods: A Case Study of Martin Margiela and the Temporalities of Fashion'. In *Fashion Studies: Research Methods, Sites and Practices*, edited by Heike Jenss, 148–59. London and New York, Bloomsbury, 2016.

Granata, Francesca. *Experimental Fashion: Performance Art, Carnival and the Grotesque Body*. London and New York: I.B. Tauris, 2017.

Green, Nancy L. *Ready-to-Wear, Ready-to-Work: A Century of Industry and Immigrants in Paris and New York*. Durham and London: Duke University Press, 1997.

Grumbach, Didier. *History of International Fashion*. Translated by © Roli Books. Northampton, MA: Interlink Publishing Group, 2014.

Gumbrecht, Hans Ulrich. *In 1926: Living at the Edge of Time*, 233–40. Cambridge, MA and London: Harvard University Press, 1997.

Gunning, Tom, and Marketa Uhlirova, eds. *Wearing Time: Past, Present, Future, Dream*. London: Fashion in Film Festival Tenth Anniversary Programme, 11–26 March, 2017.

Halberstam, Judith. 'What's That Smell? Queer Temporalities and Subcultural Lives'. *The Scholar and Feminist Online* 2, no. 1 (2003). Available at http://sfonline.barnard.edu/ps/printjha.htm (accessed 1 December 2019).

Halberstam, Judith. *In a Queer Time and Place: Transgender Bodies, Subcultural Lives*. New York: New York University Press, 2005.

Hardt, Michael, and Antonio Negri, *Empire*. Cambridge, MA: Harvard University Press, 2000.

Harris, Jonathan Gil. *Untimely Matter in the Time of Shakespeare*. Philadelphia: University of Pennsylvania Press, 2009.

Hartog, François. *Régimes d'historicité: Présentisme et expériences du temps*. Paris: Seuil, 2003.

Harvey, David. *The Condition of Postmodernity: An Inquiry into the Origins of Cultural Change*. Oxford: Basil Blackwell, 1989.

Havlin, Laura. 'A History of Female Afrofuturist Fashion'. *Another Mag*, 16 September, 2015. Available at https://www.anothermag.com/fashion-beauty/7791/a-history-of-female-afrofuturist-fashion (accessed 28 November 2019).

Holland, Eugene. 'Non-Linear Historical Materialism; Or, What is Revolutionary in Deleuze and Guattari's Philosophy of History?'. In *Time and History in Deleuze and Serres*, edited by Bernd Herzogenrath, 17–30. New York and London: Continuum, 2012.

Horyn, Cathy. 'Why Raf Simons Is Leaving Christian Dior'. *The Cut*, 22 October, 2015. Available at https://www.thecut.com/2015/10/raf-simons-leaving-christian-dior.html (accessed 22 June 2018).

Hoskins, Tansy E. *Stitched Up: The Anti-Capitalist Book of Fashion*. London: Pluto Press, 2014.

Howlader, Ramij, (Rajib), Monirul Islam, Sajib, Tanjibul Hasan and Prasad, Ripon Kumar. 'Practically Observation of Standard Minute Value of T-shirt'. *International Journal of Engineering and Computer Science* 4, no. 3 (March 2015): 10685–89.

Ichikawa, Sabine. 'Creative Industries: The Case of Fashion'. In *Cultures and Globalization Series 2: The Cultural Economy*, edited by Helmut K. Anheier, and Yudhishthir Raj Isar, 253–60. London: Sage, 2008.

Jameson, Fredric. *The Seeds of Time*. New York and Chichester: Columbia University Press, 1994.

Jardine, Alice. 'Introduction to Julia Kristeva's "Women's Time"'. *Signs* 7, no. 1 (1981): 5–12.

Jenkins, Keith, ed. *The Postmodern History Reader*. London: Routledge, 1997.

Jenss, Heike. *Fashioning Memory: Vintage Style and Youth Culture*. London and New York: Bloomsbury, 2015.

Jones, Jennifer. *Sexing La Mode. Gender, Fashion and Commercial Culture in Old Regime France*. Oxford and New York: Berg, 2007.

Julier, Guy. 'Introduction: Material Preference and Design Activism'. *Design and Culture* 5, no. 2 (2013): 145–50.

Julier, Guy. 'From Design Culture to Design Activism'. *Design and Culture* 5, no. 2 (1 July, 2013): 215–36.

Kansara, Vikram Alexei. 'Tweets and Tribes'. *The Business of Fashion*, 16 March, 2009. Available at http://www.businessoffashion.com/2009/03/fashion-20-tweets-and-tribes.html (accessed 15 October 2012).

Kansara, Vikram Alexei. 'Fashion 2.0 | New York Fashion Tweek'. *The Business of Fashion*, 10 September, 2009. Available at https://www.businessoffashion.com/articles/fashion-tech/fashion-2-0-new-york-fashion-tweek (accessed 7 October 2018).

Kawamura, Yuniya. *The Japanese Revolution in Paris Fashion*. Oxford and New York: Berg, 2004.

Kennedy, Randy. 'Revising Art History's Big Book: Who's In and Who Comes Out'. *New York Times*, 7 March, 2006.

Kern, Stephen. *The Culture of Time and Space, 1880–1918*. Cambridge, MA and London: Harvard University Press, 2nd ed, 2003.

Koselleck, Reinhart. *The Practice of Conceptual History: Timing History, Spacing Concepts*. Stanford: Stanford University Press, 2002.

Kracauer, Siegfried. *Georg*. In *Schriften*, 7. Frankfurt am Main: Suhrkamp, 1973.

Kracauer, Siegfried. 'Photography'. *Frankfurter Zeitung*, 1927. Translated by Thomas Y. Levin, *Critical Inquiry* 19, no. 3 (Spring 1993): 421–36.

Kracauer, Siegfried. *The Mass Ornament*. Translated and edited by Thomas Y. Levin. Cambridge, MA: Harvard University Press, 1995.

Kristeva, Julia. 'Women's Time'. Translated by Alice Jardine and Harry Blake. *Signs* 7, no. 1 (1981): 13–35.

Kroeber, Alfred L. 'On the Principle of Order in Civilization as Exemplified by Changes in Fashion'. *American Anthropologist*, New Series 21, no. 3 (1919): 235–63.

La Dernière Mode, no. 2 (20 September, 1874).

La Dernière Mode, no. 5 (1 November, 1874).

Lagerfeld, Karl. 'Karlism 25'. Available at www.karl.com/karlism/2013/karlism-25/#karlism-1 (accessed 12 November 2013).

Lagerfeld, Karl. 'Karl Lagerfeld on Fur (Yea), Selfies (Nay) and Keeping Busy'. Interview by Matthew Schneier. *New York Times*, 3 March, 2015. Available at https://www.nytimes.com/2015/03/05/fashion/karl-lagerfeld-on-fur-yea-selfies-nay-and-keeping-busy.html (accessed 7 May 2018).

Landow, George P. *Hypertext 2.0*. Baltimore: Johns Hopkins University Press, 1997.

Laver, James. *Taste and Fashion from the French Revolution Until Today*. London: Harrap & Co., 1937.

Laver, James. *Costume and Fashion: A Concise History*. London: Thames and Hudson, 1995.

Lazzarato, Maurizio. 'Immaterial Labour'. In *Radical Thought In Italy: A Potential Politics*, edited by Paolo Virno, and Michael Hardt, 133–47. Minneapolis: University of Minnesota Press, 1996.

Lehmann, Ulrich. *Tigersprung: Fashion in Modernity*. Cambridge, MA: MIT Press, 2000.

Lemaire, Christophe. 'On Aiming for the Ideal while Rooting for Reality'. Interview by Anja Aronowsky Cronberg. *Vestoj. The Journal of Sartorial Matters*, no. 5, On Slowness (Autumn 2014): 149–54.

Leslie, Esther. '"The Murderous, Meaningless Caprices of Fashion": Marx on Capital, Clothing and Fashion'. *Culture Matters*, 4 May, 2018. Available at https://www.culturematters.org.uk/index.php/culture/clothing-fashion/item/2809-the-murderous-meaningless-caprices-of-fashion-marx-on-capital-clothing-and-fashion (accessed 4 January 2020).

Magasin des modes nouvelles, 10ᵉ Cahier, 20 February, 1787.

Magasin des Modes Nouvelle, 19ᵉ Cahier, 20 May, 1789, 146.

Magasin des modes nouvelles, 23ᵉ Cahier, 30 June, 1787.

Magasin des modes nouvelles, 32ᵉ Cahier, 30 September, 1787.

Magasin des modes nouvelles, 4ᵉ Cahier, 20 December, 1787.

Mallarmé, Stéphane. *Oeuvres complètes*. Paris: Gallimard, 1945.

Margiela, Martin, et al. *La Maison Martin Margiela (9/4/1615)*. Rotterdam: Museum Boijmans Van Beuningen, 1997.

Martin, Richard, and Harold Koda, eds. *The Historical Mode: Fashion and Art in the 1980s*. New York: Rizzoli International, 1989.

Marx, Karl. *Das Kapital. Kritik Der Politischen Ökonomie*. Hamburg: Otto Meissner; New York: L. W. Schmidt, 1867.

Marx, Karl. *Capital Volume I*. 1867. Translated by Ben Fowkes. Harmondsworth: Penguin 1976.

Matteucci, Giovanni. 'Fashion: a Conceptual Constellation'. In *Philosophical Perspectives on Fashion*, edited by Giovanni Matteucci and Stefano Marino, 47–72. London and New York: Bloomsbury, 2016.

Mattoni, Alice. *Media Practices and Protest Politics. How Precarious Workers Mobilise*. Farnham: Ashgate Publishing Company, 2012.

Mercier, Louis-Sébastien. *Tableau de Paris*, edited by Jean-Claude Bonnet. Paris: Mercure de France, 1994.

Michaud, Yves. *L'art à l'état gazeux. Essai sur le triomphe de l'esthétique*. Paris: Stock, 2003.

Montesquieu. *Lettres persanes*, edited by Paul Vernière. Paris: Classiques Garnier, 1992.

Morand, Paul. *L'allure de Chanel*. Paris: Hermann, 1976.

Moxey, Keith. *Visual Time: The Image in History*. Durham and London: Duke University Press, 2013.

Nielsen, Jakob. 'How Long Do Users Stay on Web Pages?'. *Nielsen Norman Group*, 12 September, 2011. Available at https://www.nngroup.com/articles/how-long-do-users-stay-on-web-pages/ (accessed 4 October 2018).

O'Neill, Alistair. 'Cuttings and Pastings'. In *Fashion and Modernity*, edited by Caroline Evans, and Christopher Breward, 175–89. Oxford and New York: Berg, 2005.

Palmer, Alexandra. *Couture & Commerce: The Transatlantic Fashion Trade in the 1950s*. Vancouver: UBC Press, 2001.

Papacharissi, Zizi. 'Audience as Media Producers: Content Analysis of 260 Blogs'. In *Blogging, Citizenship, and the Future of the Media*, edited by Mark Tremayne, 21–38. New York: Routledge, 2007.

Parker, Derek, and Julia Parker. *The Natural History of the Chorus Girl*. London: David & Charles, 1975.

Parkins, Ilya. 'Building a Feminist Theory of Fashion: Karen Barad's Agential Realism'. *Australian Feminist Studies* 23, no. 58 (2008): 501–15.

Parkins, Ilya. 'Fashion as Methodology: Rewriting the Time of Women's Modernity'. *Time & Society* 19, no. 1 (2010): 98–119.

Parkins, Ilya. *Poiret, Dior and Schiaparelli: Fashion, Femininity and Modernity*. London: Bloomsbury, 2013.

Pavlik, John V. *Media in the Digital Age*. New York: Columbia University Press, 2008.

Payne, Alice. 'Counting the Cost of Fast Fashion'. *The Conversation*, 16 February, 2012. Available at http://theconversation.com/counting-the-cost-of-fast-fashion-5297 (accessed 27 November 2019).

Peace, Richard. 'On Rereading Bakhtin'. *Modern Language Review* 88, no. 1 (1993): 137–46.

Pesce, Gaetano. 'Avanti tutta'. *Corriere della Sera*, 22 April, 2009.

Phillips, Angela. 'Old Sources: New Bottles'. In *New Media, Old News: Journalism and Democracy in the Digital Age*, edited by Natalie Fenton, 87–101. London: Sage, 2010.

Piaggi, Anna. *Anna Piaggi's Fashion Algebra*. London: Thames and Hudson, 1998.

Poiret, Paul. *King of Fashion*. 1931. Translated by Stephen Haden Guest. London: V&A Publications, 2009.

Pollo, Paola. 'E la Biagiotti punta su Pitti dopo 20 anni'. *Corriere della Sera*, 10 January, 2009: 25.

Pomian, Krzysztof. *L'ordre du temps*. Paris: Gallimard, 1984.

Ponty, Marguerite de. 'La Mode (On nous harangue et nous répondons. . .)'. *La Dernière Mode*, no. 8 (20 December 1874), 2. In *Oeuvres complètes*, by Stéphane Mallarmé. Paris: Gallimard, 1945.

Prada, Miuccia. *Schiaparelli and Prada: Impossible Conversations – Introduction with Baz Luhrmann*. Film dir: Baz Luhrmann. 2012. Dialogue by Miuccia Prada. Transcript. Available at https://www.youtube.com/watch?v=c55tCFU2Oho (accessed 5 January 2020).

Quant, Mary. *Quant by Quant*. London: Cassell & Company, 1966.

Quicherat, Jules. *Histoire du Costume en France depuis les temps les plus reculés jusqu'à la fin du XVIIIe siècle*. Paris: Hachette, 1875.

Ray, Man. 'The Age of Light'. In *Photographs by Man Ray: IOS Works 1920–34*. New York: Dover Publications, 1979.

Rees-Roberts, Nick. *Fashion Film: Art and Advertising in the Digital Age*. London and New York: Bloomsbury, 2018.

Renouvier, Charles. *Uchronie (l'utopie dans l'histoire): esquisse historique apocryphe du développement de la civilisation européenne tel qu'il n'a pas été, tel qu'il aurait pu être*. Paris: La critique philosophique, 1876.

Ricchetti, Marco, and Enrico Cietta, eds. *Il valore della moda: Industria e servizi in un settore guidato dall'innovazione*. Milan: Bruno Mondadori, 2006.

Rocamora, Agnès. 'Blogs personnels de mode: identité et sociabilité dans la culture des apparences'. *Sociologie et Sociétés* 43, no. 1 (2011): 19–44.

Rocamora, Agnès. 'New Fashion Times: Fashion and Digital Media'. In *The Handbook of Fashion Studies*, edited by Sandy Black, Amy de la Haye, Joanne Entwistle, Regina A. Root, Agnès Rocamora, and Helen Thomas, 61–77. London and New York: Bloomsbury, 2013.

Roche, Daniel. *The Culture of Clothing: Dress and Fashion in the 'ancien regime'*. Translated by Jean Birrell. Cambridge: Cambridge University Press, 1994.

Rohy, Valerie. *Anachronism and Its Others: Sexuality, Race, Temporality*. Albany: State University of New York Press, 2009.

Rosa, Hartmut. *Accélération: Une Critique Sociale du Temps*. Paris: Découverte, 2010.

Rosner, Daniela K. *Critical Fabulations: Reworking the Methods and Margins of Design*. Cambridge, MA and London: MIT Press, 2018.

Rovelli, Carlo. *The Order of Time*. Translated by Erica Segre and Simon Carnell. London: Allen Lane, 2018.

Rovine, Victoria L. *African Fashion, Global Style: Histories, Innovations, and Ideas You Can Wear*. Bloomington and Indianapolis: Indiana University Press, 2015.

Safi, Michael, and Dominic Rushe. 'Rana Plaza, Five Years on: Safety of Workers Hangs in Balance in Bangladesh'. *Guardian*, 24 April, 2018. Available at https://www.theguardian.com/globaldevelopment/2018/apr/24/bangladeshi-police-target-garment-workers-union-rana-plaza-five-years-on (accessed 7 July 2018).

Sampson, Ellen. 'Creases, Crumples, and Folds'. *Fashion Studies Journal*, 2017. Available at http://www.fashionstudiesjournal.org/2-visual-essays-2/2017/4/2/creases-crumples-and-folds-maps-of-experience-and-manifestations-of-wear (accessed 10 July 2018).

Sandino, Linda. 'Oral Histories and Design: Objects and Subjects'. *Journal of Design History* 19, no. 4 (2006): 283–93.

Sandino, Linda. 'Here Today, Gone Tomorrow: Ancient Materiality in Contemporary Cultural Artefacts'. *Journal of Design History* 17, no. 3 (2004): 283–93.

Schiaparelli, Elsa. 'Foreword'. In *Shocking Life*. London: J. M. Dent, 1954.

Segre Reinach, Simona. 'Antropologia e studio della moda'. In *Moda. Storia e storie*, edited by Maria Giuseppina Muzzarelli, Giorgio Riello, and Elisa Tosi Brandi, 105–15. Milan and Turin: Bruno Mondadori, 2010.

Sem [Goursat, George], *Le Vrai et Le Faux Chic*. Paris: Succès, 1914.

Serpica Naro. 'Il Metabrand'. *Serpica Naro*, 30 July, 2012. Available at https://www.serpicanaro.com/metabrand-license (accessed 4 January 2020).

Serpica Naro. 'La Licenza'. *Serpica Naro*, 6 January, 2013. Available at https://www.serpicanaro.com/la-licenza-del-marchio (accessed 4 January 2020).

Serpica Naro. 'Il Media Sociale'. *Serpica Naro*, 27 January, 2013. Available at https://www.serpicanaro.com/serpica-story/serpica-naro-il-media-sociale (accessed 4 January 2020).

Serres, Michel. *Atlas*. Paris: Éditions Julliard, 1994.

Serres, Michel. *Genesis*. Translated by Geneviève James and James Nielson. Ann Arbor: University of Michigan Press, 1995.

Serres, Michel, and Bruno Latour. *Conversations on Science, Culture and Time*. Translated by Roxanne Lapidus. Ann Arbor: University of Michigan Press, 1995.

Shahani, Nishant. *Queer Retrosexualities: The Politics of Reparative Return*. Bethlehem: Lehigh University Press, 2012.

Sherman, Stuart. *Telling Time: Clocks, Diaries, and English Diurnal Form, 1660–1785*. Chicago: University of Chicago Press, 1997.

Shove, Elizabeth, Frank Trentmann, and Richard Wilk. *Time, Consumption and Everyday Life: Practice, Materiality and Culture*. London: Bloomsbury, 2009.

Simmel, Georg. 'Fashion'. 1904. Translated and reprinted in *The American Journal of Sociology* 62, no. 6 (May 1957): 541–58.

Simpson, Bennett. 'Techiques of Today: Bernadette Corporation'. *Artforum* 43, no. 1 (2004). Available at http://www.bernadettecorporation.com/introduction.htm (accessed 20 December 2019).

Skov, Lisa. 'Snapshot. Fashion Week'. In *Fashion Worldwide*, 230–31. Part 4 of *Global Perspectives*. Vol. X, *Berg Encyclopedia of World Dress and Fashion*, edited by Joanne B. Eicher, and Phyllis G. Tortora. Oxford and New York: Berg, 2007.

Skov, Lisa. "Fashion". In *The Cultural Intermediaries Reader*, edited by Jennifer Smith Maguire and Julian Matthews (London and Los Angeles: Sage, 2014), 113–24.

Smelik, Anneke. 'Fashioning the Fold: Multiple Belonging'. In *This Deleuzian Century: Art, Activism, Life*, edited by Rosi Braidotti and Rick Dolphijn, 37–55. Leiden and Boston: Brill-Rodopi, 2015.

Smelik, Anneke. 'Gilles Deleuze: Bodies-without-Organs in the Folds of Fashion'. In *Thinking Through Fashion: A Guide to Key Theorists*, edited by Agnès Rocamora and Anneke Smelik, 165–83. London: I.B. Tauris, 2016.

Smith, Wendy Ligon. 'Reviving Fortuny's Phantasmagorias'. PhD diss., The University of Manchester, Manchester, 2015.

Steele, Valerie. *Paris Fashion: A Cultural History*. Oxford: Berg, 1998.

Steele, Valerie. 'Fashion Futures'. In *The End of Fashion: Clothing and Dress in the Age of Globalization*, edited by Adam Geczy and Vicki Karaminas, 5–18. London: Bloomsbury, 2019.

Stern, Radu. *Against Fashion: Clothing as Art, 1850–1930*. Cambridge, MA and London: MIT Press, 2003.

Strauven, Wanda. 'Media Archaeology: Where Film History, Media Art, and New Media (Can) Meet'. In *Preserving and Exhibiting Media Art. Challenges and Perspectives*, edited by Julia Noordegraaf, Cosetta G. Saba, Barbara Le Maître and Vinzenz Hediger, 59–79. Amsterdam: Amsterdam University Press, 2013. Available at https://www.academia.edu/37493500/Media_Archaeology_Where_Film_History_Media_Art_and_New_Media_Can_Meet (accessed 31 December 2019).

Tétart-Vittu, Françoise. 'Naissance du couturier et du modéliste'. In *Au paradis des dames: Nouveautés, modes et confections, 1810–1870*, edited by Françoise Tétart-Vittu and Jean-Pierre Vittu, 36–39. Paris: Paris-musées, 1992.

Thomas, Samuel Patrick. 'Anrealage S/S/A/W 2014–15 – Subverting the Seasonal Construct'. *Tokyo Telephone*. 9 April, 2014. Available at http://tokyotelephone.com/ anrealage-ssaw-2014-15-subverting-the-seasonal-construct/ (accessed 10 December 2018).

Thompson, E.P. 'Time, Work-Discipline, and Industrial Capitalism'. *Past & Present* 38, no. 3 (December 1967): 56–97.

Tomlinson, John. *The Culture of Speed*. London: Sage, 2007.

Toussaint, Lianne, and Anneke Smelik. 'Memory and Materiality in Hussein Chalayan's Techno-Fashion'. In *Materializing Memory in Art and Popular Culture*, edited by László Munteán, Liedeke Plate and Anneke Smelik, 89–101. New York and London: Routledge, 2017.

Troy, Nancy J. *Couture Culture: A Study in Modern Art and Fashion*. Boston: MIT Press, 2003.

Tyler, David J. *Materials Management in Clothing Production*. London: BSP Professional Books Press, 1991.

Vaccari, Alessandra. 'The Daily Wardrobe – The Chronometer of Fashion'. In *Fashion at the Time of Fascism: Italian Modernist Lifestyle 1922–1943*, edited by Mario Lupano and Alessandra Vaccari, 60–64. Bologna: Damiani, 2009.

Vaccari, Alessandra. 'Hussein Chalayan. Morphing the Century'. *ZoneModa Journal*, 1 (2009): 12–19.

Vaccari, Alessandra. *La moda nei discorsi dei designer*. Bologna: CLUEB, 2012.

Valentino. 'Press Release Haute Couture spring/summer 2016'.

Van de Peer, Aurélie. 'So Last Season: The Production of the Fashion Present in the Politics of Time'. *Fashion Theory. The Journal of Dress, Body & Culture* 18, no. 3 (2014): 317–34.

Vanni, Ilaria. '"Why Save the World When You can Design It?" Precarity and Fashion in Milan'. *Fashion Theory. The Journal of Dress, Body & Culture* 20, no. 4 (2016): 441–60.

Vanni, Ilaria, and Marcello Tarì. 'On the Life and Deeds of San Precario, Patron Saint of Precarious Workers and Lives'. *Fibreculture*, no. 5 (2005). Available at http://five. fibre- culturejournal.org/fcj-023-on-the-life-and-deeds-of-san-precario-patron-saint- of-precarious-workers-and-lives/ (accessed 20 January 2013).

Veblen, Thorstein. *The Theory of the Leisure Class: An Economic Study of Institutions*. New York: Macmillan, 1899.

Vinken, Barbara. *Fashion Zeitgeist: Trends and Cycles in the Fashion System*. Oxford and New York: Berg, 2005.

Vreeland, Diana. 'Foreword'. In *Art into Fashion*, by Sonia Delaunay. New York: George Brazilier, 1986.

Walden, George. *Who's a Dandy?* London: Gibson Square Books, 2002.

Waldman, Diane. *Collage, Assemblage and the Found Object.* London: Phaidon, 1992.

Weinswig, Deborah. 'Fast Fashion Speeding Toward Ultra Fast Fashion'. *Fung Global Retail and Technology,* 19 May, 2017. Available at https://www.fungglobalretailtech. com/research/fast-fashion-speeding-toward-ultrafast-fashion/ (accessed 4 July 2018).

Welters, Linda, and Abby Lillethun. *Fashion History: A Global View.* London: Bloomsbury, 2018.

White, Sarah. 'Fashion Firms Dither over Instant Shopping on the Catwalk'. *Reuters,* 20 February, 2018. Available at https://www.reuters.com/article/us-fashion-retail/ fashion-firms-dither-over-instant-shopping-on-the-catwalk-idUSKCN1G40RY (accessed 27 November 2019).

Williams, Andrew P. *The Restoration Fop: Gender Boundaries and Comic Characterization in Later Seventeenth Century Drama.* Lewiston, NY: Edwin Mellen Press, 1995.

Wilk, Richard. 'Consumer Goods as Dialogue about Development'. *Culture and History* 7 (1990): 79–100.

Wilk, Richard. 'Colonial Time and TV Time: Television and Temporality in Belize'. *Visual Anthropology Review* 19, no. 1 (1990): 94–102.

Wilson, Elizabeth. *Adorned in Dreams; Fashion and Modernity.* 1985. Revised edition. London: I.B. Tauris, 2003.

Wissinger, Elizabeth. 'Modelling a Way of Life: Immaterial and Affective Labour in the Fashion Modelling Industry'. *Ephemera* 7, no. 1 (2007): 250–69.

Witherbee, Amy. 'New Conceptions of Time and the Making of a Political-Economic Public in Eighteenth-Century'. PhD diss. (Boston: Boston College University, 2009).

Wohlfarth, Erwin. 'Et cetera? The Historian as Chiffonier'. *New German Critique* 39 (fall 1986): 142–68.

Woodward, Sophie. *Why Women Wear What They Wear.* London: Bloomsbury, 2007.

Woodward, Sophie, and Tom Fisher. 'Fashioning Through Materials: Material Culture, Materiality and Processes of Materialization'. *Critical Studies in Fashion & Beauty* 5, no. 1 (2014): 3–22.

Woolf, Virginia. 'The Narrow Bridge of Art'. In *The Collected Essays of Virginia Woolf,* edited by Leonard Woolf, 2. London: Chatto & Windus, 1966–69: 218–20.

Wu, Juanjuan. *Chinese Fashion: From Mao to Now.* Oxford and New York: Berg, 2009.

Yomango. '¿Qué Fue de Yomango?'. *Yomango,* 2011. Available at http://yomango. info/2011/07/¿que-fue-de-yomango/ (accessed 4 January 2020).

Young, Agnes Brooks. *Recurring Cycles of Fashion, 1760–1937.* New York and London: Harper & Bros, 1937.

Zborowska, Agata. 'Invoking the Spirit of Fashion'. *Czas Kultury*, no. 173 (2013): 151–63.
    Available at http://czaskultury.pl/en/wp-content/uploads/2017/02/AZborowska_
    InvokingTheSpiritOfFashion_CzasKultury_2_2013.pdf (accessed
    6 November 2019).
Zerubavel, Eviatar. *Hidden Rhythms: Schedules and Calendars in Social Life*. University
    of Chicago Press, Chicago 1981.

Index

www.ingramcontent.com/pod-product-compliance
Lightning Source LLC
Chambersburg PA
CBHW050444280326
41932CB00013BA/2242